# Mobile Media Practices, Presence and Politics

As an example of convergence, the mobile phone—especially in the form of the smartphone—is now ushering in new promises of seamlessness between engagement with technology and everyday common experiences. This seamlessness is not only about how one transitions between the worlds of the device and the physical environment, but it also captures the transition and convergences between devices as well (i.e., laptop to smartphone

This volume argues, however, that these transitions are far from seamless. We see divisions between online and offline, virtual and actual, here and there, taking on different cartographies, emergent forms of seams. It is these seams that this volume acknowledges, challenges and explores—socially, culturally, technologically and historically—as we move to a deeper understanding of the role and impact of mobile communication's saturation throughout the world.

**Kathleen M. Cumiskey** is an associate professor at the College of Staten Island—City University of New York, U.S.

**Larissa Hjorth** is an artist, digital ethnographer and associate professor at Royal Melbourne Institute of Technology, Australia.

# Routledge Studies in New Media and Cyberculture

# Mobile Media Practices, Presence and Politics

The Challenge of Being Seamlessly Mobile

**Edited by**
**Kathleen M. Cumiskey and**
**Larissa Hjorth**

Routledge
Taylor & Francis Group

NEW YORK AND LONDON

First published 2013
by Routledge
711 Third Avenue, New York, NY 10017

Simultaneously published in the UK
by Routledge
2 Park Square, Milton Park, Abingdon, Oxfordshire OX14 4RN

First issued in paperback 2014

*Routledge is an imprint of the Taylor and Francis Group,
an informa business*

*Library of Congress Cataloging-in-Publication Data*

Mobile media practices, presence and politics : the challenge of being
    seamlessly mobile / edited by Kathleen M. Cumiskey & Larissa Hjorth.
        pages cm. — (Routledge studies in new media and cyberculture ; 12)
    "Simultaneously published in the UK"—Title page verso.
    Includes bibliographical references and index.
    1. Mobile communication systems—Social aspects.    2. Mobile
communication systems—Political aspects.    3. Digital media—Social
aspects.    4. Digital media—Political aspects.    5. Cell phones—Social
aspects.    6. Cell phones—Political aspects.    7. Information society.
I. Cumiskey, Kathleen M., 1970–    II. Hjorth, Larissa.
    HM1206.M626    2013
    302.23'1—dc23
    2012051238

ISBN  978-0-415-82127-8 (hbk)
ISBN  978-1-138-92213-6 (pbk)
ISBN  978-0-203-56587-2 (ebk)

Typeset in Sabon
by Apex CoVantage, LLC

# Table of Contents

# Figures

# Tables

# Acknowledgements

The authors would like to acknowledge Scott Campbell, Yi-Fan Chen, Lee Humphreys and Rich Ling for their assistance in the creation of this volume.

# 1 Between the Seams

## Mobile Media Practice, Presence and Politics

### *Kathleen M. Cumiskey and Larissa Hjorth*

## INTRODUCTION

Once solely a mode of telephonic communication, the mobile phone has grown to encompass numerous forms of communication and media.[1] As an example of convergence par excellence, the mobile phone—especially in the form of the smartphone—is now ushering in new promises of seamlessness between engagement with technology, Internet access and everyday common experiences.[2] Up until now, the terms "convergence" and "seamlessness" have been used relatively unproblematically in industry to highlight design innovation in mobile technology. Seamlessness has been focused on as a means of making communication more efficient and the coordination of tasks more streamlined. Yet design innovation has also yielded social and psychological consequences of the engagement with technology, just as existing forms of media practice and intimacy have informed design features.[3] Here convergence is not just a technological phenomenon, but it also has social and cultural dimensions. This volume attempts to expand upon understandings of "seamlessness" as a mode for negotiating various forms of presence, identity, politics and place in an age of so-called smartphones through cultural, psychological and media studies perspectives.

When one encounters seamlessness from a user's perspective is it often experienced as a feeling of co-presence. Co-presence has been defined as a locative and social experience of two or more humans feeling "accessible, available, and subject to one another"[4]. The design of mobile media has offered the potential of co-presence while, at the same time, rehearsing older mediated intimacies.[5] This phenomenon is so pervasive that debates about intimacy today are often conflated with the introduction of mobile media.[6] From affording burgeoning locative-based services to allowing for the creation of new social media micronarratives while on the go, mobile media present particular questions about the nature of "mobile seamlessness" today. What it means to be mobile, with a dialectical relationship to immobility, takes various forms. Mobile media reflect technological, social, cultural and economic mobilities at the same time as amplifying older intimacies and communicative rituals.[7] When combined with the idea of seamlessness, mobility highlights paradoxes around modes of presence, convergence and entanglements of place. This seamlessness is not only about how one transitions between the worlds of the device and the physical environment, but it also captures the transition and convergences between devices as well (i.e., laptop to smartphone). While seamlessness is the ultimate goal of ubiquitous technologies, it is also perpetually undermined by a variety of factors: expectations of use, co-presence, telepresence and net presence. These breaks in seamlessness are exemplified by mobile games in which interruptability has become a key element in gameplay, ensuring the growing success of mobile gaming.

In this way, the mobile experience is specific to the material and immaterial affordances of mobile media. However, we see the specters of earlier debates, especially issues around co-presence and embodiment, as outlined in early Internet studies such as feminist debates around cyberculture.[8] Through mobile media, the relationship of being online versus offline has shifted, creating new types of engagement and co-presence, and because of the mobile nature of such media, seams that either limit or enhance these experiences become evident. As a result, we see divisions between online and offline, virtual and actual, or here and there taking on different cartographies. But, as the challenges within the industry suggest, these new maps are far from seamless. Rather, just as place and accessibility has always mattered to mobile media, and intimacy via these media has always been mediated,[9] we are seeing emergent forms of seams in our ability to psychologically and socially connect via these devices. These seams are not clearly defined by networks or infrastructure. It is these more subtle and elusive seams that we want to acknowledge, challenge, explore and experience throughout this volume as we move to a deeper understanding of the role and impact of mobile communication's saturation throughout the world. Our hope is that analyzing seamlessness from this perspective will serve to inform industry and design in meeting some of its challenges as well.

The study of mobile communication is therefore at a crossroads. In one direction, mobile communication studies—as a vehicle for convergence and seamlessness—needs to distinguish itself from other disciplines, such as Internet, media and game studies. In the other direction, as a vehicle for twenty-first century convergent media practice, the interdisciplinary nature of mobile communication studies can help to expand upon some of the shortcomings of debates in these various disciplines. With mobile media increasingly becoming the key, if not the only, site for social, locative and mobile media practices, new questions about co-presence, place and embodiment arise. While not everyone has access to a computer, mobile media is providing access to the Internet to a diverse group of users. Users of mobile media vary based not only on demography but on geography as well. Contextualizing use and the variety of means for accessing the Internet reminds us of the saliency of locality in informing mobile media practice.

The debates around co-presence and what we are calling seamlessness—especially in the form of negotiating offline and online spaces—continue to haunt various disciplines in their analysis of mediation. Presence was a key concept in much of the early scholarship on the sociocultural uses of the internet. Building on existing scholarship around presence and co-presence as a way to understand intimacy and place, theories around mobile communication have served to further underscore the continued importance of presence as a crucial concept in an era of smartphones.[10] As co-presence is broadly defined in the present context, presence can be understood as referring to "the degree to which geographically dispersed agents experience a sense of physical and/or psychological proximity through the use of particular communication technologies".[11] The authors in this volume clearly demonstrate that the intimacy generated by the use of mobile devices shifts our notions of space, distance and separation. For example, the notion of perpetual contact and seamless communication takes on a different emphasis when discussing how mobile technology can be used in crisis communication and to support the health of women and children living in remote areas of the world.

In early Internet scholarship on presence, there was considerable semantic debate, specifically around attempts to differentiate between technologically mediated and unmediated forms of presence. For a number of critics participating in these debates, any such distinction was untenable; this is because, as Giuseppe Mantovani and Giuseppe Riva have noted, it fails to acknowledge that "presence is always mediated" and that it is culturally constructed.[12] Just like intimacy, presence has always been mediated, if not by technologies, then by gestures, language and memory. Mobile technologies, for Christian Licoppe, "provide a continuous pattern of mediated interactions that combine into 'connected relationships', in which the boundaries between absence and presence eventually get blurred".[13] Mobile communication inflects presence on diverse levels in which "the ways absent ones make themselves present have been many" and in which "copresent interactions and mediated communication seem woven in a seamless web".[14]

These mediated interactions and connected relationships are maintained through the use of mobile media. Who we are becomes reflected in our devices.[15] How much we share then becomes a new point of contention. Locality, economy and social capital are but a few of the fabrics that create tensions around the experience of seamless and seamful co-presence.[16] If presence and absence are blurred, then the psychological experience of always being "on" can make one question whether or not private and/or anonymous space exists. We use mobile media to create representations of our daily activities and ourselves.[17] Locative media like Foursquare and the use of microblogging can make users see cartographies between online and offline places and experiences overlaid in new ways, and forms of augmented reality are created.[18] As we emerge, we leave behind digital archives and electromagnetic traces of where we have come from, where we currently are and where we are going. The personalization of mobile media through the use of social media apps can make it seem like each user has a great amount of autonomy, but as we move into spheres of acknowledgement that we are constantly being kept track of (by multinational corporations as well as our closest friends and family), can we actually say that we are in full control of our daily lives? What's worse is that when we have come to develop a dependency on the use of mobile media in this way, how do we recover in moments when it falls apart—when the seams are revealed? Increasingly, differences between seams and seamlessness highlight the uneven distributions and usage of mobile media globally. The world is far from a homogeneous global village, and mobile media amplifies the tenacity of place in informing media practice.[19]

Seams, like the seams on our clothes, are necessary places of joining that allow for the garment to be complete and functional; however, they are often a source of annoyance and difficulty. A fraying of the seams could indicate the loss of functionality of a garment, and so if we were to apply this metaphor to the use of mobile communication devices and mobile media, the seams are the point at which we understand how these devices facilitate our mobile media-enhanced experiences, but the seams are also the point where these experiences can annoyingly and frustratingly fall apart. To aspire to be seamless is ultimately to aspire to be continuous, to be simultaneous, to have flow, unfettered access to information and to other people in a fast-paced and ever-changing world.[20] Mobile media devices are promoted to users as having these amazing powers of creating opportunities for seamless interaction and a growing oneness with those close to us and with those with whom we share a common vision and who have access to resources that we need.[21] We often imagine our devices to be able to function way beyond their technological capabilities. In the context of this volume, we will be using the notion of seams as an organizing structure around which we can examine some of the limitations of mobile technology. We use the idea of seamlessness as a state and a relationship to technology that most users desire and imagine that they have. Having such a ubiquitous tool in one's pocket, users want it to work to fulfill all of their needs as they arise in their current context and to satisfy many of the wants and desires of remote others.

As the world moves unevenly toward smartphone uptake, how we experience, practice and imagine seamlessness, co-presence and mobility is changing. In *Mobile Media Practices, Presence and Politics: The Challenge of Being Seamlessly Mobile*, we are capturing these transformations as well as putting them into context: socially, culturally, technologically and historically. With new essays from leading scholars in the interdisciplinary area of mobile communication and mobile media, *The Challenge of Being Seamlessly Mobile* adds to a growing discipline that aims to continually question and reflect upon what kind of impact the integration of this technology is having on our lives.

## SEAMS OF ADHERENCE, ACCESS AND EQUALITY

Despite some of the challenges that accompany it, access to mobile phones is improving the lives of many people in some of the remotest places on earth.[22]

It is not only allowing there to be more contact between all the people on this planet, but it is generating a psychological shift in how expansive we perceive the world to be. We know and understand that we can access most places in the world through the use of mobile technology and the availability of Internet access and mobile devices.

Mobile technology has been called upon to answer some of the most difficult challenges when it comes to disaster prevention, emergency relief, and threats to public health, safety and vitality. However, as Michael J. Palenchar and Karen Freberg point out in their chapter, there is a gap or seam between what people expect the new technology to be able to do during a disaster and what the actual needs and expectations are once the disaster hits. Despite these challenges, to many people, especially those such as the people of rural Uttar Pradesh, India, featured in the chapter by Kapadia-Kundia et al., access to mobile phones has proven to increase the health and well-being of communities. Simple improvements in communication between hospitals and citizens in remote areas have saved lives. When asked about what motivates most people to get a mobile phone, time and time again, the world over, people will respond that mobile phones are good "in case of an emergency".[23] Users literally envision their mobile phones to be lifelines, and yet not everyone has the privilege to be able to rely on such a commodity. A fantasy and hope of seamless communication becomes a literal lifeline to some, and when the infrastructure becomes unreliable the consequences can literally be a matter of life or death.

The chapters written by Tracey M. Benson and Marian Stewart Titus grapple with seams around how literacy and cultural differences may limit use and access to mobile media. Benson draws from a case study of indigenous Australians and the limited access to mobile communication that they have as the country rolls out its highly problematized National Broadband Network (NBN). She highlights the far-from-seamless nature of being online that clearly separates indigenous and nonindigenous populations in Australia. Alternatively, Titus provides an ambitious cross-cultural case study involving 30 countries, over nearly a decade, to draw out the relationship between adult literacy, education and income and its impact on mobile media practice. Here again the seams of access and ability appear to be a stumbling block for equity in the use of mobile services.

In Jonathan Donner and Cecile Bezuidenhoudt's chapter, cultural assumptions around mobile media use are put into question, especially in light of its strongly Anglophonic/ Eurocentric models for online participation.[24] Expanding upon Rich Ling and Heather Horst's critique of Anglophonic readings of media usage through their *New Media & Society* (2011) special issue on mobile phones in the Global South, Donner and Bezuidenhoudt draw on fieldwork in Kenya, Ghana and Tanzania. They argue that mobile media methods need to offer not only no implicit/default privilege to the PC but also clear conceptual separation between devices, channels, venues and uses.

Taken together, when these chapters embrace the lens of seamlessness and mobile phone saturation throughout the world, the notion of the "digital divide" is in fact reimagined in that no longer is there a total separation between users and nonusers. Understanding the impact of limited access and whether or not users embrace certain forms of mobile media reveals the often-unpredictable nature of the emergence of seams in communication and overall use.

## SEAMS OF INTIMACY, IDENTITY AND CONNECTION

The ubiquitous nature of mobile media and its fantasy of seamlessness often means that users imagine their mobile devices to be an extension of themselves.[25] People spend time, money and energy in personalizing their devices. Their collection of apps and the ways in which they use their mobile phone is a reflection of how they choose to define themselves.[26] The mobile phone most often is used to maintain ties between close friends and relatives. The nature and use of the phone can project to others how familiar you are with them, and the demand for reciprocity as it relates to the use of the mobile phone indicates that the device is now crucial not only in communicating logistics and information but also in communicating closeness, intimacy and primacy of relationship.[27] The seams of mobile communication are revealed here in the negotiation between those with whom the user is face-to-face in one's physical environment and those whom they are accessing via their mobile device, platform and/or virtual environment. Seamlessness is embraced in the ways in which people choose to integrate the technology into the flow of their daily tasks and the ways in which these "real" experiences may be enhanced by the use of mobile media tools.

In the chapter by Ditte Laursen, the mechanics of communication are explored to indicate the differences between traditional landline telephone calls and mobile phone calls. This chapter details how communication among young people seems to be quite seamless via the mobile phone and how there is an expectation on the part of the caller as well as the called that there will be minimal use of formal openings and that constant accessibility is expected. Intimacy is communicated via the maintenance of this high degree of presence and the sense that the conversation between intimates is never truly over and that because the communication device is mobile, one can almost expect to remain "in the mind" of the other.

Meng Di takes us into the world of microblogging via women's use of smartphones in Hong Kong to reveal the intricacies of self-representation via mobile media. She points out the seams of authenticity around such performances of self. Self-discovery and disclosure, the idea of broadcasting an inner dialogue, can be at once liberating and controlled. Mobile media provide an endless source of data around questions that sociologists and social psychologists have studied for years. Mobile devices blur the boundary between what is "onstage" and what is "offstage" behavior. The creation of semivirtual worlds, augmented realities, that are shared online and with known and unknown others, as Meng points out, is rife with charges of cultivating narcissism as everyone becomes a microcelebrity.

There is no better example of the creation of microcelebrity than that which is generated through the popular application Foursquare. As a key example of gamification—that is, the adding of gaming elements to a nongaming context to encourage people to behave in certain ways, locative media games have the ability to render urban spaces into playful places.[28] Raz Schwartz, in his chapter, takes us on a trip through the Foursquare experience and then moves on to challenge the notions of the seamlessness of social interactions in real life and the virtual sphere that such apps promise to generate. Kelli S. Burns, in her chapter, wisely sobers us up by calling into question how seamlessness can lead to violations of privacy and growing privacy concerns. Many of these concerns are generated by the Web platforms themselves that no longer allow for the maintenance of anonymity or of a truly "offline" life.

Together these chapters invite the reader to explore the ways in which users often desire seamlessness as a means of never feeling separated from the familiar people and places in their lives. Smartphones have become an integral part of maintaining social relationships. There are definite growing social expectations around responsiveness and accountability in cultures where mobile media use is ubiquitous. The seams of this form of communication are revealed when users are frustrated by drops in service and lack of responsiveness to messages sent or received. The rich area of the social consequences of such psychological and emotional dependency on mobile media is just beginning to be explored in this section.

## Reading Between the Seams of Expression and Sharing

The design and development of mobile media (phones, apps, platforms) have centered on the tasks of expression, communication and sharing. MobileTV, the development of camera phones and the incorporation of Web browsers and readers into smartphones are moving us toward thinking of mobile media as an all-in-one source for fulfilling all of our information and communication desires when we are away from home or away from other devices that may serve in a similar capacity. The seams of mobile communication are illuminated here when expectations for entertainment, engagement and information are not met. Seamlessness in this area is desired when users are focused on using their smartphones as a means of escape and of pure enjoyment.

Veronika Karnowski and Claudia Riesmeyer explore the more technical and design-oriented aspects of the development of MobileTV in Germany and Austria as a means of discussing what happens behind the scenes when a platform is promoted and when it fails. Oscar Westlund and Jakob Bjur focus their attention on creating an explanatory model for the way that youth do or do not use their mobile device to access news and information. They discover that based on an analysis of use, a variety of types of deployment emerge. Quite often mobile media use among the young could be labeled as either diversionist or connected. Diversionist users use their phones as a means of becoming disconnected from their current context. Diversionists use their phones to do things like listen to music and play games. Connected users use mobile media to broadcast experiences, share photos and use MMS (Multimedia Messaging Service). How these users weave access to the Internet into a seamless web of support for both their need for communication and their need for information and news while sometimes desiring to disconnect is explored in their chapter.

Troels F. Bertel and Gitte Stald also focus on youth and the ways in which they use features on their smartphones. Their chapter paints a rich description of how young people weave the use of their phones into their everyday lives. They focus on some of the more straightforward responses that people give for why they use the device in the ways that they do. The simple answer of "because I can" speaks volumes to how youth feel empowered through their ownership and use of mobile phones. This chapter highlights how the mere size, convenience and accessibility of the device itself makes it a preferable tool when compared with a laptop. This chapter plays with the simple notion that most mobile devices, just by being handheld, can open up a world of roles for mobile phones to play in the lives of youth and adults alike. Mobile phone use is less conspicuous than laptop or tablet use when trying to check e-mail or update one's Facebook page. Through the use of mobile devices, users can move seamlessly between the demands of their current physical context and the demands and desires of their virtually remote worlds. Bertel and Stald also astutely point out that the negotiations do not stop there. In addition to the use of mobile devices, we are also often juggling the presence of other platforms that demand our attention (i.e., tablets, laptops, desktops, etc.), and so the user is often stuck between worlds and platforms; therein lies the challenge of seamlessness.

There is no denying that the dynamics and the demands of the mobile phone are unlike those of PC-based platforms. The mobile phone is personal and portable and is used to maintain the fantasy of a seamless connection with loved ones.[29] Sharing experiences is now easier than ever through the use of a mobile camera and mobile video. Mikko Villi guides us through individuals' experiences of taking and sending pictures via the mobile device. For Villi, these experiences underscore the idea that Castells et al.[30] put forward arguing that connectivity, rather than portability, is the key feature of mobile communication.

The future of mobile media is quite expansive and yet to be defined. As we adjust to the integration of mobile devices into our daily lives and our interaction with others, we adapt to the ruptures and tears in what we used to understand as "experience".[31] Mobile technology has moved us beyond virtual reality and instead allows for us to create hybrids—technology-enhanced versions of our most desired realities and experiences. Our fantasies of seamlessness center on our desire to have tools of mobile communication always at our disposable—fully functional, never losing a signal. The desired state of seamlessness means that we are always connected to known others and to a vast web of relationships and information; that we have created a sense of oneness with the technology and then with each other. There are ways and means of using mobile technology to disconnect from that which is around us, yet even from that perspective we are still acknowledging that we are connected to a vast system of files, music tracks, games and videos all ready and waiting for us to consume. In this phenomenon, one must not forget that the technology itself is an ambiguous medium upon which we project our highest hopes as well as our deepest fears.[32] Our dependency on this technology needs to be continually examined, and we must continue to weigh the costs and benefits of all the promises that these media provide. A focus on the seams can lead to a more user-driven assessment of the limitations and expectations of the use of mobile media. The seams revealed in this volume as well as the expressed desire for seamlessness indicate a desire for true integration of mobile media into everyday life. In this way, these chapters reveal the ways in which mobile media, in its practice, its presence and its politics, has the potential to enhance what we do as well as to provide a medium, portal, context and site to inform existing as well as emerging forms of intimacy, sociality and communication.

## NOTES

1. Gerard Goggin and Larissa Hjorth, eds., *Mobile Technologies: From Telecommunications to Media* (New York: Routledge, 2009); James E. Katz, ed., *Handbook for Mobile Communication Studies* (Cambridge, MA: MIT Press, 2008).
2. Lynne Hamill and Amparo Lasen, eds., *Mobile World: Past, Present and Future* (London: Springer, 2005).
3. James E. Katz, ed., *Machines That Become Us: The Social Context Of Personal Communication Technology* (New Brunswick, NJ: Transaction, 2003).
4. Erving Goffman, *Behavior in Public Places* (New York: Free Press, 1963), 22.
5. Larissa Hjorth, "Locating Mobility: Practices of Co-Presence and the Persistence of the Postal Metaphor in SMS/MMS Mobile Phone Customization in Melbourne", *Fibreculture Journal* 6 (2005), accessed January 23, 2011, http://journal.fibreculture.org/issue6/issue6_hjorth.html; Larissa Hjorth, "Mobile Specters of Intimacy: A Case Study of Women and Mobile Intimacy", in *The Mobile Communication Research Series: Volume II, Mobile Communication: Bringing Us Together or Tearing Us Apart?*, ed. R. Ling and S. Campbell (Edison, NJ: Transaction Books, 2011), 37–60; Noah Arceneaux and Anandam Kavoori, eds., *The Mobile Media Reader* (New York: Peter Lang, 2012).
6. Sherry Turkle, *Alone Together: Why We Expect More from Technology and Less from Each Other* (New York: Basic Books, 2011).
7. Larissa Hjorth, *Mobile Media in the Asia-Pacific: Gender and the Art of Being Mobile* (New York: Routledge, 2009).
8. A.R Stone, *The War of Desire and Technology at the Close of the Mechanical Age* (Cambridge, MA: MIT Press, 1995); Sherry Turkle, *Life on the Screen: Identity in the Age of the Internet* (New York: Simon & Schuster, 1995).

9. Mizuko Ito, "Mobiles and the Appropriation of Place", *Receiver* 8 (2002); Hjorth, "Locating Mobility"

10. Peter Glotz, Stefan Bertschi and Chris Locke, eds., *Thumb Culture: The Meaning of Mobile Phones for Society* (New Brunswick, NJ: Transaction, 2005).

11. Milne, E. *Letters, Postcards, Email: Technologies of Presence* (London: Routledge, 2010), 165.

12. Giuseppe Mantovani and Giuseppe Riva, " 'Real' Presence: How Different Ontologies Generate Different Criteria for Presence, Telepresence and Virtual Presence", *Presence: Teleoperators and Virtual Environments* 1, no. 1 (1998): 540–550.

13. Christian Licoppe, " 'Connected' Presence: The Emergence of a New Repertoire for Managing Social Relationships in a Changing Communication Technoscape", *Environment and Planning Design: Society and Space* 22, no. 1 (2004): 135–156.

14. Licoppe, " 'Connected' Presence", 135.

15. Leopoldina Fortunati, James E. Katz and Raimonda Riccini, eds., *Mediating the Human Body: Technology, Communication, and Fashion* (Mahwah, NJ: Lawrence Erlbaum, 2003).

16. Barry Brown, Nicola Green and Richard Harper, eds., *Wireless World: Social and Interactional Aspects of the Mobile Age* (New York: Springer-Verlag, 2001).

17. Rich Ling and P. E Pedersen, eds., *Mobile Communications: Re-Negotiation of the Social Sphere* (London: Springer, 2005).

18. Larissa Hjorth and Kay Gu, "Placing, Emplacing and Embodied Visualities: A Case Study of Smartphone Visuality and Location-Based Social Media in Shanghai, China", *Continuum* 26, no. 5 (2012): 699–713.

19. Kystof Nyíri, ed., *A Sense Of Place: The Global and The Local in Mobile Communication* (Vienna: Passagen Verlag, 2005).

20. Manuel Castells, Mireia Fernández-Ardèvol, Jack Linchuan Qiu and A. Sey, *Mobile Communication and Society: A Global Perspective* (Cambridge, MA: MIT Press, 2007).

21. Kathleen M. Cumiskey, "Mobile Symbiosis: A Precursor to Public Risk-Taking Behavior?" in *The Mobile Communication Research Series: Volume II, Mobile Communication: Bringing Us Together or Tearing Us Apart?*, ed. R. Ling and S. Campbell (Edison, NJ: Transaction Books, 2011),17–36; Richard Harper, L. Palen and Alex Taylor, eds. *The Inside Text: Social, Cultural and Design Perspectives on SMS* (Dordrecht: Springer, 2005).

22. Rich Ling and Heather Horst, "Editorial", *New Media & Society*, October 2011.

23. Kathleen M. Cumiskey, " 'Simply Leaving My House Would Be Even Scarier': How Mobile Phones Affect Women's Perception of Safety and Experiences in Public Places", *Media Asia* 37, no. 4 (2011): 205–214.

24. Mark McLelland and Gerard Goggin, eds., *Internationalizing Internet Studies* (London: Routledge, 2009); Goggin and Hjorth, *Mobile Technologies*.

25. L. Srivastava, "Mobile Phones and the Evolution of Social Behaviour", *Behaviour and Information Technology* 24, no. 2 (2005): 111–129.

26. Fortunati, et. al., *Mediating The Human Body*; Ito, "Mobiles and the Appropriation of Place".

27. Ilkka Arminen and Alexandra Weilenmann, "Mobile Presence and Intimacy: Reshaping Social Actions in Mobile Contextual Configuration", *Journal of Pragmatics* 41, no. 10 (2009): 1905–1923; Katz, *Machines That Become Us*.

28. Adriana de Souza e Silva and Larissa Hjorth, "Urban Spaces as Playful Spaces: A Historical Approach to Mobile Urban Games", *Simulation and Gaming* 40, no. 5 (2009): 602–625.

29. Mizuko Ito, Misa Matsuda and Daisuke Okabe, *Personal, Portable and Pedestrian: Mobile Phones in Japanese Life* (Cambridge, Massachusetts: MIT Press, 2005).
30. Castells et al., *Mobile Communication and Society.*
31. L. Barkhuus and V. E Polichar, "Empowerment Through Seamfulness: Smartphones in Everyday Life", *Personal and Ubiquitous Computing* 15 (2011): 629–639; Goggin and Hjorth, *Mobile Technologies.*
32. Kathleen M. Cumiskey, "Mobile Fantasies on Film: Gathering Metaphoric Evidence of Mobile Symbiosis and the Mobile Imaginary", *Psychnology Journal 5*, no. 1, 2007: 83–99.

# Section I

# The Digital Divide Reimagined

## Seams of Adherence, Access and Equality

# 2 Conceptualizing Social Media and Mobile Technologies in Risk and Crisis Communication Practices

*Michael J. Palenchar and Karen Freberg*

## INTRODUCTION

The evolution of the mobile device has taken center stage in the communication technology realm, shaping the network communications framework and the ways people connect. Professional predictions point to the remarkable power of the handheld device in the future. For example, a Morgan Stanley analyst suggested that the world is currently in the midst of the fifth major technology cycle of the past half-century, predicting that within the next five years more users will connect to the Internet over their mobile devices than via desktop personal computers.[1]

At the same time, however, research shows that many organizations are struggling to define the best practices for using social media and mobile communication devices during a risk or crisis event.[2] So the question is, how can risk and crisis managers make the most effective use of new mobile communication technologies in response to the latest types of risk facing individuals, organizations, communities and governments?

Crises are by their very nature chaotic, filled with uncertainty, dread and outrage, and thus a great opportunity for rumors, misinformation and misperceptions to spread. Digital handheld devices provide a number of advantages to professionals in a disaster or crisis situation, including the ability to maintain continuous communication and to better manage the flow of information.[3] Along with these advantages, however, come new classes of risk that must be anticipated and managed.

New technologies allow the entire online community to obtain information that can potentially create more problems for those tasked with managing a crisis. For example, professionals using mobile devices in a crisis situation must be prepared with adequate training; otherwise they might inadvertently consume the entire available bandwidth or cause a complete network crash.[4] In another example, officials might experience *sousveillance*, in which bystanders use their phones to record video or take photos of emergency personnel who are not acting professionally.[5] Under the stress of a crisis, the immediacy of digital communication might result in false information being communicated to stakeholders.[6] In addition, stakeholders can use digital technologies to create and disseminate their own influence, decentralizing the dissemination of information and reducing official control. While technology plays an important role in managing communication with all stakeholders, those stakeholders now have access to more voices.

With this in mind, the purpose of this research project is to examine existing analyses through an exhaustive literature review and industry document review of social media and the use of digital handheld mobile devices in risk and crisis situations as these practices become more ubiquitous. Two specific issues will be examined regarding social media and digital handheld communication devices: (1) the use of mobile communication devices for transmitting hazard and risk warnings to members of the public who principally rely on these devices for news and communication; and (2) the implications of mobile technologies on public risk and crisis perceptions from the perspective of risk and crisis communicators.

Potential issues and implications, such as control, security, right to know, constant change, speed, training, intentionality, transparency, interoperability, information push, privacy, self-efficacy, leveraging stakeholders' communication, policies and guidelines, trust and authenticity, and information overload facing emergency management and risk communication professionals are identified and discussed throughout the chapter. Potential issues and implications facing emergency management and risk communication professionals are also identified, including: (1) the intersection of social media, mobile technologies, and risk and crisis communication; (2) the increasing use of mobile communication devices during crises; (3) significant opportunities provided by mobile devices in risk and crisis events; and (4) significant challenges raised by the use of mobile devices in risk and crisis events.

## OVERVIEW OF MOBILE DEVICES

The mobile device has transformed over the years from simply a mobile telephone to a sophisticated communication and information technology that includes many computing functions similar to powerful personal computers. In addition, mobile devices have the capability to manage location-based applications and systems (GPS). Use of the devices continues to grow at a very rapid pace. According to the United Nations Foundation Report on Technology and Emergency Management,[7] the number of individuals using mobile phones in 2010 had increased to four billion, or 61 out of every 100 people worldwide.

Mobile phones offer a number of pathways for effective communication. Traditional one-to-one verbal communication has been augmented with other variations. In one-to-many communication, a sender can broadcast information directly to a large segment of the population or to a large stakeholder group. The information can be disseminated in various forms, including visual information (photos and videos) and textual information (short messaging services [SMS] and short press releases). In many-to-many communication, the mobile device is used to connect groups of people using mobile Internet capabilities and social networking sites, including Facebook, Twitter, Google+, Instagram and Pinterest.

Foursquare and other location-based applications like the now defunct, Gowalla, are particularly well suited to the mobile device because they combine location-based features such as geographical information with social networking capabilities. The implications of such location applications can be both concerning, from a potential risk perspective, as well as incredibly useful for people to find out about each other if their location becomes part of a risk or crisis event.

The use of mobile devices, especially smartphones, has increased recently, and this is evident in recent reports. As of the fourth quarter 2011, 46% of U.S. mobile consumers had smartphones, and that figure is growing quickly.[8] Mobile devices support traditional connectivity while expanding the influence of the individual among larger communities. Mobile devices not only enhance the communication individuals have with their personal contacts, but the technology also forges connections with an entire online virtual community.[9] Users not only receive information through the devices, but they can also use the technology to create their own content or forward content to others. By doing so, users contribute directly to the media by providing eyewitness perspectives through video, photos, or texted accounts of an event, often bypassing the professional reporters on the scene and providing unfiltered views of what is happening in the world.[10]

## INTERSECTION OF SOCIAL MEDIA, MOBILE TECHNOLOGIES, AND RISK AND CRISIS COMMUNICATION

While a thorough review of risk and crisis communication literature is not the purpose of this chapter (for more details, see the *Handbook of Risk and Crisis Communication*, 2009), the explosive growth in risk and crisis communication literature since September 11, 2001, as well as the demand for research into social media and mobile technologies, has led to an ideal environment for these fields to integrate.

The Environmental Protection Agency established risk communication as a means to facilitate open, responsible, informed, and reasonable scientific and value-laden discussion of risks associated with personal health and safety practices involved in living and working in close proximity to harmful businesses and toxic substances.[11] A more progressive view of risk communication looks at the infrastructural approach to risk communication created within a dialogic community environment. "Risk communication provides the opportunity to understand and appreciate stakeholders' concerns related to risks generated by organizations, engage in dialogue to address differences and concerns, carry out appropriate actions that can reduce perceived risks, and create a climate of participatory and effective discourse".[12] Tied closely to the concept of risk, Lerbinger defined a crisis as "an event that brings, or has the potential for bringing, an organization into disrepute and imperils its future profitability, growth, and possibly, its very survival".[13]

In his review of the history of risk communication practice and study, Leiss identified the current era of risk communication that features social relations[14] and that integrates well with social media and mobile media platforms. Risk communication based on a shared, social relations, community infrastructural approach works to achieve a level of discourse that can treat the content issues of the risk—technical assessment—and the quality of the relationships along with the political dynamics of the participants.[15] This and other more recent approaches to risk and crisis communication highlight the importance of a dialogic, relationship-building approach to dealing with the concerns and perceptions of community residents and employees, often through new and mobile communication technologies.

The new form of risk and crisis communication, however, is often impeded by the lack of institutions that are responsive to the needs, interests, and level of understanding of the publics affected by the potential or ostensible risk and the new ways in which they communicate and create communities of risk bearers and risk advocates. People often encounter a maze of agencies, do not know where to acquire information, and suffer data dumps that provide huge amounts of information in ways that make it difficult to interpret. Those institutional barriers often include a lack of utilization of new media technologies.[16]

Overall, social media characteristics are about openness, conversation and dialogue, relationship development, multiple voices and getting the message to stakeholders. One recent example demonstrates the possible role of social media and mobile technologies during a risk or crisis event. Alerts about and details concerning the rare 2011 U.S. 5.8-magnitude Virginia–east coast earthquake that shook Washington, D.C., and surrounding areas was reported on Twitter before it was announced via mainstream media. Twitter topped out at 5,500 hits per second—more than were generated by the Japanese tsunami and earthquake crisis or Osama bin Laden's death.[17] "Tweets began pouring in from D.C. nearly 30 seconds before we felt the quake at our headquarters in New York City and well before any reports about the quake emerged from the media".[18]

Within social media during risk and crisis events, there is an incredible opportunity to use digital handheld communication devices for transmitting hazard and risk warnings to the public. Though in the past these devices have been principally designed for news and communication, they are more and more being used for information sharing, real-time coverage of events, dissemination of information to family and friends about a crisis, location and safety updates of family members and other loved ones, directions away from certain natural or man-made disasters, and other communication facets that relate to crisis and risk communication. For example, residents of Sutton, California,who experienced the 2007 Southern California wildfires, sought information using mobile phones to contact friends and family, including the use of information portals and websites advertised in traditional media, individual blogs, Web forums, photo-sharing sites such as Flickr and Instagram, and microblogs such as Twitter. Residents also used mobile technology devices to fill in the information dearth and get more detail that wasn't available in traditional media.[19]

A 2010 American Red Cross online survey of the U.S. population over age 18 showed that about half of respondents would sign up for emails, text alerts, or applications to receive emergency communication, including the location of food and water (53%), evacuation routes (52%), shelter locations (50%), road closures (50%), location of medical services (50%) and how to keep yourself safe during an emergency (48%). About half of those who use social media also said they would post emergency information on their sites. More than half would send a text message to a responsible agency if someone they knew needed help. Also, during an emergency nearly half would use social media to let loved ones know they are safe.

However, the challenge is in social media's use and application, taking into considerations technical challenges and security concerns, as well as access.[20] Yet some of the early work in this area shows promise for social media and mobile devices to play a constructive role in risk and crisis communication. Palen, who, along with a group of researchers at the University of Colorado and Colorado State University who study social media and crisis from a multidisciplinary platform, has argued that "Investigation of recent disasters reveals use of online social media as an emergent, significant, and often accurate form of public participation and backchannel communication".[21]

## INCREASING USE OF MOBILE COMMUNICATION DEVICES DURING DISASTERS

Disaster or crisis situations are "non-routine events that result in a host of non-routine behaviours and new social arrangements. Modern disaster and crisis situations reveal such innovative behaviour extending to online settings".[22] Both domestically and internationally, mobile devices have become more affordable and integrated into various cultures and societies, changing the ways people communicate with each other in a disaster situation.

Mobile devices play an increasingly important role in emergency situations by providing users with three capabilities: to be reachable anywhere and at any time, to obtain information while in an outreach situation; and to be visible and traceable through a device enabled with GPS capabilities.[23] Mobile devices are helpful in disaster situations because they are "more readily available than battery-operated radios, as an increasing number of residents carry them everywhere. Further, they can serve as both input and output devices, facilitating one-to-one, many-to-one, and many-to-many communication".[24]

An analysis of crisis situations occurring over the last decade helps to illustrate the opportunities and challenges of using mobile devices in a crisis. In this section, we review a number of case studies that have focused on the role of new technologies in disaster and crisis situations, including the Southeast Asia Tsunami catastrophe in 2004, the 2005 London bombings, U.S. university shootings during the 2000s, Mumbai terrorist attacks of 2008, and the Haiti earthquake of 2010.

On December 26, 2004, an earthquake hit the Indian Ocean, creating a tsunami that caused an extensive amount of damage and devastation in the region. The main areas impacted included Indonesia, Malaysia, Sri Lanka, India and Thailand. The total amount of destruction left more than 250,000 people dead, millions homeless, and damage to the region of approximately $7 billion.[25] Photo-sharing capabilities and features were used to document events and to provide dramatic visual eyewitness accounts, including a poignant and frightening video of an incoming wave taken from the abandoned camera of one of the victims.[26] After this traumatic event, the governments of Sri Lanka and other countries in the region established their own Disaster Management Center to monitor potential natural disasters and create short messages to be delivered to their respective populations for updates on disasters. This disaster also saw the initiation of the use of mobile technologies to solicit and receive donations for relief efforts.[27]

Mobile devices played key communication roles during the 2005 terrorist attacks in the London subways.[28] Gordon argued that in spite of some challenges, mobile devices were useful tools for coordinating the dissemination of information during this event to affected populations.[29] In this particular case, the initial use of mobile devices was to communicate verbal information in the form of text (SMS), followed by visual information. Mobile devices soon forwarded pictures of the impact of the bombings on train stations to the London community, the media, and to the rest of the world.[30]

Shootings occurring on university campuses, including Virginia Tech and Northern Illinois University, provided further insight into the impact of mobile media use on disasters. People were beginning to use mobile media more extensively to communicate with others and give real-time accounts on what was going on during these traumatic events. Palen and Vieweg analyzed online communication that was occurring during the Virginia Tech and Northern Illinois University (NIU) shootings and found that people were using virtual communities (such as social networking sites) to interact with others, seek information regarding the crisis, share experiences, form online relationships with others, and build community and awareness of the tragic events.[31] In the aftermath of these shootings, many colleges and universities instituted mobile telephone services used to communicate safety alerts to students, faculty and staff. As a result of the Virginia Tech shootings, many state and local governments are now creating their own social networking sites. For example, in February 2008 the Virginia Department of Emergency Management launched a YouTube channel to reach state residents with emergency-related information and public service announcements. The site was developed in partnership with Google.

Mobile phones also played a significant role in the Mumbai terrorist attacks in 2008, by raising awareness through eyewitness accounts. On November 27, 2008, a series of coordinated terrorist attacks across the city of Mumbai hit several hotels, a café, a train station, and a Jewish center, resulting in the deaths of 195 people.[32] What was unique in this particular case was the fact that the traditional news media were obtaining most of their information from sources on the ground in Mumbai. Citizen journalists were reporting events during the sixty-hour terrorist ordeal using tweets, Flickr pictures and videos posted on YouTube from their mobile devices for the world to see.[33]

Most recently, the Haiti earthquake disaster of 2010 provided further insight into the power of communication via mobile devices during an emergency. On January 12, 2010, a 7.0 magnitude earthquake hit Haiti, leaving millions of people without food, water and shelter. The country's communications systems were impacted to the point where residents were almost completely isolated from the rest of the world.[34] Following the earthquake, mobile devices were used to allow people from all over the world to donate to relief efforts using text messages, or SMS. This type of fund-raising effort, first seen following the 2004 tsunami disaster in Southeast Asia, increases the awareness of the power of nonprofit organizations as a communication channel in a disaster situation.

The Haiti earthquake disaster highlighted a more mature use of SMS text messages to communicate first response aid to individuals needing immediate medical attention, or who were trapped under buildings and other fallen structures. Mobile phones were used to communicate first aid information and to provide information about where to go for shelter, food, water and other health assistance.[35] Examples of some of the messages that were being sent via these mobile devices included information for medical care ("Hospital Sacre-Coeur in Milot says it has capacity for patients and asks people to make their own way there"), search and rescue ("Though the government says the search and rescue phase is over, SAR teams are still available. If you know someone is trapped call + 870 764 130 944, email haiti.opc@gmail.com or contact MINUSTAH"), and general advisories on other issues of relevance [36]. The growing prevalence of mobile phone ownership and use, even in very poor countries like Haiti, makes rescue efforts possible that would have been unthinkable ten years ago.

Thelwall and Stuart examined three crises (the London attacks, Hurricane Katrina and the Pakistan-Kashmir earthquake) and demonstrated that bloggers used Web 2.0 resources such as Wikinews, Wikipedia and Flickr (a picture-sharing site) for information, though these still played a minor role in comparison with mass media. All the newest technologies whose use was mentioned were Web 2.0. "The precise mix of technologies seems to depend on the nature of the crisis".[37] Last, the American Red Cross has started using Twitter to exchange real-time data about local disasters with those affected, and the U.S. Geological Survey operates a site called Did You Feel It? where people can report local earthquake activity. These case studies show a linear progression in the use of mobile technologies by both crisis managers and victims to obtain and share information. While these events have helped transform how disaster responders use mobile technology, progress towars maximizing the benefits of the technology has been somewhat slower than expected.[38]

## OPPORTUNITIES PROVIDED BY MOBILE
## DEVICES IN DISASTER SITUATIONS

Mobile devices provide many opportunities for more effective communication in disaster situations. With their immediacy, nearly universal prevalence, and relative immunity from the failure of other types of infrastructure in an emergency, mobile technologies allow rapid and proactive disaster relief responses. Professionals operating in disasters have greatly improved remote access to information, along with the ability to communicate with their home base or others onsite.

People have been very adaptive in using new forms of technologies, including mobile devices. New mobile forms of technology "provide a broad, multi-faceted and interactive connection with the outside world. In fact, the very promise of being informed and connected seems to motivate high rates of communication technology adoption and appropriation in times of disaster".[39] In this way the mobile device (smartphone or tablet) might be the most personalized mobile communication and information tool available in crisis communications. Risk bearers are able to determine what information they want to see and what applications they want to download and use professionally, and they have the ability to create, curate and disseminate user-generated content one-to-one or one-to-many.

The combination of mobile communication devices and access to the online community through the Internet allows emergency managers and risk communication professionals a gateway to handle a disaster more effectively. Emergency center operators, police, military and medical personnel have learned to actively use new forms of technology to communicate in a disaster or crisis situation.[40] The ability of a single responder to disseminate information to large groups of people reduces the workload on emergency staff. Compare the information sent in text message form to Haiti mobile devices to previous methods, such as laboriously going door to door.

Mobile communication channels also serve as a valuable resource for the community, providing information, contributing to a sense of normal life, and supplying ways to pass the time until the situation returns to normal.[41] In a disaster situation, people experience uncertainty and anxiety in addition to the challenges resulting from the particular disaster. Mobile devices help to reduce fear and anxiety by allowing people the means to obtain the information they need.[42] Mobile devices have empowered people with the opportunity to establish connections with others during a disaster situation, while obtaining access to the information and knowledge they need in order to act themselves. Stakeholders can collaborate and assist each other, enhancing their personal sense of control and further reducing the load on official emergency responders.

The use of mobile technology has the potential to facilitate reciprocal communication between responders and large groups of people impacted by a disaster or crisis. "The combination of mobile telecommunications devices and the Internet, however, has the potential to provide higher capacity and more effective service, as well as create interactive communication mechanisms that can facilitate just-in-time communication and collaboration among large numbers of residents and responders".[43]

Social mobile media has not only provided an increased access to emergency response information, but has also increased the ability of risk bearers to disseminate such information. Social media aids people in weighing conflicts of interest in risk and crisis communication and building networks among affinity groups related to a crisis; it gives them the ability to witness debates and to participate in chat rooms and other social media outlets. One example is Twitter adoption and use during emergency events. A study conducted by Hughes and Palen suggests that Twitter messages sent during mass crisis events contain even more information broadcasting and brokerage than typical microblog messages, and that Twitter is evolving toward having a more information-sharing purpose.[44] Early evidence from their research also showed that Twitter users who joined during an emergency for information-sharing purposes are more likely to become long-term adopters of the technology, which could be beneficial to long-term risk communication campaigns.

## SIGNIFICANT CHALLENGES RAISED BY THE USE OF MOBILE DEVICES IN DISASTERS

In spite of the many advantages provided by mobile devices in an emergency, the history of responses to disasters in the era of new technologies demonstrates that this is a rapidly changing landscape requiring constant analysis and proactive planning. Recognizing the challenges to planners, responders and victims posed by the use of mobile media during a crisis will allow crisis managers to anticipate problems and maximize performance.

Although personal use of mobile media is quite common, leading to relatively high levels of competence, emergency planners should not assume that all personnel have the knowledge and training to use the technology appropriately during a disaster situation. According to a Communications

Capabilities survey, the majority of emergency management respondents (73%) said that their best means of communication with one another is one-to-one.[45] All personnel on the disaster scene (e.g., team leaders, dispatchers) should be equally skilled in the use of technology, making the users of the devices interchangeable in the field.[46] Training should also minimize the likelihood that unskilled users will consume the available bandwidth, which might be stretched very thin during an emergency.

Organizations need to provide training as well. Cloudman and Hallahan examined public relations practitioners' training in crisis communication and found a lack of emphasis on overall training. Most crisis and risk communication training focused on briefings and spokesperson training, but did not take advantage of training in other techniques or technologies.[47] They argued for an increase in training, since users are commonly one of the weakest links in an information system.

Inadequate equipment will hinder efforts to use mobile technologies during an emergency. The Communications Capabilities survey found that 58% of emergency managers did not have cameras on their mobile devices, and fewer than 30% of the emergency managers surveyed could see the location of others on their dispatch screen.[48] A sound infrastructure for mobile devices supports all new features, allowing for the exchange of photos, videos and data among responders on the disaster scene, as well as with others in relevant organizations.[49] A critical aspect of a sound mobile infrastructure is the need to make security a top priority.

Emergency management professionals appear to be lagging behind in the implementation of mobile media in their communication plans.[50] Although mobile technologies are improving rapidly and access to mobile devices is common, risk communication professionals and emergency managers need to remember that not everyone in the population will have access to one of these devices. Alternate means for reaching these individuals must be included in any crisis plan.

Mobile communication not only allows agencies to disseminate messages about a disaster, but it also allows stakeholders to communicate with each other while bypassing the information gatekeepers in agencies and traditional media. Today's stakeholder groups expect to be informed rather than controlled or commanded. The reduced official control of information due to mobile media raises the likelihood that stakeholders might receive false information regarding a situation.[51] Digital information sent via mobile devices can spread virally in a matter of seconds, and receiving rumors or false information during a disaster can be catastrophic for all of those involved. Responders should also be aware that any mistakes or inappropriate behaviors would be communicated widely and instantaneously to the world audience. Also, news stories can spread incredibly fast and negative online comments can fan the flames, causing erroneous reputational damage.[52] Ultimately, used thoughtfully, mobile devices can improve the communication efforts in a disaster situation greatly.

## DISCUSSION

The primary issue facing emergency managers is a gap between expectations for the performance of new mobile technologies in a disaster and the needs and expectations of those impacted by the disaster. There are certainly challenges that need to be taken into consideration based on previous disasters and acts of terrorism.

Taking full advantage of the opportunities provided by mobile devices while avoiding the potential pitfalls associated with these technologies requires careful, thoughtful analysis long before any disaster emerges. Emergency managers should monitor potential issues while establishing crises communication plans that reside on both static and mobile devices. As issues are identified, research conducted on potential audiences should identify their trusted sources of information. Emergency managers and responders need to be proactive instead of reactive to take full advantage of the immediacy provided by mobile media.

The disaster communications and risk communications action plan should include policies specific to the use of mobile devices. A thorough risk assessment needs to be implemented to determine the challenges and opportunities of using mobile devices in specific disaster situations and the appropriate action steps that need to be taken to address any identified risks. All employees should have thorough education on these devices. It is crucial that everyone involved understands the nature of these devices, how they are used, and expected behavior by individuals using these devices in a disaster situation. Policies and measures for securing these devices should be in place. Potential issues arising in this area could be the loss of the device or a security breach on the communication channel by a third party.

Information supplied by emergency managers and first responders should be consistent, providing individuals with the information that they need to reduce uncertainty and receive necessary help while managing information overload. Emergency managers need to build a mobile communications and online community where stakeholders can engage with others and obtain contact information for media outlets and other crisis communication representatives. Empowering stakeholders in a crisis situation can work to everyone's advantage.

While this is true, the proliferation of cellular phone technology, especially data transmission via cell phones and other portable devices, puts an added stress on that system. While we need to keep wireless systems operational for emergency services, risk communicators need to use wireless systems to quickly share information with community residents, media, key stakeholders and emergency responders.

There are other concerns with the use of handheld digital devices as a fundamental communication infrastructure in risk and crisis situations. Traynor's research about the technical capabilities of emergency text messages as part of emergency alert systems (EAS) brings up issues with adopting

technology without thinking about such risks.[53] As university and other organizations have subscribed to more and more of these text messaging EAS
systems, there are problems with technology, speed of information, systems
overloads and blocking the delivery of critical information between emergency responders or the public and 911 services. "Such 'always on' connectivity may one day create new opportunities for the dissemination of critical
information during an emergency. However, as demonstrated in this study,
modern cellular networks are simply not capable of providing such a service, whether through voice calls or text messages".[54]

Mobile devices implemented in emergency communications plans will
allow a more even distribution and coordinated effort that will be beneficial
for all parties involved in the disaster situation. Emergency managers can be
actively communicating via text message or can post other information (e.g.,
videos, photos, etc.) to establish credibility and authority as a primary source
of information in a disaster situation for impacted communities. Connecting
online and using these mobile devices effectively will establish a stronger virtual community that will be more informed and engaged in the disaster recov-
ery and implementation process. Technology is not always the answer, but the
combination of sound online emergency management and communication
practices integrated with the new technology is the ultimate communication
goal for the next decade. What is scary for many organizations and risk and
crisis communicators is that mobile media speeds up communication, speeds
up awareness, and often speeds up awareness of mistakes—the real question
is whether it speeds up response and appropriate behavior.

## CONCLUSION

As people move toward a more fully integrated use of mobile devices as computer platforms to satisfy their needs while experiencing or managing a risk
or crisis event, digital mobile communication devices should immediately be
integrated into risk and crisis communication plans. Digital handheld communication devices should be used as an additional communication tool,
and not a replacement of traditional media and crisis communication tools,
for transmitting hazard and risk warnings to members of the public who
principally rely on these devices for news and communication, engaging in
dialogue to address risk and crisis perceptions, as well as for communicating
with traditional and new media communication outlets.

However, while there is strong anecdotal evidence that suggests that mobile technologies, and in particular social media communication via mobile
communication devices, can provide numerous opportunities to better manage risk and crisis communication during an event, there is, unfortunately,
little empirical research to support this contention. In addition to the limited empirical research, since new media technology is rapidly advancing,
it is difficult for any organization to develop a policy that can catch up with,

let alone keep pace with, the uncertainty and ever-expanding use of social media platforms for risk and crisis communication. At a macro level, the integration of mobile devices and computer platforms is dramatically changing what it means to be online or offline during a crisis, with tremendous social consequences related to health, safety and the environment for those who bear and suffer risk and crisis events, as well as for those who manage such events.

## NOTES

1. Mathew Ingram, "Mary Meeker: Mobile Internet Will Soon Overtake Fixed Internet", *Gigaom*, April 12, 2010, accessed October 24, 2012, http://gigaom.com/2010/04/12/mary-meeker-mobile-internet-will-soon-overtake-fixed-internet.
2. Shari Veil, Tara Buehner and Michael J. Palenchar, "A Work-in-Process Literature Review: Incorporating Social Media in Risk and Crisis Communication", *Journal of Contingencies and Crisis Management* 19, no. 2 (2011): 110–122.
3. W. David Stephenson and Eric Bonabeau, "Expecting the Unexpected: The Need for a Networked Terrorism and Disaster Response Strategy", *Homeland Security Affairs* 3, no. 1 (2007): 1–9.
4. Ibid.
5. Ibid.
6. Sarah Vieweg et al., "Collective Intelligence in Disaster: Examination of the Phenomenon in the Aftermath of the 2007 Virginia Tech Shooting", in *Proceedings of the 2008 Information Systems for Crisis Response and Management Conference*, ed. Frank Fiedrich and Bartel Van de Walle (Washington, DC: ISCRAM, 2008), 44–54.
7. Diane Coyle and Patrick Meier, "New Technologies in Emergencies and Conflict Reports", *United Nations Foundation*, March 1, 2010, accessed October 24, 2012, http://www.unfoundation.org/who-we-are/impact/our-impact/health-data-disaster-relief/communications.
8. "More US Consumers Choosing Smartphones as Apple Closes the Gap on Android", *Nielsenwire*, January 18, 2012, accessed October 24, 2012, http://blog.nielsen.com/nielsenwire/consumer/more-us-consumers-choosing-smart-phones-as-apple-closes-the-gap-on-android.
9. Leysia Palen, "Mobile Telephony in a Connected Life", *Communications of the ACM* 45, no. 3 (2002): 78–82.
10. Janey Gordon, "The Mobile Phone and the Public Sphere: Mobile Phone Usage in Three Critical Situations", *Convergence* 13, no. 3 (2007): 307–319.
11. National Resource Council, *Improving Risk Communication* (Washington, DC: National Academy Press, 1989).
12. Michael J. Palenchar, "Risk Communication", in *Encyclopedia of Public Relations*, ed. Robert. L. Heath (Thousand Oak, CA: Sage, 2005), 752–755.
13. Otto Lerbinger, *The Crisis Manager: Facing Risk and Responsibility* (Mahwah, NJ: Erlbaum, 1997).
14. William Leiss, "Three Phases in the Evolution of Risk Communication Practice", *Annals of the American Academy of Political and Social Science* 545 (1996): 85–94.
15. Ibid.
16. Susan Hadden, "Institutional Barriers to Risk Communication", *Risk Analysis* 9, no. 3 (1989): 301–308.
17. Blance Bosker, "DC Earthquake Dominates Social Media Sites: 5 Must-See Stats, *Huffington Post*, August 23, 2011, accessed October 8, 2012, http://www.

huffingtonpost.com/2011/08/23/dc-earthquake-social-media-stats_n_934796.
html#s337503&title=Twitter.

18. Lauren Indvik, "East Coasters Turn to Twitter During Virginia Earthquake", *Mashable*, August 23, 2011, accessed February 5, 2012, http://mashable.com/2011/08/23/virginia-earthquake.

19. Jeannette Sutton, Leysia Palen and Irina Shklovski, "Backchannels on the front lines: Emergent uses of social media in the 2007 southern California wildfires", in *Proceedings of the 2008 Information Systems for Crisis Response and Management Conference*, ed. Frank Fiedrich and Bartel Van de Walle (Washington, DC: ISCRAM, 2008): 624–632.

20. American Red Cross, "Web Users Increasingly Rely on Social Media to Seek Help in a Disaster", *American Red Cross,* August 9, 2010, accessed January 8, 2011, http://www.redcross.org.

21. Leysia Palen, "Online Social Media in Crisis Events", *Education Quarterly* 3 (2008): 76–78.

22. Leysia Palen and Sarah Vieweg, "The Emergence of Online Widescale Interaction in Unexpected Events: Assistance, Alliance and Retreat, in *Proceedings of the ACM 2008 Conference on Computer Supported Cooperative Work*, Bo Begole and David W. McDonald (Eds.) (San Diego, CA: CSCW, 2008), 117–126.

23. Elizabeth Avery Gomez, Katia Passerini and Karen Hare, "Public Health Crisis Management: Community Level Roles and Communication Options", in *Proceedings of the 3rd International ISCRAM Conference*, ed. Baretel Van de Walle and Murray Turoff (Newark, New Jersey: ISCRAM, 2006), 435–443.

24. Paul T. Jaeger et al., "Community Response Grids: E-Government, Social Networks, and Effective Emergency Management", *Telecommunications Policy* 31, no. 10/11 (2007): 592–604.

25. Coyle and Meier, "New Technologies in Emergencies".

26. Leysia Palen, Sarah Vieweg, Jeannette Sutton, Sophia B. Liu, and Amanda Hughes, op. cit.

27. Coyle and Meier, "New Technologies in Emergencies".

28. Gordon, "The Mobile Phone and the Public Sphere".

29. Ibid.

30. Sophia Liu et al., "In Search of the Bigger Picture: The Emergent Role of On-Line Photo-Sharing in Times of Disaster", in *Proceedings of the Information Systems for Crisis Response and Management Conference*, ed. Frank Fiedrich and Bartel Van de Walle (Washington, DC: ISCRAM, 2008), 140–149.

31. Leysia Palen and Sarah Vieweg, "Online Social Media in Crisis Events", *Education Quarterly* 3 (2008): 76–78.

32. United Nations Foundation, "Communications Saves Lives, Brings Hope After Haiti Earthquake", *News and Media*, n.d., accessed October 24, 2012, http:www.unfoundation.org/who-we-are/impact/our-impact/health-data-disaster-relief/communications.

33. Ibid.

34. Ibid.

35. Ibid.

36. "Information in a crisis: text messages beamed to earthquake survivors in Haiti", *The Guardian,* June 18, 2010, 1–2.

37. Mike Thelwall and David Stuart, "RUOK? Blogging Communication Technologies During Crises", *Journal of Computer-Mediated Communication* 12, no. 4 (2007): 189–214.

38. Judith Woodhall, "The Future of Emergency Response: Need for Technology Enabled Process Transformation" *National Science Foundation Conference: Educational Programs for Emergency Response Technology, March 2007, 1–7*).

39. Irina Shlovski, Leysia Paylen and Jeannette Sutton, "Finding Community Through Information and Communication Technology in Disaster Events", in *Proceedings of the ACM 2008 Conference on Computer Supported Cooperative Work,* Bo Begole and David W. McDonald (Eds.) (San Diego, CA: CSCW), 1–10.
40. Ibid.
41. Ibid.
42. Ibid.
43. Jaeger et al., "Community Response Grids", 593.
44. Sarah Hughes and Leysia Palen, "Twitter Adoption and Use in Mass Convergence and Emergency Events", *International Journal of Emergency Management* 6, no. 3/4 (2009): 248–260.
45. "Communication Capabilities: Survey Executive Summary", *Emergency Management* 1, February 2012, accessed October 23, 2012, http://media. govtech.net/Resource%20Centers/EM%20Sprint%20RC%2010%20Q1/ EM10_EXEC_SUMM_Sprint_Q1_V.pdf 2010.
46. Y. Yuan and B. Detlor, "Intelligent Mobile Crisis Response Systems", *Communications of the ACM* 48, no. 2 (2005): 95–98.
47. Reghan Cloudman and Kirk Hallahan, "Crisis Communication Preparedness Among U.S. Organizations: Activities and Assessments by Public Relations Practitioners", *Public Relations Review* 32 (2006): 367–376.
48. "Communication Capabilities: Survey Executive Summary".
49. Woodhall, "The Future of Emergency Response".
50. Russell Nichols, "Emergency Text Messaging Signals Evolution in Public Safety Communication", *Strategy and Leadership in Critical Times: Emergency Management,* June 7, 2010, accessed October 12, 2012, http://www.emergencymgmt. com/safety/Emergency-Text-Messaging-Public-Safety-Communication.html.
51. Vieweg et al., "Collective Intelligence in Disaster".
52. Julia Aherton, "Frontline Online: Crisis Planning in the Digital Age", *International Public Relations Association,* n.d., accessed October 18, 2012, http:// www.ipra.org/secciones.php?sec=7&fid=232&mes2=10&anio2=2009.
53. Patrick Traynor, "Characterizing the Limitations of Third-Party EAS over Cellular Text Messaging Services", September 2008 (Atlanta: Georgia Institute of Technology).
54. Ibid., 26.

# 3 Is mHealth a Silver Bullet to Improve Maternal and Child Health in Rural Uttar Pradesh, India?

## Results of a Health Information Needs Assessment

*Nandita Kapadia-Kundu, Tara M. Sullivan, Basil Safi, Geetali Trivedi and Sanjanthi Velu*

## INTRODUCTION

In a world where people from all economic strata own and use mobile phones,[1] the opportunity arises to leverage mass access to mobile technology for improving health care and health outcomes. Systematic information needs assessments are important to ensure that mobile health (mHealth) programs are driven by local information needs rather than by the technology available.[2] Often, mHealth approaches focus more on the technical component, phones and software applications and less on the nature of the content required by the user. The effectiveness of mHealth interventions can be substantially increased if information needs can be understood from an emic perspective. This study identified information needs that are locally and culturally relevant to the ASHA (Accredited Social Health Activist), the village-level health worker, and shifts the knowledge management perspective from *access* of information to *usability* of information.

## MATERNAL AND CHILD HEALTH INDICATORS

Of India's population of nearly 1.2 billion people, 69% live in rural areas. One-quarter of these rural people live below the poverty line; literacy levels are low and poor health is common.[3] With 167 million people, Uttar Pradesh (UP) is India's most populous state. UP's maternal mortality ratio (MMR) is 359 per 100,000 live births, compared with India's MMR of 212 and the Millennium Development Goal of an MMR of 109 by 2015.[4]

UP's infant mortality rate (63 deaths per 1,000 live births) and under-five mortality rate (96 per 1,000 live births) are among the highest in India.[5] The state also has one of the highest total fertility rates (TFR) in India, 3.8, compared with India's 2.6, and use of modern family planning methods is low.[6]

UP's maternal health care coverage is also very low, with half as many women receiving three or more antenatal visits as the national average (26% compared with 52%).[7]

## THE ROLE OF THE ASHA

India's health system operates at national, state, district and block levels. At the block level, the medical officer in charge and the health education officer oversee the work of auxiliary nurse-midwives (ANMs) and the ASHA, the village-level health worker. The National Rural Health Mission (NRHM) introduced ASHAs in 2005. The ASHA, which means "hope", is a female health worker with a minimum eighth-grade education. India had more than 800,000 ASHAs as of June 2010, of which approximately 130,000 are in UP.[8] In rural UP, ASHAs work closely with the community and are most people's first line of contact with the health system. People ask ASHAs questions on a broad range of health issues related to any of the national health programs under NRHM. Evidence of effectiveness of community-based workers and their impact on neonatal mortality demonstrates that the ASHA-type worker can play a major role in the reduction of infant mortality.[9]

## MOBILE REVOLUTION IN INDIA

India's mobile phone industry is the fastest growing in the world. Mobile phone penetration expanded from 1% in 1998 to 28% in 2008 and may reach 82% by 2018. As of November 2009 mobile phone subscribers numbered 57 million.[10] Projections indicate that India will have a 'billion plus' mobile users by 2015.[11] Urban penetration in 2009 was already 97%. The 16.6 million new mobile phone customers each month come from India's rural areas.[12] These data suggest a growing opportunity to improve rural health care through mHealth.

The technical sophistication of mobile phones is rapidly improving, and many low-cost phones in India support the Android system, some for less than $100 (USD). Most have Bluetooth capability that enables easy information exchange. Also many mobile handsets support a microSD chip with a two- or four-gigabyte card. This card costs two dollars (USD) and can hold an enormous amount of informational and persuasive content in audio and video formats. Changes in the capabilities of mobile handsets rapidly redefines the way people use mobile phones and the way they communicate.

## POTENTIAL ROLE OF MHEALTH

The mHealth concept includes health-related uses of mobile telecommunication and multimedia technologies for health services and information.[13]

Earlier, the Internet was seen as the best way to rapidly transmit critical health information to resource-poor settings,[14] but now mobile phones provide wider and quicker reach. Studies show that mHealth interventions can improve treatment compliance and disease diagnosis and tracking, increase public awareness of health issues, improve disease management, enhance quality of care and facilitate health systems strengthening.[15]

The widespread availability of mobile phones has led to a situation whereby large numbers of workers in remote areas can have access to need-based informational content. Mobile phones can also bypass Internet and computers through the use of information and data sharing technologies such as Bluetooth and microSD chips. The concept of "seamlessly mobile" is here in more ways than one. Content can be tailored for health workers and updated or changed every month via Bluetooth or the microSD chip. Also, instead of "generalized" Google access to information, data sharing technologies have the potential to provide need-specific, timely access to simplified information.

## PURPOSE OF THIS STUDY

This study looks at the role and needs of the ASHA in UP in relation to the various levels of the health system. The research was designed to assess health information needs, current information flow within the health system, and barriers to and opportunities for accessing and sharing information. Mapping detailed information needs can feed into the design of need-based knowledge management and mHealth applications that can substantially improve reproductive, maternal and child health indicators. The study also assessed the access, use and ownership patterns of mobile phones among ASHAs. The chapter also analyzes the ASHAs' information needs from an "actionability" perspective, using five parameters: language, timeliness, simplicity, amount of information and accessibility.[16] The actionability parameters were applied to ensure focused and useful mHealth interventions for ASHAs.

## METHOD

To enable a comprehensive understanding of health information needs and barriers across all levels of the health care system, the Knowledge for Health project at the Johns Hopkins Bloomberg School of Public Health conducted a needs assessment in Lucknow district. Three of the district's eight community blocks (Mahilabad, Mohanlalganj and Sarojini Nagar) were selected for the study. Some key informant interviews were conducted in New Delhi and in Lucknow, the state capital of UP, to obtain views on information needs at the national and state levels. Data collection consisted of forty-six key informant interviews and nine focus group discussions (FGDs). Study participants included state-level NRHM officials, district and block officials, ANMs, ASHAs, USAID officers, and staff of nongovernmental organizations and other professional organizations (See Table 3.1). The FGDs primarily involved village health workers (e.g., ASHAs, ANMs, Angawadi workers) and community representatives. Key informants at all levels of the system were asked about the ASHAs' information needs.

Prospective participants were informed that they could refuse to participate in the needs assessment or, if they did agree to participate, they could decline to answer specific questions. Verbal consent was obtained from participants after they were assured that all information collected would be kept confidential and that the data set would include no unique identifiers.

Data were collected between September and November 2009. A two-person team, a facilitator and a note-taker, conducted each key informant interview, and a three person team conducted FGDs (note-taker, facilitator and observer). All interviews and FGDs were audio-taped with the participants' consent and later transcribed. A senior member of the research team checked the transcriptions. After translation into English, the transcripts were analyzed with the ATLAS.ti software. A list of 134 codes was developed to reflect the main themes and subthemes.

## RESULTS

### What Is the Interpretation of 'Information'?

Several ASHAs defined the process of receiving and sharing information as "talk". In contrast, policy makers spoke of information as "evidence-based data" or "best practices". For ASHAs information serves two primary purposes: it helps with problem solving in the community, and it informs messages to villagers.

One ASHA explained, "information is about how to give a message and how to read the message". Another described the process of communicating information to villagers about maternal and child health as repetitive. She said people finally focus on the information only when they experience a related situation. Several ASHAs reiterated that how information is delivered is as important as its content; information needs to be shared with compassion

*Table 3.1*  Number and location of key informant interviews

| Level | Number | Location |
|---|---|---|
| National | 6 | New Delhi |
| State | 10 | Lucknow |
| District/block | 11 | Mahilabad, Mohanlalganj, and Sarojini Nagar blocks |
| Village | 9 | Mahilabad, Mohanlalganj, and Sarojini Nagar blocks |
| Network | 10 | Lucknow |
| **Total** | **46** | |

and respect. ASHAs understand that their work at the community level is not merely "provision of information" but also that of persuasion. "They [the women] should be explained properly with love . . . first [we] listen to them, and then we talk about maternal health. They agree in front of us. But later they do as they like", said one ASHA, age 38, with a tenth-grade education.

## UNDERSTANDING ASHAS' WORK

The ASHAs see themselves as responsible for the health of women, children and the community as a whole. Their main information needs, however, relate to maternal and infant health. The block-level officials understand that the ASHA plays an important role in program implementation. "Most of the work is done at lower level, which is below the district level", said a medical officer, age 42, Primary Health Centre (PHC).

Box 3.1 describes an ASHA's daily routine. It includes home visits, assisting the ANM to immunize children and responding to community members' questions, many of which she has no answer for. Many questions relate to local information, for example, the distance to the hospital from the village, how many days of hospitalization are required for a tubectomy, and how to receive Janani Suraksha Yojna benefits (financial incentive for delivering in an institution). The ASHA's description of her daily routine implies that her information needs change from one day to the next, and new information needs may arise at any time.

---

### BOX 3.1   AN ASHA'S DAILY ROUTINE

The ASHA of Hussaina village describes a day when the ANM makes her monthly visit.

**The ASHA visits Pappu's house. Pappu's wife wants to undergo a tubectomy:**

*I start at 9:30 in the morning to work. First of all I went to Pappu's place. I learnt that his wife wants to opt for a tubectomy. I asked her to come and meet ANM later in the day. We were discussing issues at Pappu's place for 5–10 minutes only.*

**Then the ASHA stops at Radheylal's house, where she finds a child who requires immunization:**

*At Radheylal's place, we learn that he has a three-year-old child who needs immunization. The ANM was there (in the village) and the child got immunized. Generally, people in the village sit outdoors so we explain to them there only. Everybody calls me didi [sister] and respects me.*

**Then she goes to Meena's house. Meena is pregnant and there is discussion about where Meena should deliver the baby:**

*We reach Meena and Sushil's place. I had a discussion at Sushil's place that Meena should come to Malihabad CHC [Community Health Center] for delivery. Dr. Khalida referred her to the Jyoti hospital (a private hospital). Dr. Khalida came during the health fair. . . . We have got other deliveries done there. That is why they were asking because they haven't got the money (to get the delivery conducted at a private hospital).*

**ASHA tells Meena about Pyarelal's family:**

*I told them that they [Pyarelal's family] got money in 2–4 days [from JSY safe motherhood scheme]. Pyarelal's family wanted the money as early as possible because their daughter-in-law is feeble and anemic; if they get money they will give good food to her. Their daughter-in-law said that her newborn is not taking her feed. She was asking whether she should give her bottle feed or not. I didn't tell her anything.*

**It is now 11:30 a.m., and the ASHA heads toward the Anganwadi. She describes the rest of the day:**

*The ANM didi comes around 10–10:15 a.m. and immunizes children. Women come to the Anganwadi till 2 p.m.; after 2 p.m. nobody comes. We discuss antenatal care, diet, nutrition, etc. with the women. It takes around one hour if we explain slowly. Then Anganwadi worker distributes panjiri [a sweet snack]. We work till ANM leaves. Then we stay there till 3:00 p.m. We reach home at 3:30 p.m. If there is any quarrel in the village, I go and solve it.*

The ASHA of Hussaina village is unable to answer the query related to what to do if a newborn is unable to latch in the first few days (Box 3.1). The ASHA encountered queries related to tubectomy, immunization, institutional delivery and breastfeeding in the course of a few hours (Box 3.1). Some ASHAs needed information related to medical emergencies. Also, they requested information about transportation, referral centers and management of immediate symptoms.

Another information need that several ASHAs identified was how to estimate the time of delivery of a woman from the onset of labor pains. In rural UP, where the ASHAs are often the first line of contact in the health system, an ASHA needs to know approximately when the delivery is going to take place after a woman starts labor pains, so that she can assess whether there is time to take the woman to a health facility. ASHAs also requested to know more about the care of newborns. Specifically, the ASHA is asking for practical demonstrations and practice for care of newborns:

An ASHA should know about . . . delivery. With how many fingers [cervical dilation] the birth takes place. How a delivery occurs. For example, a woman was about to deliver. I did not know how it would happen. . . . Show us to how to take care of newborns. They show us in the training, but we want practice. (ASHA, age 30, tenth-grade education, Rajkheda village, focus group)

## HOME VISITS

Home visits are an integral part of the ASHA's work. A representative of an international organization working in Lucknow describes it this way:

"Work of ASHA is to visit homes and explain to people. Basically ASHA takes care of pregnant and lactating mothers. They have a book that was given to them during training . . . ASHAs give information to people during home visits".

The needs assessment found that ASHAs generally conduct two types of home visits. First, there are routine home visits to pregnant women and children. As a 45-year-old ANM from Sarojini Nagar block explains, "ASHAs visit houses where deliveries are due or have taken place".

Second, ASHAs visit homes when they receive a call to see a person who is unwell. The ASHAs provide basic treatment, suggest preventive remedies or recommend appropriate referrals. Although this type of home visit is not part of the ASHAs' official job descriptions, they seem to occur often. For example, an ASHA from Mohanlal Gunj Community Health Center (CHC) described what happened during one such visit:

> A person came and said that his pregnant wife is suffering from a stomach-ache. I went to his house and observed that the pain is at right side of the abdomen. I corrected the position of fetus with my hand. Then came back home at 5 o'clock.

Another ASHA from Bharswa village described how she was called to a home where a young man was suffering as a result of stomach pain:

> In the evening when the rain stopped, a woman told me that a patient in her home is suffering from stomach-ache. Then I went and told him about the benefits of ORS [Oral Rehydration Salts] solution. He was cured the next day.

These types of house calls seem to be routine for ASHAs. As the ASHA from Hussaina village explained,

> Everybody calls us [to visit their homes], like pregnant women, if somebody's child is ill, men are ill. We go at least two to four times a week. We go and visit pregnant ladies daily.

Sometimes ASHAs must deal with the neighbors as well as the patient, since they may influence health-related decisions. A 35-year-old ASHA with an eighth grade education recounted the following story:

> Today I went to a woman's house as she was ready for delivery. When I reached there, many women were standing near her. Some were advising her not to go to the hospital and the others were suggesting her to go to the hospital. I told her, when the government is giving so many facilities, you should avail them.

## TIMELY ACCESS TO INFORMATION

The needs assessment recorded several cases where the ASHA told a woman that she would provide the required information later—but then could not. An ASHA from Govindpur village related this incident:

> On Saturday a woman stopped me in the middle of the street and asked about how to obtain forms for Janani Suraksha Yojna [financial incentive offered by the government for delivering in an institution]. I do not remember her name. She asked about family planning, too. I told her that I shall explain to her on Monday. We talked further about BCG vaccination [vaccine for prevention of tuberculosis]. I spent 15 minutes talking to her. I reached home at 4 o'clock.

Since the ASHA has already forgotten the woman's name, it is unlikely that she will return to her on Monday to provide the information requested.

## PRACTICAL INFORMATION

At the grassroots level, the ASHAs require more practical information that is local and is of immediate relevance to their daily work. Table 3.2 provides some examples of the "practical" information needs of the ASHAs that can promote better health seeking and treatment seeking behaviors. Indeed, timely information related to transport, referral centers and management of medical emergencies can make the difference between maternal and infant life and death in rural settings.

Findings indicate that health workers at the district level and below need more than technical or research-based information; they also require

*Table 3.2*   Examples of practical information that ASHAs need

Information on maternal and infant health needed to answer queries of village women and their household members

Guidelines for program implementation issued by state and district officials

Information on location, clinic hours, and phone numbers of private and government hospitals

Information on how to manage a medical emergency

Information on transport options in the village

practical information for their daily work, especially during home visits and in the community. A 30-year-old grassroots worker from Kaithala village stated that she shared with women in a group meeting all that was taught to her at the PHC. But women kept asking questions based on their experience, for which she had no answers.

As this report suggests, practical information is dynamic, changing constantly in response to health workers' needs. A mechanism is needed to both increase the technical capacity of the ASHA and to speed up delivery of information.

## SOURCES OF INFORMATION, SHARING OF INFORMATION AND INFORMATION-SEEKING STYLE

According to in-depth interviews and FGDs, the ANM is the primary source of information for ASHAs. ASHAs said that often the ANM is the "only source of information". ASHAs also get information from training, monthly meetings and booklets. Lack of mechanisms for information sharing is a barrier, as ANMs can often be the only source of information (i.e., practical information) for ASHAs.

A passive approach to information sharing is especially pervasive at the grassroots level. There is no system in place to ensure that new information routinely reaches grassroots workers:

> The only problem is we need to ask for information. It does not come automatically. And if we do not ask, then there is no information. (ASHA, age 35, tenth-grade education, Sarojini Nagar block)
>
> No special effort is made to share the latest information. (ASHA, age 26, eighth-grade education, Mirzagunj village)
>
> We do not put in special effort to get any information. (AWW, age 24, twelfth-grade education, Mirzagunj)

This passive approach suggests the ASHAs need information delivered in easy-to-use formats through a convenient and acceptable channel that does not immediately rely on the consistent presence of a more knowledgeable individual (e.g., ANM).

## MOBILE PHONES AND ICT

Data collection teams showed study participants a picture of a computer and asked them to identify it. In a focus group discussion with eight ASHAs, six participants could not identify the picture as a computer.

In contrast, ownership of mobile phones was almost universal among ASHAs and is widespread at the grassroots level. Study participants estimated that five to eight of every ten households have mobile phones. They also described a norm of sharing mobile phones with people who do not have one. A 38-year-old ASHA from the Mahilabad block explained, "Mobile is not there in all the houses. Those who don't have mobiles, they use their neighbor's mobile. Our village has unity about it".

At the grassroots level, health workers mostly used their mobile phones for voice calls and some, for SMS—although many did not know how to use SMS. According to a former director of the state training institute, ASHAs use mobile phones more than ANMs:

> Earlier, ANMs were there, and now ASHAs also come into the picture to provide health facilities, ASHAs are using the mobile more than ANMs. In comparison to ANM, ASHAs have more mobile numbers of patients than ANMs. Almost all the ASHAs who come to us have and use mobiles.

Not everyone appreciates SMS. A district health information officer said she does not use SMS often because "much is to be written [to send an SMS]; in the same time we can talk". Furthermore, mobile phones often are not equipped with SMS functions in Hindi. A health education officer from Saronjini Nagar block explained: "Messages are sent in English. Those who do not know English cannot understand the message. If SMS can be done in Hindi, it would be beneficial. We don't have the know-how to update the SMS to Hindi".

There was a consensus that grassroots workers have limited knowledge of SMS. A study participant said that "ASHAs have mobiles, but their knowledge of SMS is only 5%", and another participant expressed skepticism about the ability of ANMs and ASHAs to use SMS. Overall, voice-based communication was preferred over text-based communication. Grassroots health workers, especially older workers, want training to help them use mobile phones more effectively in their work.

Study participants described how the ability to be connected and instantly transmit or receive information has led to many changes. For example, ASHAs can now call hospitals and check the availability of beds, investigations and medical officers. As ASHAs in a FGD in Kasmandi Khurd explained,

> We use mobile phones to talk to hospitals. Women in villages also contact us over the phone. I get to know things in advance so I can be prepared. If the hospital is crowded on a particular day, I can get news about it [by making a phone call].

Health workers across the health system described in myriad ways how information and communication technologies have changed the way they work and function. The ability to be connected and transmit or receive information instantly has led to many changes. ASHAs state, as the quote above demonstrates, that they can now call hospitals and check out availability of beds, investigations and medical officers. As it was mentioned in the focus groups, mobile phones are "very useful during emergencies".

Some study participants expressed concern about the harmful health effects of long-term use of mobile phones. A block-level manager said, "It was shown on TV that mobile phone gives out dangerous rays, so I kept it away from me". Other concerns include network problems, recharging problems and nuisance calls. Grassroots health workers, especially older workers, want training to help them use mobile phones more effectively in their work.

## STATE, DISTRICT AND BLOCK PERSPECTIVES ON ASHAS' WORK

State-level participants perceive the ASHAs' information needs in terms of technical, text-based information. They believe that if the ASHA tells villagers what to do, people will listen and change their behaviors. For example, a representative of an international organization working in UP said:

> It is enough if the ASHA encourages women for check-ups during pregnancy and lactation, tells them about precautions to be taken during delivery, nutrition and care to be taken by the mother and give out information on Janani Suraksha Yojana (JSY). *She has all the information which is sufficient to give out* [emphasis added].

This is also the approach taken during ASHAs' training courses, which provide information on ideal health behaviors, such as the ideal diet for a pregnant woman or the ideal rest period. Rarely does training take a problem-solving approach or discuss the barriers to ideal behaviors in detail.

As the ASHAs describe their work, however, it becomes apparent that this approach does not match the reality of their work. ASHAs do not merely tell people what they are supposed to do, ideally. They respond to their fears and misconceptions, which form barriers to behavioral change; answer a barrage of questions, large and small; and address nontechnical issues such as son preference and false pregnancy. The general manager of NRHM identified a core issue that should be addressed in the context of the ASHAs' information needs. He said:

> The ASHA has information, but *it is important how she uses it* [emphasis added]. Training is going to take place, it is important to see what they [the ASHAs] do after the training.

Block-level officials interviewed for the needs assessment understand the important role of the ASHA in program implementation and consider them one of their main responsibilities. "Most of the work is done at the lower level, which is below the district level", said a 42-year-old medical officer from Mohanlalganj Block. The Mahilabad health education officer agreed: "ASHA is our good worker. She stays in the village. She has good information. ASHAs have a good role, they contribute a lot". All three Block health education officers acknowledged the ASHAs' potential to transform the health status of women and children in rural UP.

One of the ASHA's vital tasks is to follow up with different target groups. The general manager of NRHM gave some examples:

> It is very important for ASHAs to follow up their work. Like, if they did immunization and later the patient got fever, or after pregnancy the patient gets some infection. If follow-up is not done then problems arise. Currently our ASHAs are not fit for such type of problems.

An ANM from Mohanlalganj Block gave another example:

> ASHAs have IFA [Iron Folic Acid] tablets. They give 100 iron tablets to a pregnant woman. But they do not check whether she has taken those tablets or not. . . . The ASHA has the work of checking the women before delivery and after delivery. Also they should see whether breast-feeding is done to the baby or not. But the ASHA does not go at all.

While this ANM expressed skepticism about the ASHAs' competence, overall the ANMs in the study feel that the ASHAs are of help: "ASHAs have now come in to do good work. Some ASHAs are doing good work".

Local requirements and contexts dictate the information needs of grassroots workers. The general manager of NRHM felt that "the ASHAs should ask ANMs about their local requirements and their solutions. . . . We need information from each area and thus they should give information keeping in view local needs".

## APPLYING "ACTIONABILITY" CRITERIA TO DEVELOP MHEALTH APPLICATIONS FOR ASHAS

The crucial step between assessing information needs and making information "actionable" is the adaption of information to differing local contexts and users. MHealth applications should fulfill five criteria of actionability: language, timeliness, simplicity, amount of information and accessibility.[17]

MHealth applications need to ensure that the informational content is in the local *language*. This applies to both text- and voice-based content. The study has shown that *timeliness* of information is a core concern for the ASHA as she strides through her village on her daily rounds. She is asked many questions and has a few answers. A voice-based application of "frequently asked questions" (FAQs) can be loaded on the phones of ASHAs. The ASHAs can access these FAQs on their mobile phones and overcome the timeliness barrier. The FAQs should be based on real queries that ASHAs receive at the village level and not on what an expert thinks "an ASHA should know". A helpline for ASHAs can also provide timely information (See Box 3.2). A third element of actionable information is *simplicity*. The content for mHealth applications needs to be framed in simple manner. Simplicity requires adaptation of complex informational content. *Amount* of information is a barrier for grassroots workers. Too much information becomes excessive and its strategic value is lost. Mobile phones offer an opportunity for information specialists to limit their words. Information should be provided in small digestible amounts. Finally, *accessibility* determines the level of actionability. Here the mobile phones score very well, as they can be carried everywhere. For fulfilling ASHAs' information needs there is no requirement of Internet. Instead practical information and persuasive films can be loaded on mobile phones and remote areas can be accessed.

## DISCUSSION

This analysis raises several key questions and suggests some answers. What kind of information do ASHAs need? How should information for ASHAs be packaged? Is there an mHealth-based solution to better link the ASHA to the information she needs? And how can information be made readily accessible to the ASHA when she needs it?

The needs assessment indicated that the ASHAs have information needs primarily in three areas:

1. Information requirements during home visits for identification of pregnancy, understanding signs and symptoms of reproductive and childhood illnesses, contraceptive need, etc. Here the ASHA has to provide guidance that relates to referral and prevention.
2. Information requirements when the ASHA is called to assess the signs and symptoms of a child or adult who is feeling unwell.
3. Information requirements on how to manage medical emergencies.

The information needs assessment enabled identification of needs that are locally and culturally relevant to the ASHA, the village-level health worker. These information needs can be converted into "informational content" that can be disseminated through mHealth platforms and blended with existing print resources. Most importantly the focus shifts from access of information to usability of information. The five criteria for actionable information provide mHealth planners with parameters with which to make information more usable.

While it is often assumed that frontline health workers need technical content, the reality for the ASHAs is that they often need practical information that helps solve immediate problems and answer questions on a wide range of topics from the hours and fees charged by local referral facilities to arguments against son preference. Regardless of topic, the ASHAs expressed the need for timely access to information at the point of care. The information should be packaged in short, simple, actionable 'bites' (e.g., in a question and answer format), so that ASHAs can quickly act on it. Given the circumstances of their work and the fact that they already have and use the technology, the most promising way to make information accessible in this way may be via mobile phones.

The needs assessment indicates that the seamlessly mobile concept has enormous potential for changing the way we approach health workers' information needs. The small three- to four-inch handset that has become an integral part of the daily lives of many individuals can in fact become a job aid, a decision tool or a motivator, provided that practical, need-based, timely information is included. The device, in the hands of a human, enables the option of simultaneous mediated mass and interpersonal communication.

With these advances in technology and program design, the seamlessly mobile concept is fast becoming a reality for promoting maternal and infant health with the availability of low-cost smartphones in resource-poor settings.

With these rapidly expanding options for communications, traditional theoretical communication constructs are being turned upside down. For example, it is assumed that electronic mass media refers to mediated communication where the audience cannot not directly interact with the media source. However, with mobile phones, it is possible to view thirty-second TV spots on the handset of a health care worker, pause, ask questions, interact with the health care worker and view the TV spot again. Such a scenario was not imaginable even a decade ago.

At the same time, new theoretical frameworks will be required to identify the facilitators, barriers and process-oriented indicators for mobile mediated communication and information sharing. Sense-making theory provides a basis that will enable the exploration of multiple challenges for mobile phone and knowledge management joint efforts.[18] A key finding from this study resonates with the sense-making theory that advocates viewing information exchange or sharing as involving a person(s) *in a situation* and looks toward understanding information flows.[19] In the case of the ASHA, her situation and context are constantly changing as she encounters different health issues and scenarios on a daily basis. Her information needs are dynamic and need to be viewed from the perspective of the community with which she works. Sense-making embeds the enquiry of information needs into the reality of the context within which the knowledge-seeking or -sharing interaction occurs.[20] Importantly, it provides a role for emotion in the information provision and sharing situation. Emotion has a crucial role in the Indian cultural context, where *sahradaya* (compassion) and *rasa* (emotional response) are two of five core constructs for "real" communication to occur.[21] Further research on health information needs of grassroots workers should include the dimensions suggested by the sense-making theory.

The need for *practical* information has been highlighted in this chapter.[22] Once again, the analytical perspective changes when information needs are viewed within a real-world context that is embedded in a live ecosystem that has its own layers and complexities. These findings also point toward the need for further research regarding the motivation levels of the ASHA and how motivation can impact her information-seeking and -sharing processes and skills.[23]

This systematic assessment of health information needs and usage patterns is a crucial first step to assuring the adoption of any mHealth strategies for community-level workers. MHealth must be used strategically, responding to audience needs and being viable and sustainable in the local context.[24] Further, mHealth applications should complement other programs, products and services, such as job aids and other print resources. For example, existing resources in UP can be repackaged to provide clinically robust and culturally relevant content for an ASHA helpline for newborn survival and reduction of neonatal mortality.[25]

Mobile technologies can extend the reach of health information resources to remote areas that are in "information dark" zones. More importantly, they can play a cost-effective role in saving lives of mothers and infants through the timely availability of action-oriented information.[26] The ASHA can use the mobile phone to persuade households to change their health behaviors, to refer women for institutional deliveries, to manage medical emergencies and to follow up her clients. A helpline for the ASHA can address in a timely manner the myriad changing information needs that she encounters daily.

The needs assessment indicates that voice-based applications are best for ASHAs. SMS is not a viable option. Most handsets in rural areas do not yet support Indian language scripts, and those that do can be difficult to use. Interactive voice response communication is an attractive option for low-literacy audiences and can be customized for local languages and seem natural to use.[27] Box 3.2 illustrates how mHealth applications can be used to improve maternal and infant health programs using voice applications.

## BOX 3.2 DESIGNING AN MHEALTH APPLICATION TO IMPROVE MATERNAL AND INFANT HEALTH

The needs assessment indicates that voice applications are more suitable than SMS at the grassroots level. One application includes mobile technologies to promote specific behavior change in maternal, newborn and infant health through voice prompts (IVRS). Electronic "flip-books" are another application that can be loaded on the ASHAs' mobile phones. Low-end mobile phones can support electronic flip-books with "voice-overs." ASHAs could use these effectively during home visits.

A telephone helpline for ASHAs is proposed. ASHAs from throughout the state could call in to a toll-free number. The ASHA requires information in "small and specific" amounts according to the immediate need. Printed practical information on all the above topics should be compiled to help the helpline operators answer her questions. At the same time there should be a medical practitioner available at the helpline desk to guide ASHAs through maternal and infant health emergencies. Also, a set of FAQs (frequently asked questions) that include people's questions asked of the ASHA can be loaded on the mobile phone (not requiring a call).

In addition, mobile phone numbers can be recorded for every pregnant woman with access to a mobile phone. Voice prompts to the woman and her family will continue all through her pregnancy and until her child is one year old. A computer program can routinely send out the prompts based on the mother's stage of pregnancy or the child's age.

In this manner, customized messaging can be sent in an automated fashion. Appropriately timed voice prompts could cover:

—Number and timing of ANC check ups
—Taking iron–folic acid tablets
—Eating at least four times a day
—Eating an iron-rich and vitamin C-rich diet
—Registration for institutional delivery
—High-risk signs and symptoms
—Provision of colostrums
—Postnatal care
—Immunization visits 1, 2, 3, 4 and 5
—Starting complementary feeds at 6 months
—Number of complementary feeds
—Date and time of Village Health and Nutrition Day
—Motivation for family planning
—Where family planning services are available (place, time, etc.)

The potential for using mobile technologies to increase information sharing and use is enormous and unprecedented. MHealth is an emerging field and requires more testing and evaluation of a variety of approaches. Most evaluations of mHealth applications center on SMS.[28] However, this study highlights the importance of voice communication, and there are almost no evaluations of mHealth applications using voice. This chapter suggests how an information needs assessment can inform mHealth programming, where mHealth is not considered a silver bullet, but rather a particularly appropriate channel to reach rural health workers effectively with actionable information they need to improve their interactions with clients at the point of care and, ultimately, maternal and infant health in UP.

## NOTES

1. Carole Leach-Lemens, "Using Mobile Phones in HIV Care and Prevention", *HIV & AIDS Treatment in Practice* 137 (May 21, 2009). C. McNab, "What

Social Media Offers to Health Professionals and Citizens", *Bulletin of the World Health Organization* 87, no. 9 (2009): 566.

2. Leach-Lemens, "Using Mobile Phones in HIV Care".
3. International Institute for Population Sciences (IIPS) and Macro International, *National Family Health Survey (NFHS-3), 2005–06: India: Volume I* (Mumbai: IIPS, 2007).
4. Office of Registrar General India. "Special Bulletin on Maternal Mortality in India 2004–06: Sample Registration System", April 2009, accessed March 25, 2011, http://www.mp.gov.in/health/MMR-Bulletin-April-2009.pdf.
5. Ibid.
6. International Institute for Population Sciences, *National Family Health Survey.*
7. Ibid.
8. National Rural Health Mission (NRHM), "Accredited Social Health Activist", 2011, accessed March 21, 2012, http://www.mohfw.nic.in/NRHM/asha.htm#abt.
9. Abhay Bang, RA Bang, SB Baitule, MH Reddy and MD Deshmukh, "Effect of Home-Based Neonatal Care and Management of Sepsis on Neonatal Mortality: Field Trial in Rural India", *Lancet* 354 (1999): 1955–61; Andy Haines, D. Sanders, U. Lehmann, AK Rowe, JE Lawn, S. Jan, DG Walker and Z. Bhutta, "Achieving Child Survival Goals: Potential Contribution of Community Health Workers", *Lancet* 369 (2007): 2121–31; Vishwajeet Kumar et al., "Effect of Community-Based Behaviour Change Management on Neonatal Mortality in Shivgarh, Uttar Pradesh, India: A Cluster-Randomised Controlled Trial", *Lancet* 372 (2008): 1151–62.
10. Telecom Regulatory Authority of India, "Information Note to the Press, (Press Release No. 20/2010)", April 26, 2010, accessed February 22, 2013, http://www.breezecom.biz/doc/Telecom%20Regulatory%20Authority%20of%20India.pdf.
11. Economic Times, "India to Have Billion Plus Mobile Users by 2015: Executive", November 18, 2009, accessed June 2010, http://economictimes.indiatimes.com/News/Economy/Finance/India-to-havebillion-plus-mobileusers-by-2015-executive/articleshow/5242284.cms.
12. Telecom Regulatory Authority of India, "Information Note to the Press".
13. Jody Ranck, *Health Information and Health Care: The Role of Technology in Unlocking Data and Wellness—A Discussion Paper* (Washington, DC: United Nations Foundation & Vodafone Foundation Technology Partnership; Earth Institute, 2011). Patricia Mechael et al., *Barriers and Gaps Affecting mHealth in Low and Middle Income Countries: A Policy White Paper* (Washington, DC: mHealth Alliance, 2010).
14. B. Lown, F. Bukachi and R. Xavier, "Health Information in the Developing World", *Lancet* 352, Supplement 2 (1998): S34–S38.
15. Vital Wave Consulting, mHealth for Development, *The Opportunity of Mobile Technology for Healthcare in the Developing World.* (Washington, D.C. and Berkshire, UK: UN Foundation-Vodafone Foundation Partnership, 2009.)
16. Nandita Kapadia-Kundu et al., "Understanding Health Information Needs and Gaps Within the Health Care System in Uttar Pradesh, India", *Journal of Health Communication* 17, S2 (2012): 30–45.
17. Brenda Dervin, "Sense-Making Theory and Practice: An Overview of User Interests in Knowledge Seeking and Use", *Journal of Knowledge Management* 2 (1998): 36–46.
18. Kapadia-Kundu et al., "Understanding Health Information Needs".
19. Dervin, "Sense-Making Theory and Practice".
20. Ibid.

21. Nandita Kapadia-Kundu, "An Empirical Test of the Sadharanikaran Theory of Communication to Defecation Hygiene Behaviour: An Evaluation of a Child-to-Community Intervention in Maharashtra, India" (PHD Thesis, submitted to Johns Hopkins School of Hygiene and Public Health, 1994).

22. R. Savolainen, "Everyday Life Information Seeking: Approaching Information Seeking in the Context of 'Way of Life'". *LISR* 17 (1995): 259–294.

23. A. Weiler, "Information-Seeking Behavior in Generation Y0 Students: Motivation, Critical Thinking, and Learning Theory", *Journal of Academic Librarianship*, 31, no. 1 (2004): 46–53.

24. AC Norris, RS Stockdale and S. Sharma, "A Strategic Approach to mHealth", *Health Informatics Journal* 15, no. 3 (2009): 244–253.

25. V. Kumar, S. Mohanty, A. Kumar, RP Misra, M. Santosham, S. Awasthi, AH Baqui, P. Singh, V. Singh, RC Ahuja, JV Singh, GK Malik, S. Ahmed, RE Black, M. Bhandari, GL Darmstadt, Saksham Study Group, "Effect of Community-Based Behaviour Change Management on Neonatal Mortality in Shivgarh, Uttar Pradesh, India: A Cluster-Randomised Controlled Trial", *Lancet, 372(9644),* (2008), 1151–62; Young Infants Clinical Signs Study Group, "Clinical Signs That Predict Severe Illness in Children Under Age 2 Months: A Multicentre Study", *Lancet,* 371 (9607) (2008): 135–42.

26. Zhou-wen Chen et al., "Comparison of an SMS Text Messaging and Phone Reminder to Improve Attendance at a Health Promotion Center: A Randomized Controlled Trial", *Journal of Zhejiang University* 9, no. 1 (2008): 34–38.

27. M. Heisler, L. Halasyamani, K. Resnicow, M. Neaton, J. Shanahan, S. Brown and JD Piette, " 'I Am Not Alone': The Feasibility and Acceptability of Interactive Voice Response-Facilitated Telephone Peer Support Among Older Adults with Heart Failure", *Congestive Heart Failure* 13 (2007): 149–157.

28. A. Rodgers, T. Corbett, D. Bramley, T. Riddell, M. Willis, RB Lin, et. al., "Do You Smoke After Txt? Results of a Randomized Trial of Smoking Cessation Using Mobile Phone Text Messaging", *Tobacco Control*, 14 (2005): 255–261; Kevin Patrick et al., "A Text Message–Based Intervention for Weight Loss: Randomized Controlled Trial", *Journal of Medical Internet Research* 11, no. 1 (2009); Richard Lester, "Effects of a Mobile Phone Short Message Service on Antiretroviral Treatment Adherence in Kenya (WelTel Kenya1): A Randomised Trial", *Lancet* 376, no. 9755 (2010): 1838–45; Victoria Franklin et al., "Patients' Engagement with 'Sweet Talk'—A Text Messaging Support System for Young People with Diabetes. *Journal of Medical Internet Research* 10, no. 2(2008), e20.

# 4  Remotely Connected

## Is There a Seamless Solution to Address the Digital Divide in Remote Indigenous Communities?

*Tracey M. Benson*

## INTRODUCTION

It has often been stated that Australians pick up on new technologies early, in particular those that assist with communications across distances. Since the adoption of the telegraph that linked communities in Australia in the 1860s and then to the outside world in the 1870s, the implementation of telecommunications technologies is part of the nation-building narrative of Australian history.[1]

Despite a real or imagined national identity as global innovators in the digital space, there have been significant barriers for many people when it comes to accessing the Internet in urban, regional and remote locations. This is primarily because Internet access may be limited depending on where one lives, with many remote communities having no access via phone line modem, broadband cable, satellite or Next G mobile phones. Distance is a great challenge in many remote areas, as there may be hundreds of kilometres between towns, making the provision of essential infrastructure and services difficult.

This chapter scopes some of the strategies and technologies being used in remote and rural Australia to leapfrog the digital divide, and documents some key findings of recent research focused on a number of remote Indigenous[2] communities and their access to the Internet and mobile phone networks. The chapter is focused on developing a best practice approach to engaging with remote Indigenous communities to collaboratively develop effective information communications technology literacy skills and improved access to communications technology. It is also a documentation of an evolving understanding of the many challenges people face in remote areas and the significant impact of the digital divide, specifically in smaller remote Indigenous communities.

In this chapter, the idea of a world that is seamlessly mobile is advocated, and it is recognised that other steps need to be taken to reach that goal. For example, the cross-fertilisation and integration of tools and technologies enable flexible modes of communication and information sharing and gathering. In the case of remote Indigenous communities, it is also necessary to look at how technology impacts communities in terms of employment, creative skills development and literacy. For some communities, access to 3G Internet capacity is limited, as is access to broadband, making the goal of seamless mobility a real challenge. The other overriding issue that has a direct impact on accessing the Internet is the reliable supply of power. Many remote Indigenous communities use diesel to generate electricity, and this creates a range of issues, including affordability, travel to purchase diesel and availability of supply. On this topic there have been a number of excellent energy and sustainability initiatives targeted at addressing this community need, and some of these are discussed later.

The focus is specifically on a number of communities in the Central Australia region, mainly Yuendumu, Papunya and more broadly Anangu Pitjantjatjara Yankunytjatjara (APY).[3] These communities, although all in the Central Australia region, are members of different regional Indigenous media associations, reflecting the complexity of telecommunications capabilities in remote Australia.[4] There are also a number of relevant government and community-based programs that cut across communities in this region, which will be explored to provide a demonstration of the network of activities that traverse this huge geographical area.

Access to health, education and technology are all critical elements for ensuring equitable social outcomes for people living in remote communities. Moreover, this chapter addresses how flexible and seamless access to media can and does assist in terms of building social capital and supporting health and education agendas.

## IDENTIFYING A POTENTIAL NEED

As mentioned earlier, there are still significant limitations to online access in regional and remote locations, let alone access to mobile networks in smaller communities. In a recent study titled "Home Internet for Remote Indigenous Communities" it was noted that Indigenous social policy is trending towards the centralisation of services into larger settlements.[5] Policies under the Closing the Gap (2011) reforms direct funding to twenty-nine larger communities (Territory Growth Towns[6]) with the "expectation that residents of smaller communities will travel between locations, or move to larger towns to access government services".[7] The "Home Internet for Remote Indigenous Communities" report states that

> The Council of Australian Governments (COAG) National Partnership Agreements and the NT [Northern Territory] Government's "Working Future" strategy aim to develop the infrastructure and services in this group of "priority communities" or "growth towns" (the Governments' respective terms for these) to the point where they are comparable with those in equivalent sized regional towns. While the Commonwealth and

NT Government groups are not identical, there is a high degree of over-lap, and the total number of communities thus targeted in the NT is 20. All of these communities are upwards of 300 in population. These policies do not directly fund the smaller communities and outstations. The rationale is that the transport links between the "hub" target towns and the smaller communities in their sphere of influence will be upgraded, with a view to encouraging and assisting residents of these smaller communities to utilise the hub services.[8]

There is much talk of 'closing the gap' between Indigenous and non-Indigenous Australians, and government initiatives have implications on a range of issues, most significantly by addressing challenges related to access to health, housing and education services, as well as other basic needs like reliable access to power and communications channels.

Closing the Gap is an Australian Government social policy framework that is aimed at addressing Indigenous social disadvantage. In June 2009 a COAG agreement was made to improve remote Indigenous public Internet access. The intergovernmental agreement Closing the Gap: National Partnership Agreement on Remote Indigenous Public Internet Access committed to investing in a number of priority locations around Australia, including communities discussed later—Papunya and Yuendumu.[9]

Under the previous Labor Prime Minister Kevin Rudd, the Australian federal government started the process of implementing a National Broadband Network (NBN), which would not only provide much-needed broadband Internet access in the remote locations of Australia, but would also speed up Internet connections in urban areas. But is this the best method for the majority of remote Indigenous communities?

Other countries have leapfrogged optic fibre for satellite broadband access to the Internet, and this would appear the most practical option for some remote areas. In a number of communities, including Papunya, satellite broadband is already being used, but the funding for supplying this service is not guaranteed after 2012.

Communities need to be able to identify opportunities, and because of limited computer literacy, there is sometimes a lack of recognition that having access to computer technology is a positive step. For example, research in the 2011 "Home Internet for Remote Indigenous Communities" report identified that one of the most significant barriers was cost, closely followed by computer literacy and English literacy.[10] People who had little exposure to computers were far less likely to see them as a part of daily life and interaction, which is one possible reason why progress is slow.

The other crucial issue is the cultural sensitivity surrounding working with Indigenous people. For example, it is not appropriate to go to communities uninvited, and the invitation must be made by elders in the community. There are also cultural laws around what material people can see and record, for example many ceremonies are only for the eyes of a specific group, and this also proves a challenge in terms of archiving culture. Cultural law also has implications for recording images of traditional lands, as certain places are tied to culture and ritual. Some remote Indigenous communities have chosen to break with cultural law to ensure that the culture is preserved, by recording ceremonies and publishing them on YouTube.

The Northern Territory Library is responsible for managing the rollout of the Remote Indigenous Public Internet Access (RIPIA)[11] program, which sits under the Closing the Gap initiative. There are a range of tools being implemented, including a secure site for cultural and community heritage and a conferencing and training tool. RIPIA is being implemented in forty communities in the Northern Territory, twenty-nine of which have already been provided with access. In addition, school students in remote communities are entitled to an XO-1 laptop as part of the Closing the Gap initiative, supported by the One Laptop Per Child (OLPC) nonprofit organisation. The XO-1 is an inexpensive subnotebook computer intended to be distributed to children in developing countries around the world, to provide them with access to knowledge and opportunities to "explore, experiment and express themselves".[12] The laptop was developed by OLPC and manufactured by Quanta Computer. The XO-1 laptops are designed for sale to government-education systems, which then give each primary school student their own laptop. More recently the XO-1 has become available for purchase by the general public.

Executive director of OLPC Australia Rangan Srikhanta stated that the organisation is hopeful the laptops will help the school children preserve and sustain their local culture, language and way of life. He commented, "In Australia this means helping children in remote communities cross the 'digital divide' by giving them laptops that are not only fully loaded with educational and entertaining programs to help them learn, but that can also be connected to the Internet so they can share their experiences with the rest of the world and, likewise, learn from others".[13]

## SOME FACTS AND FIGURES

To provide a snapshot of Australia in terms of Internet usage, the Australian Bureau of Statistics (ABS) reported that in December 2010 there were 10.4 million active Internet subscribers in Australia, compared with 9.6 million in June 2010. On June 30, 2012, there were 5.9 million mobile wireless broadband connections in Australia, an increase of 7% since the end of December 2011. Mobile wireless broadband was again the most prevalent Internet technology in Australia, accounting for 49% of all connections.[14] What is revealing in the ABS data is that the volume of users accessing the Internet with wireless and mobile devices has been significantly increasing since 2006. According to the data published on the ABS website in December 2010, the use of broadband and wireless/mobile access is almost on par, whereas satellite access has remained static.

On the distribution of the Indigenous population, ABS data revealed that "In 2008, just over two-thirds (68%) of Indigenous people lived outside the major cities, with 44% living in regional areas and 24% living in remote (or very remote) areas. More than half of the Indigenous population lived in either New South Wales (30%) or Queensland (28%), with another quarter living in either Western Australia (13%) or the Northern Territory (12%)".[15] There are 1,187 discrete Indigenous communities across Australia. Of these 865 (73%) have a population below 50, and 987 (83%) have a population below 100. The average size of those communities with populations under 100 is 20 people. The majority of the communities identified as remote or very remote are located in the Northern Territory, Queensland and Western Australia. All of the government's twenty-nine priority communities have a population of more than 300 people.[16]

The statistics on the social gaps between Indigenous and non-Indigenous people in Australia is testament of the need for development in the area of health and education. For example, the infant mortality rate among Indigenous people is three times higher than the national average, or 15.2 deaths per 1,000 births compared with five per 1,000.[17]

Education is another area where Indigenous people often fall behind the national average. Mick Gooda, the Aboriginal and Torres Strait Islander social justice commissioner of the Australian Human Rights Commission, commented in 2010 that "We do not enjoy the same standards of education. In 2008, only 63% of year five Indigenous students achieved the national minimum standard for reading compared with 93% of non-Indigenous students—a gap of 30%."[18]

In terms of cultural diversity, there are more than 200 Australian Indigenous languages. Although fewer than twenty languages are widely spoken, the regions where these languages are spoken are either remote or very remote. Many languages in southern Australia are now extinct and many are currently under threat of extinction.[19]

## REGIONAL FOCUS

For the purpose of this chapter, the Central Australia region is the major focus. This is primarily because of the diversity of what is happening in this inland region in terms of issues related to communications, reliable access to power and sensitivity to climate change. What is notable is that there is an uneven distribution of communications capability. For example, Papunya is a community that has had limited access to communications technology until recently.

In 2009, the Papunya Computer Room (PCR) was established, which has had a significant and positive effect on the community. Yuendumu, on the other hand, has been working with communications technology for many years, with experimentation with pirate radio and video production starting in the early 1980s. Experimentations also started relatively early in APY communities; for example, a number of Pitjantjatjara and Yankunytjatjara communities have been digitising their culture and language for a number of years.

## NEED FOR APPROPRIATE CULTURAL ENGAGEMENT

It is critical to approach working with Aboriginal people in a respectful way. Since European settlement, there has been a plethora of laws and interventions for and about Indigenous Australians without any consultation. For example, Aboriginal people in Australia did not get the right to vote in elections until 1962 and were granted full citizenship rights only after constitutional changes that were the result of a referendum in 1967. Previous to this change in legislation Aboriginal and Torres Strait Islander people's citizenship was dictated by a complex web of state-based laws.

The continuing issue with much government policy implementation for people living in remote communities is the lack of consultation about issues that affect Aboriginal people directly and profoundly. Governance and the need for local decision making is seen as a critical issue in the September 2012 RemoteFOCUS report titled: "Fixing the Hole in Australia's Heartland: How Government Needs to Work with Remote Australia", where the need for alignment of local, state and federal policy is identified. [20]

On the other hand, a number of organisations are making legitimate and serious efforts to engage with Aboriginal people respectfully and sensitively. For example, volunteers with the nonprofit organisation Indigenous Community Volunteers (ICV) are trained in detail on how to collaborate with Indigenous communities in a culturally appropriate way. This training includes addressing sensitive issues like photographing the landscape while "on country" (a term commonly used to describe being on traditional lands). Projects are initiated and owned by the respective community and are focused on sustainable community development outcomes—education, employment, building and health. Volunteers go to communities to share skills and to assist in the delivery of priority projects in the community. The approach used by ICV empowers the community to drive the project and build skills and resources for their community and its people, long after the volunteers have left. [21]

Other organisations are wholly owned by Indigenous communities and cross many geographical locations, a number of which will be explored later. Some of these examples will provide more detail around the history, guiding principles and governance arrangements of Indigenous media ownership that have contributed to the development of telecommunications infrastructure in the Central Australian region.

## RELEVANT RESEARCH PROJECTS

There have been number of research papers published that focus on the area of Internet and communications technology access for remote Indigenous communities. The research that has been undertaken has varied results, demonstrating the unevenness of online and mobile capability in these remote areas. For example, in the 2009 research paper about communities in remote North Queensland titled *Report to Wujal Wujal Aboriginal Shire Council on Mobile Technology in the Bloomfield River Valley*, it was documented that 55% of Indigenous residents interviewed in a survey had owned at least one mobile phone, compared with non-Indigenous residents, who had 71% ownership. This report also evinced that there was reliable reception in some areas, around 50% of the region identified.[22]

What was surprising in the Wujal Wujal report was the relatively low percentage of home-based Internet, which was 9.5%, with only 7% of private dwellings having a fixed phone line. Another point of interest was that many respondents had the perception that there was widespread use of mobile phones. This may be attributed to families sharing phones, creating an impression that "just about everyone has them".[23]

Both of these findings are a clear indication of the way in which people in remote communities live together by sharing resources across the community. The notion of individual ownership that is centred in Western societal values is not appropriate in the context of Aboriginal communities and cultures, whether urban, regional or remote. The "Home Internet for Remote Indigenous Communities" report refers to a practice known as 'demand sharing', which is described as follows:

> For individuals living in remote Indigenous communities, economic decision making is often influenced by factors that most Australians do not experience, notably, the system of "demand sharing". Simply put, Aboriginal people may frequently give away resources in circumstances when non-Indigenous Australians would consider it wiser to hold on to that resource. Anthropologists have identified this form of behaviour as one of the defining qualities of Aboriginality, common to groups of people living in urban, region and remote contexts. Known as "demand sharing", or colloquially as "humbugging", this form of exchange is said to have foundations in traditional lifestyle when sharing was a matter of survival in a situation of scarcity and unpredictable food supply.[24]

This presents a real issue when considering the rollout of the NBN, as the expectation of the Australian government is that access will be primarily provided to individuals and families at a defined location (i.e., at home), rather than a community-based location.

In contrast, the "Home Internet for Remote Indigenous Communities" report focused on three communities, Kwale Kwale, Mungalawurru and Imangara, all of which currently have no mobile phone coverage despite 30% of people owning a mobile phone.[25] The people from these communities who own mobile phones purchased the phone to use in town, where there is access to 3G capability. Around 30% of this group used mobile phones to access the Internet for music downloads and to chat. Of these three communities only 6% of total residents had a laptop or a home computer, although 58% of people have used a computer at some time. Only two-thirds of this group had ever been online, and 75% of Internet users were under 30 years of age. This report also documented that the 2006 census revealed that only 20% of Indigenous households in remote and very remote Australia have an Internet connection, compared with 60% of non-Indigenous people in the same statistical area.[26]

This report is the first output of a three-year study that is a collaboration between Australian Research Council Centre of Excellence for Creative Industries and Innovation (Swinburne University of Technology), the Centre for Appropriate Technology (CAT) and the Central Land Council (CLC).

Both of these reports are very timely, given the government's agenda to roll out the NBN, as both reports signal the importance of providing alternatives to the NBN. The "Home Internet for Remote Communities" report recommends that a broadband assistance program be established to assist in the implementation of satellite broadband access and Wi-Fi networks. The Wi-Fi network would be available community wide, providing access to any dwelling as a shared resource. The Wujal Wujal report recommends extending coverage in the area, providing reliable access to computers, training local people in managing mobile phones providing an equitable Universal Service Obligation.

These reports highlight that there is still a long way to go to address the digital divide for remote residents. Because mobile phone uptake is much higher than individual home access to the Internet, people are vulnerable to mobile phone companies installing transmitters so they have reliable access to mobile networks. It has also been mentioned in the media and via word of mouth reports that mobile phone companies are exploiting customers in remote areas because of limited literacy and are capitalising on a lack of awareness of the details in the phone contracts being entered into.[27]

A world that is seamlessly mobile has the ability to integrate voice, text, image and geophysical site easily with other forms of media. It has the capacity for broadcasting as well as narrowcasting. For the communities discussed in this chapter, attention needs to be made to what other elements are needed to construct a world that is seamlessly mobile. For example, online teleconferencing tools can be used across devices—mobile, laptop and desktop—making the exercise in developing community hubs vital to stepping people in remote communities towards being connected in a more seamless way.

As mentioned earlier, one initiative will undoubtedly benefit many young people living in remote communities in terms of providing access to technology. The OLPC program's mission is "to enhance learning opportunities for over 500,000 primary school aged children by providing each one with a connected XO laptop as part of a sustainable training and support program, by 2020".[28]

Despite the fact that there is uneven access to communications channels, there has been significant investment in media production and broadcasting by Aboriginal people in remote Australia over the last thirty years, and this is explored in the next section.

## INDIGENOUS-RUN MEDIA PRODUCTION

The notion of being "seamlessly mobile" is about the integration of diverse media channels and tools, embracing new technologies while building on existing frameworks already in place, for example, media production initiatives owned and run by Indigenous communities. For the purpose of this chapter, it is necessary to look at what initiatives are already in place in Central Australian remote Indigenous communities in order to understand the complexity surrounding access and skills in online media and media production. It is evident that in some communities there has been a lot of work done in developing community-based media and training.

For example, Yuendumu is the largest remote community in Central Australia and had relatively early uptake of communications technology. It is also a community that has relatively good mobile coverage. Yuendumu is located 290 kilometres northwest of Alice Springs and has a population of between 800 and 1.000 people. A largely Warlpiri community, it is actually located on Anmatyerr lands.[29]

Melinda Hinkson has written widely on the subject of remote Indigenous peoples access to media, and in her essay *New Media Projects at Yuendumu: Towards a History and Analysis of Intercultural Engagement* she discusses early experimentation with video production, which preceded the establishment of a "pirate" radio station in 1985. Early video production activities at Yuendumu were associated with the Warlpiri Literature Centre.

Experimentation with video work intensified with the arrival of Dr Eric Michaels, with the Warlpiri Learning Centre being formally renamed as Warlpiri Media Association in 1985 (now known as PAW Media).[30] On the PAW Media website Michaels was "firstly working with Kurt (Leonard) Japanangka Granites and then with Francis Jupurrurla Kelly he acted as a catalyst for the development of a distinctively Warlpiri approach to video".[31] Michaels reported at the time that there was insufficient access to communications as there was only an unreliable radio telephone, a telegram service the emergency radio for the Royal Flying Doctors Service, police radio, CB radio and twice-a-week mail service.[32]

By 1995, Yuendumu had access to email, video conferencing network, two television stations, two radio stations, and telephone and facsimile machine. PAW Media continues to have a strong interest in media and creative media production. The Yuendumu Community has also initiated other programs that incorporate media training for young people. For example, the Warlpiri Youth Development Aboriginal Corporation (WYDAC), formally known as the Mt Theo Program, was started by the Yuendumu Community in 1993 to address chronic petrol sniffing in Yuendumu.[33] The program has since broadened in nature and scope to provide a comprehensive program of youth development and leadership, diversion, respite, rehabilitation and aftercare throughout the Warlpiri region.

The Warlpiri Education and Training Trust Youth and Media Project started in 2007 with a focus on media training and employment across the Warlpiri region. This project aims to support Warlpiri youth to develop their sense of self, family and culture through diversionary programs with a special focus on media.

Project-based media workshops focus on developing media opportunities for young people as a diversion from antisocial behaviour and investment in future opportunities for employment and enterprise. Over time media activities have moved towards the development of employment options and media products for use in the communities involved and the wider community. Youth workers in Willowra, Yuendumu, Nyirrpi and Lajamanu communities receive ongoing training with PAW Media.

WYDAC is an excellent example of how access to media and training has positive social benefits, including a diversion from substance abuse, increased opportunities for employment and better communications capabilities. The 2012 Strategic Plan documented that currently 52% of staff employed have been "Yapa" (*Yapa* is the Warlpiri word for Aboriginal people).[34]

Another community-based initiative that has supported the preservation of Indigenous peoples culture and history in the Central Australian region is the secure networked database *Aṟa Irititja*, which was designed at the request of APY in 1994.

Located in the remote northwest of South Australia, APY is a large Aboriginal local government area that consists of a number of communities comprising the Pitjantjatjara, Yankunytjatjara and Ngaanyatjarra peoples (or Anangu), with a population of around 2,500 people. The council was formed in 1981 by the passing of the Anangu Pitjantjatjara Yankunytjatjara Land Rights Act, 1981, by the Parliament of South Australia.[35]

*Aṟa Irititja's* purpose is to prevent the loss of the history and to allow the teaching of it to others in the community. Administered through the Pitjantjatjara Council, the communities own *Aṟa Irititja*. The program delivers workstations to around 20 communities and well as a mobile library. What makes *Aṟa Irititja* unique, in terms of how it sits with other cultural digitisation projects, is that *Aṟa Irititja* is not an open, public resource; it has layers of access depending on what the cultural material is and whether you are allowed to see/hear the material. This approach protects the kinship and gender protocols that already exist for the traditional cultural owners. *Aṟa Irititja* has also shared its database software with other communities, including the "community stories" archive that is part of the RIPIA project.

In other communities not discussed in this chapter, cultural material is now being put online by some Indigenous communities who made the decision that it was more important to preserve the culture than to adhere to the customs restricting visibility.

Yuendumu and APY have a demonstrated track record with implementing community-based initiatives focused on software development and online media tools aimed at building skills and recording culture. By contrast, Papunya established a computer room in 2009, which is comparatively later. The PCR was initiated by the Central Australian Youth Link-Up Service to address a social need to facilitate adult education and provide an alternative to substance abuse. Many young people growing up in the 1990s and early 2000s were affected by petrol sniffing and missed out on school. The project is a crucial step in empowering this and future generations towards a better future. Recently, the PCR set up a separate "Kunga" room (*Kunga* being the Luritja word for woman). It is the first centre to have this arrangement in Central Australia and is proving successful.[36]

Compared with activities happening in Yuendumu there seems to be a lack of information about media access and uptake in Papunya prior to the PCR, which bears closer attention as part of the course of this research. Aside from Papunya being famous as a major centre for contemporary Aboriginal art, there are also strong links to Indigenous contemporary music, as the well-known Warumpi Band came from Papunya in the early 1980s. As a point of interest, Warumpi Band was the first rock band to perform in an Aboriginal language.

The PCR relies on donations and volunteer activity to survive and as part of the Closing the Gap initiative, the Northern Territory government is paying for satellite access for one year; after that the future is uncertain. The scenario in Papunya demonstrates how a lack of reliable communications capability limits opportunity for people to bridge equity gaps.

It is uncertain how much of the funding will be spent on communities like Kwale Kwale, although the ongoing longitudinal study by Swinburne, CAT and CLC will hopefully evince in later years whether there is any investment in small remote Indigenous communities. It is also unclear how much Papunya will benefit from this investment, despite that it is noted as a priority community.

Despite some smaller communities having limited access to communications channels, the emerging trend towards mobile technology is an interesting phenomenon in terms of the opportunities as well as the challenges. There are many benefits and services that access to an online environment can provide, including the opportunity for building skills in computer literacy and information management.

## ACCESS TO RELIABLE SOURCES OF
## POWER AND SUSTAINABILITY ACTIONS

The importance of reliable power has been identified in a number of research papers, including "Home Internet for Remote Communities", as a key barrier to the uptake of the Internet in remote Indigenous communities. The lack of access to reliable power sources also underlines a serious equity issue for people living in these areas, as it represents a lack of basic services. Many communities run diesel-powered generators, and there is much expense in sourcing and transporting the fuel, let alone the cost of the diesel itself.

The Bushlight program, based in Alice Springs, is part of CAT, an organisation working with Indigenous communities to deliver a range of services including planning and engagement, learning and development, and sustainability measures relating to water, waste, transport and energy, as well as the Desert Peoples Centre. CAT is a national Indigenous science and technology organisation, established in 1980, and is governed by an Indigenous board. CAT's website states, "CAT's vision is for happy and safe communities of Indigenous people".[37]

Bushlight specifically addresses the challenge of sustainable access to power. The program is a direct result of an audit of renewable energy systems in remote areas that was carried out between 1997 and 1999 by Australian Co-operative Research Centre for Renewable Energy and CAT. The audit found that many of the systems did not meet the power needs of residents, were installed without information and training, and did not have a regular service and maintenance regimen in place.[38]

In 2002, Bushlight was established to address these issues. They focus on informing and training communities to better understand and use energy services, working with service networks to improve delivery and designing and building renewable energy systems. To date over 140 renewable energy systems have been designed and installed in more than 120 communities.

## CONCLUSION

In scoping out the landscape of what constitutes seamlessly mobile communications technology in the very remote regions of Australia, it is fair to argue that there are many complex elements—challenges of distance, availability of technology, affordability, access to power and of course cultural engagement. There is also the clear evidence that there are wildly differing capabilities and access to communications technology across the Central Australian region. On the positive side, there seems to be growing number of networks between communities under a range of umbrella activities, for example RIPIA, Mt Theo and *Aṟa Irititja*.

At such an early point in the research project there are no significant conclusions as yet, except that there is still a significant digital divide for many people living in Australia and it will not be sufficiently rectified with the rollout of the NBN. The most vulnerable people are those living in remote areas, most specifically Indigenous communities where lack of mobile and Internet access is less of an issue than other basic needs like reliable access to power. This chapter highlights that despite the rapid uptake of new technology around the globe, there needs to be consideration made to the people who are still losing out because of their geophysical location. A level playing field is an essential ingredient in fostering the goal of being "seamlessly mobile", making it not just a technological challenge but an issue of social equity.

## NOTES

Thanks to Martin Drury, Bronwyn Pollock, Andrew Taylor, Jim Best, Metta Young, Susan Schuller, Aaron Corn, Catherine Wohlan, Clare Maclean, Fiona Sivyer and Liam Campbell.

1. "What Do We Mean by the Term "Telecommunications" and How Is It Different from "Communications"?" *NBN Co*, n.d., accessed October 14, 2012, http://www.nbnco.com.au/for-schools/fact-sheets/history-of-telecommunications.html.
2. In this chapter the use of "Indigenous" to describe the diversity of cultures and communities in Australia is reflective of the broader discussion reflected in the references. It needs to be noted that for many native people this is not an appropriate term, their preference being Aboriginal, Torres Strait Islander, and specific regional references, e.g., Murri, Koori, Warlpiri.
3. PY Media, "Anangu Pitjantjatjara Yankunytjatjara (APY)", n.d., accessed October 29, 2011, http://www.waru.org/organisations/ap/.
4. "Remote Indigenous Broadcasting Services", Australian Government Department of Environment, Water, Heritage and the Arts, December 2008, accessed October 12, 2012, http://www.dbcde.gov.au/__data/assets/pdf_file/0016/137050/Map_showing_locations_of_Remote_Indigenous_Broadcasting_Services_RIBS.pdf.
5. Ellie Rennie et al., "Home Internet for Remote Indigenous Communities", 11, *ARC Centre of Excellence for Creative Industries, the Centre for Appropriate Technologies and the Central Land Council.* Australian Communications Consumer Action Network, 2011, accessed October 25, 2011, http://www.cci.edu.au/sites/default/files/mcummins/Home%20internet%20for%20remote%20Indigenous%20communities.pdf.
6. Bob Beadman, "A Working Future, Territory Growth Towns" (paper presented at the 4th Indigenous Economic Development Forum, Alice Springs, Australia, October 6–7, 2009), accessed August 29, 2011, http://www.rdia.nt.gov.au/__data/assets/pdf_file/0003/115653/A_Working_Future_Territory_Growth_Towns.pdf.
7. Rennie et al., "Home Internet for Remote Indigenous Communities", 11.
8. Ibid., 18.
9. COAG, "Closing the Gap: National Partnership Agreement on Remote Indigenous Public Internet Access", July 2, 2009, accessed October 12, 2012, http://www.dbcde.gov.au/__data/assets/pdf_file/0006/119679/NP_remote_indigenous_internet_access_Sig.pdf.
10. Rennie et al., "Home Internet for Remote Indigenous Communities", 15.

11. "Remote Indigenous Public Internet Access", *Introduction of Remote Indigenous Public Internet Access*, n.d., accessed August, 29, 2010, https://ntlwiki. nt.gov.au/display/RIPIA/3.+Introduction+to+Remote+Indigenous+Public+Int ernet+Access.
12. Kathryn Edwards, "OLPC Boosts Outback Education with Laptop Deployment", *Computer World*, May 27, 2009, accessed August 29, 2011, http:// news.idg.no/cw/art.cfm?id=82914112-1A64-6A71-CE4FA1189EFBFC7C.
13. Edwards, "OLPC Boosts Outback Education".
14. "8153.0—Internet Activity, Australia, Jun 2012", ABS, accessed October 21, 2012, http://www.abs.gov.au/ausstats/abs@.nsf/Lookup/5F0E5DC35F155A D3CA257A8E00127E25?opendocument.
15. "4714.0—National Aboriginal and Torres Strait Islander Social Survey, 2008", ABS, accessed October 12, 2012, http://www.abs.gov.au/ausstats/abs@.nsf/ Latestproducts/4714.0Main%20Features42008?opendocument&tabname=S ummary&prodno=4714.0&issue=2008&num=&view=.
16. Rennie et al., "Home Internet for Remote Indigenous Communities", 11.
17. "Aboriginal Children's Health", Better Health Channel, n.d., accessed February 2, 2012, http://www.betterhealth.vic.gov.au/bhcv2/bhcarticles.nsf/pages/ Aboriginal_children's_health?open.
18. Mick Gooda, "Towards a Reconciled Australia" (paper presented at the National Press Club, Canberra, November 3, 2010), accessed August 2, 2011, http://www.hreoc.gov.au/about/media/speeches/social_justice/2010/20101103_ npc.html.
19. Aboriginal Art Online, 2000, accessed August 4, 2010, http://www.aborigi nalartonline.com/culture/language.php.
20. Bruce W. Walker, Douglas J. Porter and Ian Marsh, "Fixing the Hole in Australia's Heartland: How Government Needs to Work With Remote Australia", RemoteFOCUS, September 2012, accessed September 14, 2012, http://www.desertknowledge.com.au/Files/Fixing-the-hole-in-Australia-s-Heartland.aspx.
21. Indigenous Community Volunteers, n.d., accessed August 4, 2011, http:// www.icv.com.au/.
22. F. Brady, and L. Dyson, "Report to Wujal Wujal Aboriginal Shire Council on Mobile Technology in the Bloomfield River Valley", 2009, accessed October 20, 2010, http://www.staff.it.uts.edu.au/%7Elaurel/Publications/MobileTechnology InBloomfieldRiverValley.pdf.
23. Brady and Dyson, "Report to Wujal Wujal Aboriginal Shire Council".
24. Rennie et al., "Home Internet for Remote Indigenous Communities", 54.
25. Ibid., 46.
26. Ibid., 7.
27. Kirrin McKechnie, "Stateline ABC News report", ABC, May 14, 2010, accessed August 4, 2011, http://www.abc.net.au/news/video/2010/05/14/2900122.htm? site=farnorth.
28. "Mission", One Laptop Per Child (OLPC) Australia, n.d., accessed August 2, 2012, http://laptop.org.au/.
29. "Yuendumu", PAW Media, n.d., accessed August 5, 2011, http://www. pawmedia.com.au/community/profiles#yuendumu.
30. "Paw History", Paw Media, n.d., accessed August 5, 2011, http://www. pawmedia.com.au/about-us/history.
31. "Paw History".
32. Melinda Hinkson, "New Media Projects at Yuendumu: Inter-Cultural Engagement and Self Determination in an Era of Accelerated Globalization", *Continuum: Journal of Media and Cultural Studies* 16 (2002): 201–220.

33. "The Mt Theo Program", Walpiri Youth Development Aboriginal Development Corporation, n.d., accessed 11 October, 2012, http://mttheo.org/home/wydac/.s

34. "2012 Strategic Plan", 3, Warlpiri Youth Development Aboriginal Corporation, n.d., accessed October 12, 2012, http://www.mttheo.org/home/wp-content/uploads/2011/10/WYDAC_Strategic_Plan_2012.pdf.

35. PY Media, Anangu Pitjantjatjara Yankunytjatjara (APY), n.d., accessed October 29, 2011, http://www.waru.org/organisations/ap/.

36. Caddie Brain, "Papunya Moves from Dots to Dot.com", *ABC Rural*, May 4, 2012, accessed October 12, 2012, http://www.abc.net.au/rural/nt/content/201205/s3495837.htm.

37. "About CAT" Bushlight, n.d., accessed October 12, 2012, http://www.bushlight.org.au/default.asp?action=article&ID=70.

38. "Our History" Bushlight, n.d., accessed October 12, 2012, http://bushlight.org.au/default.asp?action=article&ID=24.

# 5 Staying Connected: How Adult Literacy, Education and Income Influence Mobile Phone Use

## A Comparative Analysis of 30 Countries from 2001 to 2009

*Marian Stewart Titus*

## INTRODUCTION

It is now well established that global mobile phone penetration has occurred at a staggering rate since these devices were first introduced commercially in 1983. Mobile phones have out-diffused virtually every prior technology, including bicycles, radios, television sets, wallets, wire-line phones and wrist-watches, and in just twenty-five years.[1] This surge in global mobile phone penetration—particularly in emerging markets—warrants further study in order to better understand the penetration rates between countries with very high, medium and low levels of human development.

Mobile phones occupy a unique place in the repertoire of information and communication technologies (ICTs). With many other ICTs, such as landline telephones or fixed Internet access, physical infrastructure is required to facilitate widespread diffusion and adoption. However, even though mobile phone networks also need infrastructure, such as cell towers and electricity, to operate, users can operate mobile phones even without electricity by charging them with car batteries.[2] So people worldwide, whatever their level of income, education, literacy, geographical location, age or gender, are using these devices.

The mobile phone has become the new "universal necessity"[3] that provides people with the informal right to personal connectivity. As more people acquire mobile phones, it becomes necessary for others to have one as well, leading mobile communication expert James Katz to observe in a National Public Radio interview with E. Weiner in 2007, "You're a problem for other people if you don't have a mobile phone".[4]

## LITERATURE REVIEW

By 2009, there were 4.6 billion mobile phone subscribers and users worldwide, out of a global population of 6.7 billion.[5] Mobile phone adoption is now greatest in emerging markets such as Asia, Africa, the former Soviet Union, Latin America and the Caribbean, and is being driven primarily by prepaid mobile phone subscriptions.[6] Mobile telephony is recognized for its ability to diminish the digital divide between more technologically and less technologically developed countries.[7] Increased mobile telephony penetration can strengthen the reciprocal relationship between technology and quality of life,[8] which has major positive implications for lesser-developed countries.

The digital divide is not a homogenous phenomenon, and Internet and mobile phone digital divides are not the same.[9] The digital divide is less evident with mobile phone penetration compared with other ICTs such as the Internet and personal computing. Mobile phones have been able to overcome the barriers of inadequate landline infrastructure in many developing countries. Prepaid phones in particular have bypassed the haphazard economic condition of poorer populations who are unemployed or seasonally employed and ineligible for post-paid contracts. In addition, mobile phones have several attributes that make them very attractive to users all over the world, such as their relative advantage, compatibility with a range of lifestyles, simplicity, trialability, observability,[10] economy, affordability and portability.[11]

The literature on new-product diffusion among individuals has established that adoption is a function of consumer demographics, such as age, income and education, and other personal, psychological and product-specific factors.[12] Numerous studies support a positive relationship between education and innovativeness.[13] However, some studies have shown mixed results for the impact of demographic variables on mobile phone adoption. In the context of Western culture, Rice and Katz found that, for Americans, work status, marital status, and age were predictors for mobile phone adoption.[14] Wareham, Levy and Shi found that income, education, occupation but not age predicted mobile phone adoption.[15] Data from Asia showed similar trends, where, in Korea in particular, age, sex and education were important predictors as well.[16]

Global mobile phone penetration has attracted increased research interest. Between 1998 and 2007, fourteen studies were published on cross-country mobile telephony penetration from 1960 to 2004, using sample sizes ranging from 10 to 184 countries.[17] Among independent variables of interest to this study, thirteen of these studies included GDP per capita and one used GNP per capita as income measures; eleven used population; seven used fixed phone penetration; eight used competition; seven used cost; one used illiteracy; one used education; and one used age. Many of these studies explored country-level demographic predictors identified previously such as GDP, education and literacy. However, nearly all of these studies included a limited number of countries—only two examined more than 75—and the results were mainly descriptive, with little, if any contribution, to theory development.[18] An exception is more recent ethnographic work on mobile phone use in select Jamaican urban and rural communities, with its thick descriptions of the embeddedness of these ICTs in people's lives.[19] None of these studies included adult literacy or individual income among their independent variables. These studies showed that high wealth, high GDP per capita, competition, low user costs, a large user base, long wait times and late mobile adoption all promoted diffusion. Research results on the influence of country-level factors on mobile adoption in a global setting have been mixed, with penetration varying substantially even among the twenty-three Organization for Economic Co-operation and Development (OECD) countries of different GDP per capita.[20]

To date, there is little empirical data on mobile telephony penetration in lesser-developed countries.[21] Kas Kalba studied mobile adoption in over twenty countries and examined two cross-country databases compiled by Merrill Lynch and the International Telecommunications Union (ITU), an UN-affiliated agency.[22] He found that prepaid subscriptions made mobile communication accessible to nonsalaried individuals, who, on a worldwide basis, outnumber people with automobiles and fixed salaries. These two latter groups were the first mobile adopters worldwide. Prepaid mobile customers pay a premium for the convenience and flexibility of not wanting, or not being able to have a post-paid contract.[23] This benefit is especially germane in lesser-developed countries where landline telephone infrastructure may be limited.

## RESEARCH QUESTIONS

This study sought answers to these three questions:

> RQ1: To what extent has adult literacy contributed to greater mobile phone use in highly developed versus lesser-developed countries from 2001 to 2009?
>
> RQ2: To what extent has educational attainment contributed to greater mobile phone use in highly developed versus lesser-developed countries from 2001 to 2009?
>
> RQ3: To what extent has income contributed to greater mobile phone use in highly developed versus lesser-developed countries from 2001 to 2009?

## THEORETICAL RATIONALE

An extensive body of research links education to economic development and growth.[24] Furthermore, an educated population tends to have higher levels of literacy, and tends to drive the demand for technological innovations.[25] Therefore, the following alternative hypotheses are being proposed:

> *Hypothesis 1*: The level of a country's adult literacy will be positively related to its level of mobile phone subscriptions.

*Hypothesis 2*: The level of educational attainment of a country's population will be positively related to its level of mobile phone subscriptions.

Innovation diffusion studies have shown that early adopters tend be wealthier and can more afford to invest in new technologies.[26] Therefore, the following is being proposed:

*Hypothesis 3*: The level of male and female income of a country's population will be positively related to its level of mobile phone subscriptions.

## METHOD

### Sample

Secondary data from ten highly developed, ten medium-developed and ten low-developed countries for the years 2001, 2003, 2005, 2007 and 2009 were collected from the Human Development Reports for 2003, 2005, 2007/2008, 2009 and 2010, published by the United Nations Development Programme (UNDP), and from the website of ITU. All the data consisted of aggregated country-level figures. The UNDP human development index (HDI) is a summary measure of a country's human development.[27] The UNDP data were compiled from national censuses or surveys, data from other UN agencies and the World Bank.[28]

The thirty countries in this study were selected in a nonprobability manner in order to achieve a comprehensive representation with varying levels of development across all five continents. Countries were selected with the very highest and among the lowest HDI (Norway versus Afghanistan/Mali/Burkina Faso respectively); others in Asia with very HDI (Japan and Singapore); OECD countries such as the United States, Canada and Germany; medium HDI countries in Eastern Europe (Ukraine, Turkmenistan), the Middle East (Iran), Latin America and the Caribbean (Honduras, Jamaica, Suriname); low HDI countries in sub-Saharan Africa; and two recent and presently war-torn countries: Liberia and Afghanistan respectively. A complete list of the countries can be found in the Appendix of this chapter.

### Measures

Four independent continuous variables were selected. The first was adult literacy: the percentage of the literate population age five and above. The second was education, which comprised the combined gross enrollment ratio for primary, secondary and tertiary education expressed as a percentage, for 2001 to 2009. The third and fourth independent variables were estimated earned income for men and women respectively for 2001 to 2007. For 2009, the UNDP data were reported differently for education, as the percentage of the population age 25 and older with at least secondary education; and for income as gross national income (GNI) per capita (PPP US$), with no separate figures for male and female income. The dependent variable was mobile phone penetration per 100 inhabitants from 2001 to 2009, gleaned from the ITU.

## DATA ANALYSIS

The data were organized into three blocks of high, medium and low HDI countries, and descriptive statistics calculated for each group for each of the five years. Then for each year, histograms were created for each of the independent and dependent variables, of each block and then of all thirty countries, to visually inspect the data. Scatterplots were then created to show the relationship between each independent and the dependent variable for each block and for all thirty countries for each year. Finally, correlation analysis was carried out of each independent variable and multiple regression for all independent variables on the dependent variable for each block of ten countries by year. This process was repeated for all thirty countries by year. The results of the analyses for all thirty countries are displayed in Tables 5.1 and 5.2.

## RESULTS

### Adult Literacy

Adult literacy in high HDI and medium HDI countries demonstrated much higher levels than in low HDI countries from 2001 to 2009. Adult literacy was stable in high and medium HDI countries across the period. In the low HDI countries, it persisted at much lower levels, but increased slightly from 34.6% in 2001 to 48.2% in 2009.

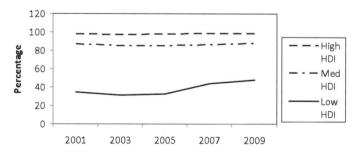

*Figure 5.1*   Mean of adult literacy in high, medium & low development countries: 2001–2009 ($n = 30$)

## Male Income

For 2001, 2003, 2005 and 2007, the UNDP data disaggregated male and female income, but for 2009, these were combined as GNI and reported as one average. For this chart, the GNI reported for 2009 was included with the estimated male income for 2001 to 2007. Male income rose in high HDI and medium HDI countries between 2001 and 2007, but much less so in low HDIs. In the high HDIs however, gains in male income peaked at US $45,254 in 2007 but declined somewhat to $37,509 in 2009 when reported as GNI. Male income grew most in medium HDIs where it more than doubled from $3,417 in 2001 to $7,461 in 2007, but in 2009, its GNI had slipped to $6,394. In low HDI countries, male income was relatively flat for the entire period and decreased in 2009 to $1,104, less than the 2001 level of $1,120.

## Female Income

There was a persistent gap between estimated male and female income from 2001 to 2007, where women earned approximately 50% less than men did in all thirty countries. This gap was widest in medium and low HDIs. Female income more than doubled in medium HDIs from $1,484 in 2001 to $3,787 in 2007. Female income increased in high HDIs as well but in low HDIs, these figures remained relatively flat at subsistence levels of less than $5,000.

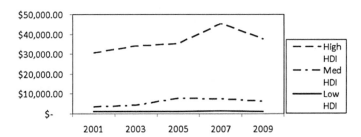

*Figure 5.2*   Mean of male income in high, medium & low development countries: 2001–2009 (*n* = 30)

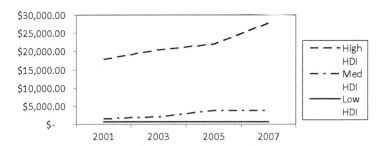

*Figure 5.3*   Mean of female income in high, medium & low development countries: 2001–2007 (*n* = 30)

## Education

For each of the three categories of countries, educational attainment was fairly stable from 2001 to 2007. Means were not calculated for 2009 as several medium and low HDIs had no data for the percentage of their populations with secondary education. For the high HDIs, there was a slight dip in 2005 to 86.06% before increasing to 91.5% in 2007. In medium HDIs, there were slight gains in 2005 to 72.2% but these declined to the 2001 level of 67.8% again in 2007. In the low HDIs, educational attainment rose slightly in 2003 (32.6%) and 2005 (33.4%) before declining to the 2001 level of 30.3% in 2007.

## Global Mobile Phone Penetration

In contrast to the previous variables, mobile phone subscriptions rose steadily and dramatically over the period in all thirty countries. These subscriptions doubled in high HDIs from 2002 to 2009. The increases in medium and low HDIs were even more dramatic, as subscriptions in these countries in 2001 were fewer than ten subscriptions per 100 inhabitants, but increased to 95.38/100 in medium HDIs and 34.55/100 in low HDIs by 2009.

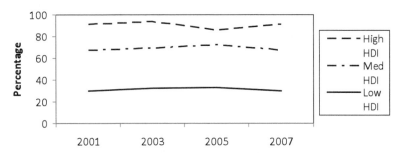

*Figure 5.4*   Mean of combined educational attainment ratio of high, medium & low development countries: 2001–2007 (*n* = 30)

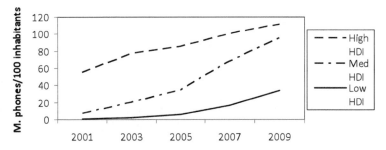

*Figure 5.5*   Mean of mobile phone subscription per 100 inhabitants in high, medium & low development countries: 2001–2009 (*n* = 30)

## Regression Analysis

What follows are the results of correlation, linear and multiple regression analyses for each of the three independent variables on the dependent variable first by each of the three blocks of countries, and then the results for all countries combined for 2001, 2003, 2005, 2007 and 2009.

## 2001: High HDI Countries

In high HDIs, male and female income (.33; $R^2 = .10$) and education (.29; $R^2 = .08$) were weakly correlated with mobile phone subscriptions, and were weak predictors as well. The weakest correlation was between adult literacy and mobile phone subscriptions (.26), with an effect size of only 7%. Multiple regression analysis showed that all independent variables combined were strongly correlated (.76) with the dependent variable, showing a 58% effect size.

## 2001: Medium HDI Countries

There was no relationship between literacy and mobile phone subscriptions. Education was weakly correlated (.24) with the dependent variable, accounting for a negligible 5% of variability. Male income (.10) was not correlated, and female income (.24) correlated very weakly with the dependent variable. Multiple regression analysis showed that all independent variables combined were moderately correlated (.53) with the dependent variable, showing a 28% effect size.

## 2001: Low HDI Countries

Male income was strongly correlated (.73; $R^2 = .54$), female income less so correlated (.49; $R^2 = .24$), and literacy very weakly correlated (.31; $R^2 = .09$) with mobile phone subscriptions. Education showed the weakest correlation (.28) with 8.3% variability. Multiple regression analysis showed that all independent variables combined were strongly correlated (.96) with the dependent variable, showing a 92.8% effect size.

## 2001: All Countries

There was a positive, but moderate, correlation between all the independent variables and mobile phone subscriptions. The strongest correlation was between male and female income and subscriptions (.88; $R^2 = .78$). Educational attainment was positively correlated with subscriptions as well (.70; $R^2 = .49$). Adult literacy and mobile phone subscriptions were correlated (.57), but this was the weakest predictor, explaining 33% of the variability in subscriptions. Multiple regression analysis of all three independent variables combined on the dependent variable showed a strong correlation

(.90), where the predictor variables explained 81% of the variability in mobile phone subscriptions.

## 2003: High HDI Countries

Male income (.13; $R^2 = .01$ ) and literacy (.22; $R^2 = .05$) were weakly correlated with the dependent variable, but female income somewhat less so (.21; $R^2 = .04$). Education showed a moderate correlation (.54), accounting for 29% of the variability. Multiple regression analysis of all three variables combined showed a somewhat stronger correlation (.66), accounting for 44% of the variability.

## 2003: Medium HDI Countries

Both literacy (.14; $R^2 = .02$) and education (.19; $R^2 = .03$) were weakly correlated with the dependent variable. Male (.37) and female (.28) income showed a weak correlation as well. Multiple regression analysis showed all independent variables as strongly correlated (.63), accounting for 40% of the variability, although 60% of this variability was unexplained.

## 2003: Low HDI Countries

Male income was strongly correlated (.69) and female income less so (.49) with the dependent variable, but education (.18) and literacy (.19) were very weakly correlated. Multiple regression analysis showed a marked increase in the strength of the correlation (.81).

## 2003: All Countries

Male income (.84) and female income (.83) showed the strongest correlations with the dependent variable, followed by education (.76) and literacy (.65). Multiple regression analysis showed an even stronger correlation (.87), predicting 76% of the variability.

## 2005: High HDI Countries

Literacy was positively correlated (.40), and female income much less so (.12) with the dependent variable. There was no relationship between male income or education on the dependent variable.

## 2005: Medium HDI Countries

Both literacy (.11) and education (.46) had very weak correlations, and male and female income had no relationship with the dependent variable.

Multiple regression analysis showed a strong correlation between literacy, income and education (.65) and the dependent variable, although accounting for 42% of the variability.

## 2005: Low HDI Countries

Male income (.54; $R^2$ = .29) and female income (.35; $R^2$ = .12) were correlated with the dependent variable, but education much less so (.11). There was no relationship between literacy and the dependent variable. Multiple regression analysis showed a strong correlation between literacy, income and education (.71) and the dependent variable, accounting for 51% of the variability.

## 2005: All Countries

Male and female income (.84), followed by education (.78) and literacy (.70) were strongly positively correlated with the dependent variable. Multiple regression analysis showed a very strong correlation between all three predictor variables (.87) and the dependent variable, accounting for 75% of the variability.

## 2007: High HDI Countries

Literacy (.54) was moderately correlated with the dependent variable, and male income (.19), education (.19) and female income (.12) showed very weak correlations. Multiple regression analysis showed a moderate correlation (.58) between the three predictor variables and the dependent variable, explaining 34% of the variability.

## 2007: Medium HDI Countries

Female income was moderately correlated (.51; $R^2$ = .26), and education very weakly correlated (.14) with the dependent variable. There was no relationship between literacy or male income and the dependent variable. Multiple regression analysis showed that all predictor variables were strongly, positively correlated (.72) with the dependent variable.

## 2007: Low HDI Countries

Male income was most strongly correlated (.74) with the dependent variable, followed by female income (.29) and literacy (.26; $R^2$ = .06). There was no relationship between education and the dependent variable. Multiple regression analysis showed a strong positive correlation between all predictor variables (.78) and the dependent variable.

## 2007: All Countries

Literacy (.72), education (.72), male income (.69) and female income (.67) were all strongly and positively correlated with the dependent variable. Multiple regression analysis revealed that all predictor variables were strongly correlated (.78) with the dependent variable, accounting for 61% of the variability.

## 2009: High HDI Countries

Literacy was moderately correlated (.49; $R^2 = .24$), the percentage of the population with secondary education (.39; $R^2 = .15$) weakly correlated, and GNI (.11) very weakly correlated with the dependent variable. Multiple regression analysis revealed a moderate correlation (.54) between these predictor variables and the dependent variable.

## 2009: Medium HDI Countries

The percentage of the population with secondary education was weakly correlated (.19; $R^2 = .03$), literacy very weakly correlated (.11; $R^2 - .01$), and GNI had no relationship with the dependent variable. Multiple regression analysis showed a weak correlation (.26) between all predictor variables and the dependent variable, accounting for 7% of the variability.

## 2009: Low HDI Countries

GNI was strongly correlated (.82; $R^2 = .67$), literacy (.32; $R^2 = .10$), and the percentage of the population with secondary education (.13; $R^2 = .09$) were weakly correlated with the dependent variable. Multiple regression analysis revealed a strong, positive correlation (.88) with the dependent variable.

## 2009: All Countries

The percentage of the population with secondary education (.59), GNI (.56) and literacy (.54) all had moderate correlations with the dependent variable. Multiple regression analysis showed a somewhat stronger correlation (.63; $R^2 = .40$) between the predictor variables and the dependent variable.

All three alternative hypotheses were supported, as simple linear regression analysis showed that there was a statistically significant, positive relationship at both the $p < .05$ and $p < .01$ levels, between adult literacy, income and education, and mobile phone subscriptions in all thirty countries from 2001 to 2007. However, except for educational attainment, adult literacy, male income and female income all weakened as predictors from 2001 to 2009. Tables 5.1 and 5.2 outline the results of the correlation and regression analyses.

*Table 5.1*    Correlation coefficients for all 30 countries: 2001 to 2009

|  | 2001 | 2003 | 2005 | 2007 | 2009 |
|---|---|---|---|---|---|
| Adult literacy | 0.57 | 0.65 | 0.70 | 0.72 | 0.54 |
| Estimated male income | 0.88 | 0.84 | 0.84 | 0.69 | |
| Estimated female income | 0.88 | 0.83 | 0.83 | 0.67 | |
| Gross national income | | | | | 0.56 |
| Educational attainment | 0.70 | 0.76 | 0.78 | 0.72 | |
| Population w/secondary education | | | | | 0.59 |
| N | 30 | 30 | 30 | 30 | 30 |

*Table 5.2*    Multiple regression results for all 30 countries: 2001 to 2009

|  | 2001 | 2003 | 2005 | 2007 | 2009 |
|---|---|---|---|---|---|
| Multiple R | .90 | .87 | .87 | .78 | .63 |
| R square | .81 | .76 | .75 | .61 | .40 |
| Adjusted R square | .78 | .72 | .71 | .55 | .34 |
| F value (*df*) | F (26.83, 4) | F (19.9, 4) | F (19.58, 4) | F (10.18, 4) | F (5.99, 3) |
| Significance F | 9.99 | 1.77 | 2.07 | 4.95 | .00 |
| Intercept | −4.04 | −11.13 | 8.11 | −10.92 | 33.79 |
| N | 30 | 30 | 30 | 30 | 30 |

Multiple regression analysis of all thirty countries—although still statistically significant—showed a weakening of the relationship between all the independent variables combined and the dependent variable, especially by 2009.

When analyzing the data within each of the three blocks, the situation from 2001 to 2009 was more nuanced, as demonstrated in Tables 5.3 and 5.4. The independent variables were much weaker predictors of mobile phone subscriptions especially in medium and low HDIs. Regarding male income, by 2007 and 2009, this was no longer correlated with mobile phone subscriptions in medium HDIs, whereas female income showed a moderate correlation with mobile phone subscriptions for this same period (.51 for 2007; .029 for 2009). In low HDIs, male income showed strong correlations and female income less so between 2001 and 2007. In medium HDIs, literacy was not associated with the dependent variable in 2001 or 2007 but showed a very weak and declining correlation from 2003 to 2009. Except for 2003, education was weakly correlated with mobile phone subscriptions in high HDIs, and weakly or not correlated in the medium and low HDIs from 2001 to 2009.

Multiple regression analysis showed a slight strengthening of these correlations, no doubt due to the inclusion of higher values for literacy, income

Table 5.3  Correlation coefficients for high, medium and low HDI countries: 2001 to 2009

| | 2001 | | | 2003 | | | 2005 | | | 2007 | | | 2009 | | |
|---|---|---|---|---|---|---|---|---|---|---|---|---|---|---|---|
| | High | Med. | Low | High | Med. | Low | High | Med. | Low | High | Med. | Low | High | Med. | Low |
| Literacy | 0.26 | 0.01 | 0.31 | 0.22 | 0.14 | 0.19 | 0.40 | 0.11 | 0.05 | 0.54 | 0.04 | 0.26 | 0.49 | 0.11 | 0.32 |
| M/income | 0.32 | 0.10 | 0.73 | 0.13 | 0.37 | 0.69 | 0.07 | 0.01 | 0.54 | 0.19 | 0.08 | 0.74 | | | |
| F/income | 0.33 | 0.24 | 0.49 | 0.21 | 0.28 | 0.49 | 0.12 | 0.04 | 0.35 | 0.12 | 0.51 | 0.29 | | | |
| Educa-tion | 0.29 | 0.24 | 0.28 | 0.54 | 0.19 | 0.18 | 0.08 | 0.46 | 0.11 | 0.19 | 0.14 | 0.07 | | | |
| GNI | | | | | | | | | | | | | 0.11 | 0.08 | 0.82 |
| Popn. w/sec. educ. | | | | | | | | | | | | | 0.39 | 0.19 | 0.13 |
| N | 10 | 10 | 10 | 10 | 10 | 10 | 10 | 10 | 10 | 10 | 10 | 10 | 10 | 10 | 10 |

Table 5.4  Multiple regression results for high, medium and low HDI countries: 2001 to 2009

| | 2001 | | | 2003 | | | 2005 | | | 2007 | | | 2009 | | |
|---|---|---|---|---|---|---|---|---|---|---|---|---|---|---|---|
| | High | Med. | Low | High | Med. | Low | High | Med. | Low | High | Med. | Low | High | Med. | Low |
| Multiple R | 0.53 | 0.96 | .66 | 0.66 | 0.63 | 0.81 | 0.67 | 0.65 | 0.71 | 0.58 | 0.72 | 0.78 | 0.54 | 0.26 | 0.88 |
| R square | 0.28 | 0.92 | 0.44 | 0.44 | 0.40 | 0.65 | 0.45 | 0.42 | 0.51 | 0.34 | 0.52 | 0.61 | 0.30 | 0.07 | 0.77 |
| Adj. R square | -0.28 | 0.87 | 0.00 | 0.00 | -0.07 | 0.38 | 0.01 | -0.03 | 0.13 | -0.17 | 0.14 | 0.31 | -0.04 | -0.39 | 0.66 |
| F value | 0.49 | 16.28 | 1.00 | 1.00 | 0.83 | 2.41 | 1.04 | 0.92 | 1.34 | 0.66 | 1.37 | 2.01 | 0.86 | 0.15 | 6.99 |
| df | 4 | 4 | 4 | 4 | 4 | 4 | 4 | 4 | 4 | 4 | 4 | 4 | 4 | 4 | 4 |
| Sig. F | 0.26 | 0.74 | 0.00 | 0.48 | 0.55 | 0.17 | 0.46 | 0.51 | 0.37 | 0.64 | 0.36 | 0.23 | 0.50 | 0.92 | 0.02 |
| Intercept | 544.45 | 20.55 | -0.13 | 127.43 | -12.68 | 0.57 | 636.78 | -60.26 | 3.90 | 636.78 | -60.26 | 3.90 | 1120.97 | 52.02 | -6.76 |
| N | 10 | 10 | 10 | 10 | 10 | 10 | 10 | 10 | 10 | 10 | 10 | 10 | 10 | 10 | 10 |

and education for the high and some medium HDIs, although the overall decline in the correlations' strength was still evident. Literacy, income and education combined were strongest as predictors in low HDIs.

## DISCUSSION

This study is significant because the data show that globally, the mobile phone has become a powerful tool of personal connectivity. Furthermore, this study also shows that in lesser-developed countries, the digital divide is more complicated than originally believed. The research questions asked about the extent to which adult literacy, education and income contributed to greater mobile phone use in highly developed versus lesser-developed countries from 2001 to 2009.

The alternative hypotheses proposed a positive correlation between these three variables and mobile phone subscriptions, and these hypotheses were all supported. However, the study revealed that the extent of the contribution of the predictor variables was not very dramatic. What the data also showed—by implication—is that systemic landline constraints as barriers to Internet use are no longer impediments in developing countries. Although this study did not specifically examine Internet access, there is a spinoff from owning a mobile phone, which comes with additional affordances, such as wireless Internet access. As Manuel Castells notes, as more technological convergence occurs between the Internet and wireless communication and multiple applications that distribute communicative capacity through wireless networks, more people worldwide can begin to live in a "culture of real virtuality", whatever their socioeconomic circumstances.[29] Therefore, people in lesser-developed countries have "leapfrogged" over fixed computer use and landline Internet access to gain the potential for, and access to, mobile wireless Internet.[30]

The study confirmed that literacy, income and education—all well-established predictors of innovation adoption—were statistically significant predictors of mobile phone penetration in both rich and poor countries. But these independent variables actually weakened in their predictive value or were no longer correlated with mobile phone subscriptions from 2001 to 2009 in all thirty countries, while these subscriptions grew exponentially over the same period. The multiple regression analyses of all countries for each year tended to disguise the true effects of literacy, education and income on mobile phone penetration, as the high values of these variables in high HDIs and some medium HDIs tended to act as a suppressor in the regression analysis.

### Implications

These findings differ from much of the previous literature on innovativeness and adoption. Contrary to the literature in which education and innovativeness are strongly correlated,[31] in this study, except for 2003, education was weakly correlated with mobile phone subscriptions in high HDIs, and weakly or not correlated in the medium and low HDIs from 2001 to 2009. Stump and others had a similar finding in their study of 170 countries using secondary data from the UNDP, the World Bank, the ITU and the Central Intelligence Agency Factbook, where education at the country level did not significantly affect mobile phone adoption levels.[32] Similarly in this study, in medium HDIs, literacy was not associated with the dependent variable in 2001 or 2007 but showed a very weak correlation in 2009.

Wealth (operationalized as GDP per capita), another important determinant of mobile penetration rates and consistent with the individual adoption literature,[33] was not a major predictor in this study, especially in high and medium HDIs. In fact, the study showed that in medium HDIs by 2007 and 2009, male income was no longer correlated with mobile phone subscriptions. The opposite was true for low HDIs, where male, and to a lesser extent, female income had a positive effect on the dependent variable from 2001 to 2009. Kalba, in his 2008 study cited previously, found a similar tenuous relationship between income and mobile penetration in high-income countries and a stronger relationship between income and mobile adoption in lower-income countries. Kalba, in this same study, highlights this paradoxical effect of income where he observes that the literature continues to treat income per capita as the lead indicator of a country's mobile phone penetration level, but "the declining role of GDP per capita in mobile adoption is difficult to deny", especially in countries with GDP per capita below $2,000.[34] Kalba also states that a growing number of these countries have attained mobile penetrations of 30%, 40%, 50% or higher, compared with 0.8 to 1.6 percent in developed markets.[35] In lower-income countries, the poorest households are spending more of their disposable income on mobile communication devices, which may exceed 10% in some low-income markets.[36] According to Kalba these households may be reducing their expenditure on food, clothing, transportation and other necessities, and he hypothesizes that these households may also have underreported income.[37] This author is personally aware that in the emerging market of Jamaica, which was included in the medium HDI countries for this study, there is a substantial underground economy that contributes to increased disposable income from time to time.

Why are people in medium and low HDIs willing to make this sacrifice to spend so much of their limited disposable income on mobile phones? Is their need for personal connectivity such a major imperative for them? As indicated earlier, people in these regions are already paying a premium for prepaid mobile access. The answers to these questions are beyond the scope of this study, and would require deeper country-level quantitative and/or qualitative studies of these users.

As mobile phones have become ubiquitous from 2001 to 2009, the established demographic predictors of use have become less important. The attributes of mobile phones—their portability, low cost, ease of use, and easy access—enable these devices to transcend all barriers, whether physical or demographic. The Internet, the Web and wireless communication are all means of interactive communication, rather than media in the traditional sense.[38] Therefore, people in medium and low HDI countries are no longer being locked out of the mainstream of ICT use. The mainstream is now becoming an "every-stream", so to speak, where world citizens—wealthy and poor—are living in a virtual or online culture, which is becoming embedded in their daily existence. Mobile phone distributors seem to have bypassed the constraint of cost and the systemic constraints of low literacy and education in poor countries, as these populations are subscribing just as much as those in wealthier regions.

## LIMITATIONS AND RECOMMENDATIONS FOR FUTURE RESEARCH

This study had limitations, as secondary data were used, and the UNDP cautioned that cross-country comparisons should be done with great care as the data were collected in national surveys and censuses with varying levels of rigor. There were changes in how some data were reported between 2007 and 2009, which made cross-country comparisons problematic. Nevertheless, this study raises critical questions about the reasons for the popularity of mobile phones worldwide. What is driving the ongoing surge in penetration, and has this device yet reached critical mass globally? It would be useful to examine other mobile ICTs in this cross-country context, across similar time periods, to discover whether the interrelationships among factors that influence mobile phone adoption are similar for other ICTs. It would also be valuable to explore, using quantitative and qualitative country-level studies, how mobile phones can be used to both shrink the digital divide within and between countries and enable access to more social and economic gains for populations of all countries.

# Appendix
## Countries Used in the Study
### High HDI

Norway
Canada
Sweden
Japan
USA
Singapore
New Zealand
Germany
Greece
Barbados

**Medium HDI**

Ukraine
Iran
St. Vincent and the Grenadines
Samoa
Suriname
Jamaica
Ghana
El Salvador
Turkmenistan
Honduras

**Low HDI**

Malawi
Cote d'Ivoire
Eritrea
Senegal
Liberia
Mozambique
Chad
Burkina Faso
Mali
Afghanistan

## NOTES

1. Manuel Castells, *The Rise of the Network Society* (Chichester, UK: Wiley-Blackwell, 2010), xxv; Kas Kalba, *The Global Adoption and Diffusion of Mobile Phones* (New Haven, CT: Kas Kalba, 2008), 2–3; Petri Rouvinen, "Diffusion of Digital Mobile Telephony: Are Developing Countries Different?" *Telecommunications Policy* 30 (2006): 47; Rodney Stump, Wen Gong and Zhan Li, "Exploring the Digital Divide in Mobile-Phone Adoption Levels Across Countries. Do Population Socioeconomic Traits Operate in the Same Manner as Their Individual-Level Demographic Counterparts?" *Journal of Macromarketing* 28 (2008): 397.
2. Kalba, *The Global Adoption,* 4.
3. James Katz, personal communication, with Marian Stewart Titus, March 30, 2011.
4. Quoted in Rich Ling and Jonathan Donner, *Mobile Communication* (Cambridge, UK: Polity, 2009), 145.
5. International Telecommunications Union, *Internet Subscriptions per 100 People: 2010,* http://www.itu.int/, accessed: February 23, 2013; Ronald Hill and Kanwairoop Dhanda, "Globalization and Technological Achievements: Implications for Macro-Marketing and the Digital Divide", *Journal of Macromarketing* 24 (2004): 150.
6. Kalba, *The Global Adoption,* 10.

7. Stump et al., "Exploring the Digital Divide", 398.
8. United Nations Development Programme, *Human Development Report 2007/ 2008* (New York: UNDP, 2008); Hill and Dhanda, "Globalization and Technological Achievements", 149.
9. Ronald Rice and James Katz, "Comparing Internet and Mobile Phone Usage: Digital Divides of Usage, Adoption, and Dropouts". *Telecommunications Policy* 27 (2003): 601–602.
10. Everett Rogers, *Diffusion of Innovations* (New York: Free Press, 1995), 224–250.
11. Rouvinen, "Diffusion of Digital Mobile Telephony", 7.
12. Rogers, *Diffusion of Innovations*.
13. Ibid.
14. Rice and Katz, "Comparing Internet and Mobile Phone Usage", 600.
15. Jonathan Wareham, Armando Levy and Wei Shi, "Wireless Diffusion and Mobile Computing: Implications for the Digital Divide", *Telecommunications Policy* 28 (2004): 450; Jonathan Wareham and Armando Levy, "Who Will Be the Adopters of 3G Mobile Computing Devices? A Probit Estimation of Mobile Telecom Diffusion", *Journal of Organizational Computing and Electronic Commerce* 12, no. 2 (2002): 168.
16. Hyungtaik Ahn, "A Nonparametric Method of Estimating the Demand for Mobile Telephone Networks: An Application to the Korean Mobile Telephone Market", *Information Economics and Policy* 13 (2001): 101.
17. Stump et al., "Exploring the Digital Divide", 407–408.
18. Ibid., 399.
19. Heather Horst and Daniel Miller, *The Cell Phone: An Anthropology of Communication* (Oxford: Berg, 2006), 81–99.
20. Stump et al., "Exploring the Digital Divide", 400.
21. Ibid., 399.
22. Kalba, *The Global Adoption*, 5–9.
23. Ibid., 15.
24. William Schweke, *Smart Money: Education and Economic Development* (Washington, DC: Economic Policy Institute, 2004), 5.
25. Kristopher Robison and Edward Crenshaw, "Post-Industrial Transformations and Cyberspace: Across National Analysis of Internet Development", *Social Science Research* 31 (2002): 336.
26. Rogers, *Diffusion of Innovations*, 264.
27. The UNDP HDI measures the average achievements in a country based in three basic dimensions: a long and healthy life (measured by life expectancy at birth), access to knowledge (measured by adult literacy and combined gross enrollment ratio in education) and a decent standard of living (measured by GDP per capita in purchasing power parity [PPP] U.S. dollars). These three dimensions are standardized to values between 0 and 1, with the simple average taken to arrive at the overall HDI value in the 1 to 0 range. Countries are then ranked on this value with 1 representing the highest HDI value. Countries are ranked as very high, high, medium, and low HDI. The total list of countries were for 2001: 175; 2003: 177; 2005: 177; 2007: 182; and 2009: 182. Each year, some countries rise or fall in this ranking, depending on socioeconomic circumstances.
28. According to the UNDP, due to differences in methodology and timeliness of underlying data, cross-country comparisons and comparisons over time should be made with caution.
29. Castells, *The Rise,* xxxi
30. Stump et al., "Exploring the Digital Divide", 398.
31. Rogers, *Diffusion of Innovations*, 264.

32. Stump et al., "Exploring the Digital Divide", 404.
33. Ibid., 399.
34. Kalba, *The Global Adoption*, 21–22.
35. Ibid., 20
36. Castells, *The Rise*, xxv.
37. Kalba, *The Global Adoption*, 23.
38. Castells, *The Rise*, xxvi.

# 6 In a World with Mobile Data, Survey Questions About Internet Use Should No Longer Implicitly Favor PCs

*Jonathan Donner and Cecile Bezuidenhoudt*

## INTRODUCTION

In this methods chapter, we draw upon surveys from Ghana, Kenya and Tanzania to illustrate how the widespread use of data-enabled mobile handsets presents new challenges for the measurement and theorization of Internet behaviors, particularly in resource-constrained settings where mobile-only or mobile-centric use is becoming increasingly common.

The traditional sketch of Internet 'use' as a discernible session (with a beginning, middle and end), taking place via a personal computer (PC), has steadily been losing its operational and theoretical utility to the social research and policy communities. Of course, this chapter breaks no new ground by restating this proposition; a broad community of Ubicomp researchers has been describing and developing alternative computing experiences for decades.[1] What is new, though, and worthy of discussion here, is the emergence of a parallel set of methodological and theoretical complications, coming not from the "smart homes" and "paperless workplaces" of the highly connected Global North—which constitute the traditional realms of Ubicomp research—but from everywhere else.[2] Specifically, the increasingly common use of data-enabled phones in resource-constrained communities in the Global South is also challenging how we conceptualize and measure Internet use. Thus, the most common operationalization of Internet use is under pressure from two groups—those for whom the PC has become but one of myriad methods of access, and those who use a PC rarely if at all. The research community can adjust in order to account for these groups, but only when it is willing to examine how its conventional methods for assessing and describing Internet use frequently retain an implicit or explicit default to the PC.

Among other things, there is a need for survey questions to be revised. In this chapter, we explore how, for many individuals, it is becoming increasingly difficult to respond reliably to variants of the conventional question, "How often do you access the Internet?" Researchers and policy makers face a fragmentation of platforms, affordances and contexts that are straining this common survey question. An earlier qualitative study of first-time mobile Internet use in South Africa concluded with the assertion that "the Internet is different when it is 2.5 inches wide".[3] This chapter discusses some method-ological implications of that difference. Since the Internet as experienced pri-marily or exclusively via data-enabled feature phones in pay-as-you-go bursts is not the Internet as experienced in smart households with a dozen or more seamlessly connected devices, *any survey questions that seek to encompass both (or either) of the extremes must be more carefully calibrated than before.*

To illustrate this proposition, we begin by describing our experience of analyzing secondary household survey data from Kenya and Ghana gathered by a market research firm. The firm's survey and sampling methods were world-class and have yielded some helpful insights. Nevertheless, as a subse-quent contrast with Tanzanian data from the same organization makes clear, the initial survey design limited our ability to distinguish Internet use by device and by venue. Only via the Tanzanian design were we able to isolate various permutations of Internet use: PC-only, mobile-only, and mobile+PC.

A second analysis uses the hypothetical experiences of families in more- and less-technologically connected settings to examine the wording of the "traditional" survey question "How often do you access the Internet?" A careful unpacking of the statement, in light of the rise of mobile Internet use as seen in the Tanzania data, reveals both the current implicit stance of the research community toward the notion of Internet use and the increasing complications associated with this stance.

Our discussion offers a set of concrete recommendations about survey crafting. We recommend methodological and conceptual approaches that offer (a) *no implicit/default privilege to the PC channel* and (b) *clear concep-tual separation between devices, channels, venues and uses.* We conclude by arguing that the interplay between theory and operationalization is bidirec-tional, in that simple measures (e.g., the digital divide) can take on broader policy significances. In this light, the shift to a more fluid and multifaceted operationalization of "Internet use", if widely adopted, may help reframe theoretical discussions of what it means to interact with the world's digital data networks, and how and where these interactions fit into users' lives.

## CASE STUDIES: KENYA, GHANA AND TANZANIA

Mobile-centric (or mobile-only) Internet use was first seen in Japan in the mid-2000s, with the popular I-Mode system.[4] With the drop in the cost of data-enabled handsets and the spread of mobile connectivity worldwide, mobile-centric Internet users are appearing elsewhere, particularly in de-veloping countries where PCs and landline Internet access remain relatively scarce and expensive. The world's next wave of Internet users is increas-ingly likely to have its first and primary Internet experience on a mobile phone.[5] Note, in this case, we are interested in the interface—particularly the screen—that faces the user. There are, of course, other new ways to get online, notably tablets and PCs and laptops that link to the Internet via a cellular/mobile modem or USB stick. Though common, none of these modes present the same combination of affordances and constraints as mobile handsets do. There is a small but growing research literature on mobile-centric Internet use, particularly from South Africa,[6] where there are already more mobile Internet users than "traditional" PC-based Internet users.[7] However, the practice is new and, despite the attention hype, remains under-addressed in the scholarly literature.

## GHANA AND KENYA DATA, 2009

One of the authors of this chapter chose, as part of her honors project in statistics at the University of Cape Town, to explore demographic and behavioral predictors of mobile-centric Internet use.[8] There, she had the opportunity to access representative household data gathered by the AudienceScapes project, which is run by InterMedia, the global research-based consultancy. By early 2010, with support from the Bill & Melinda Gates Foundation, the AudienceScapes project had released comprehensive data sets to the scholarly community from household surveys conducted in Ghana and Kenya during the spring and summer of 2009.[9] We were thrilled to find "mobile Internet" questions embedded in the surveys, even before mobile Internet use was likely to have spread far into Ghana and Kenya.

We wanted to use the data to identify demographic and behavioral variables that would differentiate between four cells in a 2x2 table; in other words, we wanted to distinguish PC Internet users from mobile Internet users, and, in particular to see if we could find evidence for a discrete set of "mobile only" Internet users in each nation. The primary items for our analysis were:

> C1:4 "Item available at home in working order: Internet access (e.g., on a computer, mobile phone)"
> C10:5 "How often do you use a mobile phone to: Access the Internet?"
> H1: "Apart from today, when was the last time you used the Internet?"

In Kenya (Table 6.1), 24% of respondents had mentioned using the Internet, in any form, at least once before the day of the interview; of those 24%, roughly two-thirds had also accessed the Internet via mobile. In Ghana (Table 6.2), roughly a quarter of the 17% who had accessed the Internet indicated that at least some of that access was via a mobile device. In other words, overall reported Internet usage levels were higher in Kenya than in Ghana, and the proportion of that usage that appeared to be mobile-based was also higher. This difference, relative to Ghana, is reflective of the telecommunications and social media boom underway in Kenya, which is home to initiatives like the crowdsourcing/mapping platform Ushahidi,[10] the technology incubator i-Hub, and most importantly, arguably the world's most successful "mobile money" platform, m-PESA.[11]

*Table 6.1*   2009 AudienceScapes Household Survey, Kenya

| | | C10:5 Accessed Internet via mobile | | |
| --- | --- | --- | --- | --- |
| | | Never | At least once | Total |
| H1: Apart from today, when was the last time you used the Internet? | At least once | 8% | 16% | 24% |
| | Never | 73% | 2% | 75% |
| | Total | 81% | 18% | |

n = 1,802 valid cases, with no missing data, from an original survey of 2000

*Table 6.2*   2009 AudienceScapes Household Survey, Ghana

| | | C10:5 Accessed Internet via mobile | | |
| --- | --- | --- | --- | --- |
| | | Never | At least once | Total |
| H1: Apart from today, when was the last time you used the Internet? | At least once | 12% | 4% | 17% |
| | Never | 82% | 1% | 83% |
| | Total | 95% | 5% | |

n = 1,746 valid cases, with no missing data, from an original survey of 2,051

Bezuidenhoudt drew on diffusion of innovations theory[12] to explore how demographic and behavioral predictors distinguished between those with mobile Internet access and those with exclusively traditional PC Internet access. In all, behavioral variables were better differentiators between "PC-only use" and "PC+mobile use" than were demographic variables, which limited our ability to identify a discernible group of mobile Internet users.

Yet the particular configuration of the survey items limited our ability to craft the desired 2x2—that is, to distinguish those who access the Internet *exclusively* through the mobile from those who utilize two more familiar combinations of access (PC-only, or PC+mobile). Had question C10.5 (b) been worded "How often do you use a PC to: Access the Internet?" in a format parallel to that of the question on accessing the Internet via mobile, we could have proceeded. The right ingredients (i.e., devices, venues, functions) were all present in the codebook, but this small omission complicated our inquiry.

## TANZANIA DATA, 2010

Given these setbacks with the 2009 data, we were pleased to learn of a revised survey design in AudienceScapes' 2010 Tanzania and Zambia studies, in which a general question on Internet use was followed by venue- and device-specific modifications. In case there was any confusion, the general question (H1) "How often do you use the Internet?" was accompanied by the following note: "INTERVIEWER: Please note, this includes using the Internet anywhere, including via mobile phones".[13]

Compared with Ghana and Kenya, Tanzania had a much lower incidence of Internet use overall, with only 171 (8.5%) of 2003 respondents reporting "At least once" to the question "How often do you use the Internet?" But with its revised design, the questionnaire in Tanzania was able to distinguish more finely between modes of Internet use. The 171 respondents who reported using the Internet were asked follow-up questions about use at specific locations (e.g., home, work, Internet cafes, school/ university, elsewhere, and at various locations via a mobile phone or other device). ('Mobile' was treated as a location in this design). They were also asked to identify their most frequent location for Internet use among those six locations.

We combined responses for three items in order to isolate different Internet access patterns vis-à-vis the mobile phone. Despite difficulties with missing values across eight items, we were able to identify seventy-two individuals that used the mobile phone as a means of Internet access in addition to their primary PC access, thirteen that used mobile as their primary mode of access (augmented by PC access), and five that relied exclusively on a mobile phone for Internet access. The modified 2x2 of mobile-only and mobile-primary Internet use for Tanzania appears in Figure 6.1. Most Tanzanians do not use the Internet, but among those who do, a subset relies on the mobile phone as opposed to the PC.

From these responses, we were able to identify the 13 individuals (.7% of Internet users in Tanzania) who used the mobile as their primary mode of Internet access (mobile-primary) as well as those who used only the mobile phone—in this case, the 5 respondents (.3 % of Internet users in Tanzania) who said they used the Internet on their handset and nowhere else. Represented using the base of all (valid) respondents, the modified 2x2 of mobile-only and mobile-primary Internet use for Tanzania appears in Figure 6.1. Most Tanzanians do not use the Internet, but among those who do, a subset relies on the mobile as opposed to the PC.

At this stage, it is best not to dwell on the exact sizes of the cells. The five mobile-only and thirteen mobile-primary users in the Tanzanian data were too few to be 'predicted' by demographic or behavioral variables in any statistically meaningful way. The numbers are small and likely to change quickly as data-enabled handsets become more popular, as they have become in neighboring Kenya. A replication of this grid with data from Kenya, South Africa or Armenia (as Pearce et al. have recently done)[14] would yield 2x2s with higher proportions of mobile Internet users.

Instead, the grid is an opportunity to begin to disaggregate the concept of "Internet use" into distinct modes. These various modes of "Internet access" are unlikely to be exact substitutes. Each has strengths, weaknesses and different use cases.[15] Why do researchers continue to lump them together?

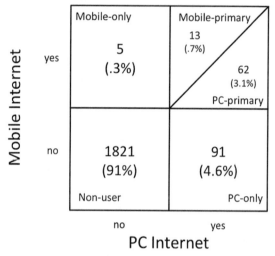

Source: Audiencescapes (2010). n excludes 11 refused/incomplete responses

*Figure 6.1*  Modes of Internet access in Tanzania, respondents (*n* = 1,992)

## RECONSIDERING THE "ACCESS/USE" QUESTION

The distinctions we observed between the 2009 and 2010 survey structures create an opportunity to contribute to an ongoing methodological conversation about how to operationalize Internet access and use. Meta-reviews of discrepancies between different methods appeared as early as 1996.[16] Others offered alternatives to early binary characterizations of "use", suggesting that Internet use was best reflected not as a divide between users and nonusers but rather as a spectrum of intensity of use or skill to use.[17] In the United States, the ongoing set of surveys from the Pew Internet & American Life project, on which Lenhart and Horrigan draw, uses a general-then-specific structure similar to the post-2010 AudienceScapes design, and thus allow for differentiation between Internet use across different platforms and locations.[18]

A basic estimate of who accesses the Internet *in general* is not without utility. There is important work do be done in the comparing of users and non-users.[19] However, the core questions supporting these estimates—namely, "how often do you use the Internet" and "how often do you access the Internet"—are pervasive enough to merit additional periodic scrutiny. Using examples from hypothetical settings in a well-connected domestic environment (e.g., an upper-middle-class family in Palo Alto) and a not-so-well-connected domestic environment (e.g., working-class Nairobi), this section reconsiders these traditional questions anew, and demonstrates how they are straining under the weight of new use cases by both the more and less (technologically) prosperous among us.

### "How Often . . ."

In more technologically connected households, the challenge may be in defining a top end to the question of frequency. When does periodic, frequent, discrete usage become simply "always"? If the more-connected family's home PC is on before anyone even wakes up, or if Mom's tablet's e-mail setting is set to "push", is the family ever offline? And, for practical purposes, should their responses be treated differently from those who are online all day at work but return in the evenings to a home with no PC?

Contrast that with a newer scenario, where, for our less-connected family, Internet connectivity may not be measured by the rhythm of a workweek or school day but rather by the availability of prepaid airtime to drive the mobile phone.[20] In earlier work in South Africa, we observed study participants who dropped in and out of connectivity based on the amount of airtime they had on their phone or whether they had a phone at all.[21]

### ". . . Do You . . ."

For more-connected families, it is becoming trickier to determine what is meant by "you". Shared DVRs, game consoles, set-top boxes, digital picture frames, appliances and electricity meters may be chatting away on 'the Internet', doing their owner's bidding via Internet Protocols (IPs). Are they "us" or merely our agents? Similarly, as individuals maintain digital identities online, on social networking sites in particular, their profiles can be viewed even when their owners are offline. If someone reads a status update after that user has logged off, is that user still, in a sense, online?

The less-connected families have issues with the subject of the question ("you"), as well. What if the family has two handsets, one of which is data-enabled and the other not? And if the family occasionally shares the devices,[22] who then is the "you"? Or, in the case of mediated access,[23] if a phone owner brings a phone to a shop and lets someone else "drive" the Internet for them, to download a song or get a ringtone, does the phone owner, who may or may not have the skills to manipulate the phone's online capabilities, get to respond to the question about her being "online"?

### ". . . Access or Use . . ."

In more-connected families, the phenomenon of fractional attention means there may be more screen hours than there are hours in a day.[24] The access question, however, seems to imply complete and undivided attention.

Or, consider a use case from someone who gives a device his full attention and yet can barely be said to be "using" it. In our earlier study with first-time mobile Internet users, we recruited women in South Africa who owned Internet-ready phones but, for the most part, did not know how to operate them. Some had pressed the Internet button or found the on-screen Internet folder but had little idea of what they were viewing.[25] Perhaps a would-be user happens to speak a language into which little or no online content has yet been encoded. If he pushes his phone's search button and is taken to the homepage of an English-language search engine, has there been "access"? Has he "used" the Internet successfully? As Warschauer[26] argues, access to and use of the Internet matters little without the skills to take advantage of the systems.

## "... the Internet?"

This has always been the slipperiest part of the phrase, and is probably getting worse as screens and form factors proliferate. More-connected families have always been able to toggle between e-mail, instant messengers, games, client programs like financial management software, and browsers. Only the browser experience necessarily utilizes the World Wide Web—the rest may only be "on the Internet", and the two are not synonymous.

The quality of hardware, software and network connections matter too. The difference between what one can accomplish in fifteen minutes, sitting in a dusty cybercafé with a few machines sharing the same dial-up connection, and what one can accomplish "back at the office" with dual monitors, multiple cores and a T1 line, is astounding.[27]

Mobile phones—as well as tablets and other devices that run downloadable applications—exacerbate these conceptual distinctions, between Web and Internet and between Internet and data, since many people are using "apps" to access content that previously or alternatively could be accessed via the World Wide Web. In our conversations with first-time, mobile-centric Internet users in South Africa, we found some individuals who were using instant messenger clients, particularly Mxit, but did know they were accessing the Internet at the time. Others even claimed to know of and use popular search engines by name but reported having never been "on the Internet".[28] One result of this fragmentation in South Africa has been Goldstuck's suggestion that the "mobile Internet" be divided into three tiers.[29]

- "Tier 1: The WAP [Wireless Application Protocol] Internet (access to WAP gateways, which includes mobile versions of brand sites, mobile versions of traditional and new media publisher sites, downloads of ringtones, games and other content, which may only involve a single link from the phone; the typical user of the WAP Internet is not always aware of using the Internet)"

- "Tier 2: The Mobile Application Internet (usage of 'stand-alone' applications on the phone that rely on data feeds, such as Mxit, Gmail, and Maps; the typical user is aware of using data, but not of fully accessing the Internet)"
- "Tier 3: Mobile Web Browsing (usage of a Web browser to access the World Wide Web from the phone—understood by most users to represent full Internet access)"

Meanwhile, efforts are underway to extend the reach of the Internet to low-resource communities by giving it "offline" skins and interfaces that would bring it even beyond Tier 1—to people with no data access at all. SMS servers and gateways can query databases[30] and services like Google, Twitter, and Facebook. Voice servers can read and write to Web pages[31] and wikis;[32] meanwhile, simpler mechanisms, like "blackboard bloggers",[33] may take online content and republish it in offline ways.

This is not to say that all cases are problematic; most people, most of the time, know when they are interacting with "the Internet" . . . but as ubiquitous computing scenarios proliferate, as, in the parlance of this volume, the "seamlessness" of Internet experiences increases to the point where awareness of online status fades, as chatty portable Internet devices store, use and broadcast our locations and activities (with or without our approval), and particularly, as tens of millions of midrange phones begin to hide the data channel behind stand-alone applications, survey respondents should not be expected to always know when they are "online".

## IMPLICATIONS FOR SURVEYS AND QUESTIONNAIRES

The scenarios and questions raised by the data analysis and explication exercise suggest that the traditional method of asking about Internet access is becoming increasingly problematic. The march toward smart homes, cloud-based computing and ubiquitous devices, from tablets to TVs to laptops, continues to strain the method from one direction, while the rapid uptake of inexpensive data-enabled handsets among those with no other forms of Internet access may soon place strain on it from another.

The single most important message to would-be questionnaire writers is to craft questions and question sequences in *a format that grants no implicit/default privilege to the PC as the means of accessing "the Internet"*. We wish to caution against designs that start with PC-based Internet use and then modify it with 'extras' such as mobile Internet use. Respondents should be able to accurately share the full sweep of their Internet behaviors, even if there is no PC in sight.[34]

## AN INCREMENTAL FIX

The first way to achieve this might be, space willing, to ensure clear conceptual separation between devices, channels, venues and uses. Questionnaire writers might still elect to do what the recent Pew and AudienceScapes surveys have done, asking first about "the Internet" in general before diving into an interlaced litany of devices and venues. As long as the items include "mobile only" and "non-PC" experiences alongside PC experiences, this should work; however, with populations having no previous PC/Internet experience, such a setup may miss those in the lower tiers of mobile Internet use who do not know they are online.

Depending on the purpose of the survey, a set of questions employing this incremental fix might include the following:

- Devices/screens
- Channels (dial-up, DSL, cable, cellular/wireless)
- Ownership/control (public, shared privately, or owned personally)
- Venues (home, telecenter/café/library, workplace, school, mobile)
- Functions (e-mail, social network, search, information processing, music entertainment, news, etc.)
- Agents (from devices that run on people's behalf to humans accessing the net on others' behalf)
- Costs (free access, pay-as-you-go, or post-paid/unmetered)

These items are likely to require conditional nesting into cascading matrices of items as required, though it is unlikely that the full multidimensional matrix will be explored.

## A REIMAGINATION

A more radical reimagination avoids representing a 'digital divide', in favor of something more like the spectrum described by Lenhart and Horrigan.[35] One brief—albeit not particularly exhaustive or accurate—route is to offer clusters or archetypes that could be shared with respondents, such as, "Which of the following is most like you? Which is least like you?"

- David never uses the Internet. He has a simple cell phone but doesn't use computers.
- Mary uses the Internet on her cell phone. She chats, does searches, and can update her social network profile via her phone. She uses a PC from time to time at work or school but doesn't own one.
- Adam has a PC at home and uses it for all kinds of things, like downloading movies and surfing the net.

- Kate's family has a DVR and downloads videos from the Internet to watch on the TV. She has a smartphone as well as a tablet and toaster that download their own software updates.

Another approach recognizes that the number of permutations and dimensions involved in Internet access may now be too numerous (and multidimensional) to capture in even a single spectrum. Instead, discrete combinations of venues, devices and purposes could be generated on the fly, like a conjoint.[36]

- Do you check e-mail from a phone at work?
- Do you watch videos on a tablet at a telecenter?
- Does a friend help you do instant messaging on a PC at home?
- Do you do searches on a PC at school?

With a big enough sample, clusters of context-specific Internet behaviors might emerge, and would provide a different conceptualization of what use looks like across a population. That new representation would come at the cost of comprehensive details about any one individual respondent; however, it is a radical fix in that it is not supportive of efforts to standardize and generalize, nor is it possible to track a figure like "the number of Internet user per 100", in the International Telecommunication Union (ITU) style,[37] if one has abandoned a single definition of 'use'.[38]

## DISCUSSION: IT MATTERS HOW WE ASK

This is not exclusively a discussion about methodological minutiae for closed-end questionnaires. These questions about frequencies and distributions of Internet access and use are reflective and reinforcing of certain theoretical, design and policy orientations toward the phenomenon of Internet access. Previously, while almost *all* Internet access was observable in discrete PC-based events (and, conversely, almost all telephonic activity occurred via landlines), these events could be aggregated and summed up into patterns of use and nonuse; the number of people "online", and the time they spent online, could be easily quantified. When those aggregations revealed consistent patterns of more use and less use between subsections of the U.S. (and later world) populations, discussion of "digital divides" naturally followed.[39]

Concurrently, and importantly, many scholars questioned the stark "binary" nature of a divide, pointing instead to a set of gradations based on skills and/or frequency of access.[40] Yet the popular metaphorical and rhetorical pull of the binary divide was strong, and, when coupled with the explosion in mobile phone use around the world, perhaps irresistible. By the middle of the first decade of the twenty-first century, some were suggesting that mobiles would "close" the divide.[41] This formulation has become quite common, so much so that a Web search in October 2012 for ["Digital Divide" + "Mobile"] in Google and Bing yielded 4.3 and 2.1 million hits, respectively. By treating access as a binary thing (and demanding metrics to assess it), the combined efforts of industry, researchers, NGOs and policy makers helped solidify a popular fixation on the question, "How often do you access the Internet?"

The overall concept of binary access needs not disappear entirely from the policy and research domains. The ITU's statistics, for example, have revealed steady but not perfectly distributed advancements in the number of landline, mobile and broadband connections per 100 people. In the future, those numbers will probably continue to mark progress toward the moment when nearly every human being has at least one way onto the Internet, but we return to the uncertainty around the answers to that core question, "How often do you access the Internet?" This chapter's central assertion has been that, thanks to more "ubiquitous" experiences in the Global North, and thanks equally to more low-functionality mobile experiences in the Global South, this question is becoming increasingly flawed.

The realistic, pragmatic, minimum implication of this flaw is that the question must be revised to treat it carefully and to craft questions and question sequences in a format that grants no implicit/default privilege to the PC as the means of accessing "the Internet". We will know we have succeeded in removing the implicit privilege afforded to the PC if the phrase "PC Internet" became as common in the literature as "mobile Internet".

The less realistic, probably radical, implication of this flaw is to abandon entirely the line of questions aiming to assess a presumed universal "Internet" experience in favor of ones that identify patterns, commonalities and interdependencies between contextually situated uses of a variety of devices, applications and systems that happen to share a reliance on some similar digital protocols, like IP and the URL. This repivot may work for some specific research projects—indeed, the input of study participants might make it possible to create context-specific instruments—but not for the broader policy community, which requires globally generalizable survey items, at least until everyone is, indeed, "online".

Both the incremental fix and proposed reimaginations do not reject the PC; rather, they reframe it as one mode among many. The irony here is that it may not be the connected family or the smart home of the future that gets us, as researchers, to a PC-neutral research frame but rather the growing numbers of less-connected households in Nairobi, Accra and so on. This brief chapter focused on the methodological implications of the spread of data-enabled handsets in the developing word for research drawing on survey instruments. As more individuals and households in these environments continue to find their way online without a PC, the least that we can do as researchers is to ensure that our instruments reflect these patterns.

These refinements to our instruments can support our theoretical endeavors. If our goal is to measure and compare Internet use across geographies and income levels, then our survey and questionnaire items need to be more nuanced and flexible. If our goal is to explore one or more of a growing heterogeneity of use cases (where "the Internet" as experienced by first-time mobile-only users in South Africa is not the same "Internet" as that which is accessible via a cable modem in a home in California or that which is accessed via a telecenter/café in Beijing), then researchers may feel empowered to deviate from that traditional "how often do you access the Internet" question. In either case, whether refining a mile-wide ITU-style sweep or sharpening the mile-deep dive, the shift to a more fluid and multifaceted operationalization of "Internet use", if widely adopted, may help reframe theoretical discussions of what it means to interact with the world's digital data networks, and how and where these increasingly diverse interactions fit into users lives.

## NOTES

Initial analysis for this paper was supported by the University of Cape Town as part of Cecile Bezuidenhoudt's honors project. We are grateful to Greg Distiller, lecturer in statistical sciences, for his comments and support. Data analyzed in this article were collected by InterMedia as part of the AudienceScapes project. The authors appreciate the assistance provided by InterMedia in making these data available. The views expressed herein are the authors' own.

1. Norbert Streitz and Paddy Nixon, "The Disappearing Computer", *Communications of the ACM* 48, no. 3 (2005): 32–35; Mark Weiser, "Hot Topics—Ubiquitous Computing", *Computer* 26, no. 10 (1993): 71–72.
2. A specific conversation about the role of the Global South in Ubicomp research occurred at "Globi-Comp: Taking Ubicomp Beyond Developed Worlds", a workshop held on September 30, 2009, in conjunction with the 2009 Ubicomp Conference in Orlando, FL. The resulting special issue is described in Gary Marsden, Lucia Terrenghi and Matt Jones, "Globicomp—Doing Ubicomp Differently: Introduction to the Special Issue", *Personal and Ubiquitous Computing* 15, no. 6 (December 14, 2010): 551–552.
3. Jonathan Donner, Shikoh Gitau and Gary Marsden, "Exploring Mobile-Only Internet Use: Results of a Training Study in Urban South Africa", *International Journal of Communication* 5 (2011): 574–597.
4. Kenichi Ishii, "Internet Use via Mobile Phone in Japan", *Telecommunications Policy* 28, no. 1 (February 2004): 43–58.
5. Morgan Stanley Research, *The Mobile Internet Report: Ramping Faster Than Desktop Internet, the Mobile Internet Will Be Bigger Than Most Think* (New York: Morgan Stanley, 2009).
6. Tanja Bosch, "Wots Ur ASLR? Adolescent Girls' Use of Cellphones in Cape Town", *Commonwealth Youth and Development* 6, no. 2 (2008): 52–69; Wallace Chigona et al., "Can Mobile Internet Help Alleviate Social Exclusion in Developing Countries?", *The Electronic Journal of Information Systems in Developing Countries* 36 (2009): 1–16; Donner et al., "Exploring Mobile-Only Internet Use".
7. Arthur Goldstuck, "The Mobile Internet Pinned Down", *World Wide Worx Reports*, 2010, accessed February 23, 2013, http://www.worldwideworx.com/the-mobile-Internet-pinned-down/.

8. Cecile Bezuidenhoudt, "The Mobile Internet in Africa with Specific Reference Made to Ghana and Kenya" (honors project, University of Cape Town, 2010).
9. AudienceScapes, "Codebook and SPSS Dataset for Ghana Survey 2009" (Washington, DC: AudienceScapes, 2009); AudienceScapes, "Codebook and SPSS Dataset for Kenya Survey 2009" (Washington, DC: AudienceScapes, 2009). The AudienceScapes website has a freely available data query tool whereby users can conduct basic analyses of Ghana and Kenya data sets, as well as 2010 data from Zambia and Tanzania. Their website was accessed February 23, 2013, http://www.audiencescapesdata.org/adscap/ASQuestions.jsp.
10. Ory Okolloh, "Ushahidi, or 'Testimony': Web 2.0 Tools for Crowdsourcing Crisis Information", *Participatory Learning and Action 59*, no. 1 (2009): 6.
11. Nick Hughes and Susie Lonie, "M-PESA: Mobile Money for the 'Unbanked' Turning Cellphones into 24-Hour Tellers in Kenya", *Innovations: Technology, Governance, Globalization 2*, no. 1–2 (April 2007): 63–81.
12. Everett M. Rogers, Diffusion of Innovations (New York: Free Press, 1962).
13. AudienceScapes, "Questionnaire for Tanzania Survey 2010" (Washington, DC: AudienceScapes, 2010).
14. Katy E. Pearce et al., "Demographics, Means of Access, and Internet Activities: How Do Mobile-only Internet Users Differ from PC-Only Internet Users?", in *International Communication Association Conference 2012 Mobile Preconference* (Phoenix, AZ, 2012).
15. Ibid.
16. Donna L Hoffman, William D. Kalsbeek and Thomas P. Novak, "Internet and Web Use in the U.S.", *Communications of the ACM 39*, no. 12 (December 1996): 36–46.
17. Wenhong Chen and Barry Wellman, "Minding the Cyber-Gap: The Internet and Social Inequality", in *The Blackwell Companion to Social Inequalities*, ed. Mary Romero and Eric Margolis (Malden, MA: Blackwell, 2005), 523–545; Mark Warschauer, *Technology and Social Inclusion: Rethinking the Digital Divide* (Cambridge, MA: MIT Press, 2003); Eszter Hargittai, "Second-Level Digital Divide: Differences in People's Online Skills", *First Monday 7*, no. 4 (2002): 1–20; Amanda Lenhart and John B Horrigan, "Re-Visualizing the Digital Divide as a Digital Spectrum", *IT & Society 1*, no. 5 (2003): 23–39.
18. Princeton Survey Research Associates International, "Spring Change Assessment Survey 2010", *Pew Research Center's Internet & American Life Project*, 2010, www.pewInternet.org/~/media//Files/ . . . /Mobile-Access-2010-topline.pdf.
19. See, for example, Ronald E. Rice and James E Katz, "Comparing Internet and Mobile Phone Usage: Digital Divides of Usage, Adoption, and Dropouts", *Telecommunications Policy 27*, nos. 8–9 (September 2003): 597–623.
20. Marshini Chetty et al., " 'You're Capped!' Understanding the Effects of Bandwidth Caps on Broadband Use in the Home", in *Proc CHI 2012* (New York: ACM, 2012), 3021–3030.
21. Shikoh Gitau, Gary Marsden and Jonathan Donner, "After Access—Challenges Facing Mobile-Only Internet Users in the Developing World", in *Proc. CHI 2010* (New York: ACM, 2010), 2603–2606; Jonathan Donner and Shikoh Gitau, "New Paths: Exploring Mobile-Centric Internet Use in South Africa", in "Mobile 2.0: Beyond Voice?" *Pre-Conference Workshop at the International Communication Association (ICA)* (Chicago, 2009).
22. Jenna Burrell, "Evaluating Shared Access: Social Equality and the Circulation of Mobile Phones in Rural Uganda", *Journal of Computer-Mediated Communication 15*, no. 2 (January 2010): 230–250.
23. Nithya Sambasivan et al., "Intermediated Technology Use in Developing Communities", in *Proceedings of the 28th International Conference on Human Factors in Computing Systems—CHI '10* (New York: ACM Press, 2010), 2583.

24. Donald F. Roberts and Ulla G. Foehr, *Kids and Media in America* (New York: Cambridge University Press, 2003).
25. Gitau et al., "After Access".
26. Warschauer, *Technology and Social Inclusion*.
27. Susan P. Wyche et al., "Deliberate Interactions: Characterizing Technology Use in Nairobi, Kenya", in *Proc CHI 2010* (New York: ACM, 2010), 2593–2602.
28. Donner and Gitau, "New Paths".
29. Goldstuck, "The Mobile Internet Pinned Down".
30. Rajesh Veeraraghavan, Naga Yasodhar and Kentaro Toyama, "Warana Unwired: Replacing PCs with Mobile Phones in a Rural Sugarcane Cooperative", *Information Technologies and International Development 5*, no. 1 (2009): 81–95.
31. Arun Kumar, Sheetal K. Agarwal and Priyanka Manwani, "The Spoken Web Application Framework", in *Proceedings of the 2010 International Cross Disciplinary Conference on Web Accessibility (W4A)—W4A '10* (New York: ACM, 2010), n.p.
32. Merryl Ford and T. Leinonen, "MobilED—Mobile Tools and Services Platform for Formal and Informal Learning", in *Mobile Learning Transforming the Delivery of Education and Training* (Edmonton, AB: AU Press, 2010), 195–214.
33. http://www.afrigadget.com/2009/03/13/liberias-blackboard-blogger/.
34. A second implication, although less central to this paper, might be to reconsider the use of the word "Internet" when we might mean "World Wide Web" or, alternately, a set of discrete human behaviors like chatting, browsing, writing, processing, storing, searching, and so on. As the ways to access Internet become more fragmented, what one does there (rather than how one gets there) might be the better place to focus.
35. Lenhart and Horrigan, "Re-Visualizing the Digital Divide".
36. Paul E. Green, Abba M. Krieger and Yoram Wind, "Thirty Years of Conjoint Analysis: Reflections and Prospects", *Interfaces* 31, Supplement 3 (May 1, 2001): S56–S73.
37. ITU, "Online Statistics, ICTeye', 2011, http://www.itu.int/ITU-D/icteye/Default.aspx.
38. Goldstuck, "The Mobile Internet Pinned Down".
39. Pippa Norris, *Digital Divide: Civic Engagement, Information Poverty, and the Internet Worldwide* (New York: Cambridge University Press, 2001); NTIA, *Falling Through the Net: A Survey of the "Have-Nots" in Rural and Urban America* (Washington, DC: United States Department of Commerce, 1995).
40. Chen and Wellman, "Minding the Cyber-Gap"; Warschauer, *Technology and Social Inclusion*; Hargittai, "Second-Level Digital Divide"; Lenhart and Horrigan, "Re-Visualizing the Digital Divide".
41. Economist, "Calling an End to Poverty", *The Economist* 376, no. 8434 (2005): 51–52; Jonathan Wareham, Armando Levy and Wei Shi, "Wireless Diffusion and Mobile Computing: Implications for the Digital Divide", *Telecommunications Policy* 28, nos. 5–6 (June 2004): 439–457.

Section II

# Mobile-Mediated Presence
## Seams of Intimacy, Identity and Connection

# 7 Organizing 'My Mind Is With You'
## Continued Interaction After Closed Interaction via the Mobile Phone

*Ditte Laursen*

## INTRODUCTION

Every interaction between people who have spoken before is continued interaction, and we know from studies of everyday conversations that just as conversation participants have techniques to create coherence between turns in the same interaction ("tying techniques"[1]), they have techniques to create coherence between different interactions. A party may, for example, very early on in a phone conversation, refer to an earlier conversation by bringing up a previous topic with the question, "How's your mother?" [2] According to Sacks, this is a way to show "my mind is with you", e.g., a way of saying that I know who you are and I know that the last time we talked your mother was sick.

This chapter examines how 14-year-olds in Denmark create coherence among different interactions in the form of mobile phone calls and text message exchanges. Hitherto, research on mobile phone communication has studied text messages and calls as isolated units of analysis. Research on text messages has focused on their discursive and linguistic features[3] and the sequential organization of exchanges.[4] Research on mobile phone calls has focused on call opening and its similarities and differences with empirical features of call opening characteristic of landline telephone calls.[5] Only one study, to my knowledge, has examined mobile phone calls and text message exchanges in interconnected communication sequences.[6] In that study, the sequences of interactions examined involved a text message preceding a call. In contrast, our study will focus on interconnected sequences in which closed interaction (by call) is *followed* by new interaction (by call or by text message). While the participants have a number of common reference points and previous topics to draw upon when they engage in the new interaction, the data demonstrate how participants continue, in their new interaction, the business of their immediate previous interaction. Using a conversation-analytic approach, we will demonstrate how interconnected communication sequences are established and maintained through the joint efforts of the participants, and we will demonstrate how this indicates the ways in which participants organize their relations.

## CONVERSATION-ANALYTIC WORK ON TELEPHONE CALLS

Conversation analysis is a methodology aimed at the systematic analysis of interaction, and was well suited for analyzing the daily mobile communication of the young people in this study. There is a long tradition of using conversation analysis to examine telephone conversations. Research on landline telephone openings is relevant to research on mobile phone openings. Four sequences in the landline telephone openings have been identified as follows: "summons-answer", "identification/recognition", "greeting-greeting" and "initial inquiries" ("How are you?").[7] All four sequences are not always present, but they nonetheless constitute the so-called canonical opening. Here's an example where all four sequences are present:

> ((summons: i.e,. phone ring))[8]
> Nancy: H'llo?
> Hyla: Hi:,
> Nancy: ↑Hi::.
> Hyla: How are yuhh =
> Nancy: = Fi:ne how er you,
> Hyla: Oka:[y,
> Nancy: [Goo:d,
> PS: (0.4)
> Hyla:.mkhhh[hh
> Nancy: [What's doin',

The canonical opening, based on U.S. landline telephone calls, has proved surprisingly robust in studies of telephone openings in other languages, but discrepancies have manifested themselves. For example, in Dutch, Swedish and Danish, unlike in American English, the callee usually identifies himself by name in his first turn.[9]

More recent research has focused on mobile phone conversations' openings, which have some distinctive features of their own.[10] In Finnish, the exchange of self-identification with name typical of landline openings is dropped in about half the cases in favor of a "greeting opening", in which the called first greets the caller, and the caller then greets the called and/or gives the reason for the call. With the British data, Hutchby and Barnett identify a "pre-voice sample identification" whereby both parties show an orientation toward identification before the other has said anything. Both observe a "where-are-you sequence", which sometimes may be part of the opening before the reason for the call is presented.

## CONTINUED INTERACTION ON THE TELEPHONE

In his studies on landline telephone openings, Schegloff also examines the special case of the callee using "yes" and "hi" in his first turn, in response to the summons. "Yes" and "hi" treat "presumptively the prospective conversation as 'foreknown', as one in which the answerer takes it he has warrantable information about the caller and the prospective course of action".[11] If the caller, in response, uses expressions whose referents are not in conversation, the call may be framed as a "call-back call":

((summons))
E: Yah?
J: Well, she doesn't *know*

In the call-back call, the parties display a "mutual orientation to 'what we know we (were) talk(ing) about' ".[12] Button has in his work with closings identified different sequence types appearing in the closing procedure.[13] One of these is the "arrangement-sequence", which puts the conversation "on a closing track", while showing the parties' orientation toward the conversation as one in a series.[14] By agreeing to meet or talk later the parties evoke a "standing relationship", making relevant this relationship as a type involving several consecutive meetings or conversations.[15] Years later, Licoppe investigated participants' collaborative work of mutual localization in mobile phone calls and showed that when this work is turned into an assessment of "co-proximity", a face-to-face encounter is projected as a relevant next action.[16]

## CONSTRUCTING RELATIONSHIPS IN OPENINGS AND CLOSINGS

Conversation analysis looks at language and interaction from a fundamentally sociological perspective. When we use language, we use it together, and a social order is brought about through our interaction. In conversation analysis, relationships are seen as being created, maintained and altered within and through interaction. This form of analysis contrasts with scholarly traditions in which relationships are taken as units that exist outside and are independent of the participants' own actions. Instead, conversational analysis takes into account that relationships change, sometimes from one moment to the next, and seeks to describe how participants construct social relationships from utterance to utterance as they converse. However, relationships are rarely foregrounded as a topic, rather, certain communicative acts, and the manner in which they are enacted, have particular implications for the relationships between the two interacting parties.[17] For example, Goodwin demonstrated that the way in which a request is made expresses a particular aspect of the relationship between conversation partners.[18]

The way in which this study's participants constructed their mobile conversations and text message exchanges as a continuous interaction had a unique impact on the relationships between the parties involved. In the opening of a text message dialogue or mobile conversation, the participants established a link with the foregoing conversation. The parties constructed their utterances in such a way that the other party could evaluate them as having some connection with a foregoing communication and some connection to a new set of actions. The manner in which the parties identified themselves to each other at the outset, the way in which they expressed recognition of the other and greeted one another, was crucial for the relationship and the ongoing interaction. Similarly, the way in which the parties concluded an interaction played a role in the construction of continuous communication, and its closing affected the way that the parties were left at the conclusion. Thus, it is in the openings and closings that the parties construct their interaction as an ongoing interaction, and it is here, too, that they demonstrate how much (or how little) they are in each other's minds. What follows is a more detailed analysis of the beginnings and endings of young people's mobile communications, through the examination of calls and text messages that continued the interaction from previous 'closed' calls.

## DATA

Recordings of mobile communication (text messages and mobile phone calls) of six 14-year-olds over a period of six weeks, during which each person was recorded for one week, were collected and analyzed. The six young people were friends belonging to the same class at a school in Copenhagen. They all use their mobile phones daily for text communication and calls. The recordings were made in cooperation with TDC Mobil, the leading Danish telecommunications company, and with the consent of both the participants and their parents. TDC Mobil was technically in charge of the recordings of calls and the logging of text messages. They used their standard equipment, normally used by order of the Danish police. The author received raw data (calls on digital audio tapes and text messages in Excel format) and TDC Mobil kept no copies. The author transcribed calls[19] and all data were coded. Names and places were changed in order to guarantee the anonymity of the persons involved. Sixty-six people are represented in the total data set, which consisted of 519 text messages, 284 conversations and 135 calls to answering machines. The focus of analysis for this chapter was on the mobile communication among thirty-one young people that consisted of 481 text messages, 173 calls and 72 calls to answering machines. In addition, the analysis for this chapter makes use of ethnographic observations dated from the time of the recordings.

Young friends in this study used their mobile phones to communicate over time in continuing, interconnected communication sequences. Their text messages and calls were often linked to other text messages and calls: 100 (out of 173) calls were parts of a series of calls, and 24 calls were preceded by a text message; another 24 calls were followed by a text message. Consequently, the calls and the text messages could not be dealt with in isolated units of analysis. The analysis for this chapter was limited to examining calls and text messages following "closed" calls, i.e., calls where the conversation initiates no further communication or requests for or promise of a later call/text message.

## MOBILE PHONE CALLS FOLLOWING 'CLOSED' CALLS

In the whole data set, 100 (out of 173) calls were parts of a series of calls. Calls could be connected in a series in a variety of ways. A typical sequence across two calls is a sequence in which the conversation in the first call concludes with a request for or promise of a later call that is fulfilled by the following call. This second call is similar to Schegloff's call back mentioned above. This series of calls appears to be oriented toward a request-acceptance-fulfillment sequence:

```
(Katrine/S75)
((summons))
2661       Da:    Daniel here
2662       Ps:    (0.7)
2663  → Ka:  yes hi Daniel (0.3) could you just give me a ring?
2664       Ps:    (1.3)
2665  → Da:  °OK°
2666       Ps:    (0.6)
2667       Ka:    bye:
2668       Ps:    (1.5)
@End

(Katrine/S76)
→ ((summons))
2679       Ka:    hi Daniel
2680       Ps:    (0.4)
2681       Da:    h*i*?
2682       Ps:    (0.8)
2683       Ka:    do you know what you did today?
[. . .]
```

In the first call (S76), Katrine rang Daniel with a request that he ring her (*could you just give me a ring?*) and the request was granted (°OK°). A moment later Daniel rang Katrine (S76). Katrine answered the call with the greeting *hi Daniel*, and Daniel greeted her again and expressed recognition with the intonation of *h*i*?*. With the following pause (0.8), Daniel gives the initiative back to Katrine, who asked him to call. In Schegloff's words, the caller invokes "the relevance of a preset agenda without explicating its basis".[20] This call series is based on a social practice whereby one keeps to agreements and fulfills promises and requests. The two parties enter into mutual obligations, with an expectation to keep their promises.

In this section, I will focus on the data sets' twenty cases in which mobile phone calls followed 'closed' calls, i.e., calls in which the conversation initiated no further communication. Although the previous call was concluded without any commitment to call back, this conclusion was treated as interim in the call that followed, such as the conclusion of an act in a play without the play itself ending:

(Daniel/S135)
[. . .]

| 1609 | Ru: | e:h are you coming down to the school now? |
| 1610 | Ps: | (0.9) |
| 1611 | Da: | yeah (.) where do we meet |
| 1612 | Ps: | (0.7) |
| 1613 | Da: | the can[teen |
| 1614 | Ru: | [[(>outside at the bu-<) |
| 1615 | Ps: | (0.3) |
| 1616 | Ru: | a::t- t- at the bus I guess |
| 1617 | Ps: | (1.2) |
| 1618 | Da: | at the bus |
| 1619 | Ps: | (0.5) |
| 1620 | Ru: | yes: why not |
| 1621 | Ps: | (1.3) |
| 1622 | Da: | right right what ever |
| 1623 | Ps: | (1.0) |
| 1624 | Da: | right but then- (.) I'll get my stuff and leave |
| 1625 | Ps: | (0.3) |
| 1626 | Ru: | okay |
| 1627 | Ps: | (1.1) |
| 1628 | Da: | bye |
| 1629 | Ps: | (0.4) |
| 1630 | Ru: | bye |
| 1631 | Ps: | (0.8) |

(Daniel/S136)
((summons))

| 1642 → | Da: | ye:ah? |
| 1643 | Ps: | (0.4) |
| 1644 → | Ru: | >where are you< now |
| 1645 | Ps: | (0.9) |
| 1646 | Da: | I'm up by the: (.) steps |
| 1647 | Ps: | (0.6) |
| 1648 | Da: | over by the football pitch |
| 1649 | Ps: | (0.4) |
| 1650 | Ru: | THEN RU::N |

[. . .]

The second call (S136) between Rune and Daniel came seven minutes after the two friends had agreed in another mobile phone conversation to meet at a bus stop (S135). In this call, there was no displayed expectation that a further call would be needed before they met at the bus stop. However, Rune rang Daniel anyway, and both parties showed in the opening exchange a heightened orientation toward each other by devoting almost no time to mutual identification, acknowledgement and greeting: Daniel answered the call with *yeah?*, which indicated his orientation toward Rune and enabled them to move quickly to the purpose of the conversation, at which time Rune presented the reason for his call already in his first turn.

The call is a typical case of calls following otherwise closed calls. In twelve out of twenty examples the callee displayed recognition in his first turn, showing awareness toward the caller and her call. The callee answered the call in the following ways: *hi:: sweetie?* (S3), *he::y* (S17), ↑*ha::*↓*llo::* (S37), *wha:t* (S42), *yeah?* (S81), *hi Daniel* (S119), *yea:h?* (S136), *yea::h?* (S145), *we're on King's New Square* (S146), *yea::h?*(S152), *he:y* (S233), *hi* (S243). In all these examples, the callee showed an orientation toward the caller and allowed in various ways a quick entry to the reason for the call. Compared with the data set as a whole, this is remarkable. This demonstrates that the caller ID function is a resource that is brought into play in certain contexts. In one case, the callee even anticipated the reason for the call and responded to the summons in his first turn with *we're on King's New Square* (S146). Of the remaining cases, "yeah" is the most minimal communication—mutual identification, recognition and greetings are skipped and the caller is able to start his business in his first turn. "Hi", "hey" and "hallo" skip mutual identification and recognition, but prompt a return greeting before the reason for the call is introduced. "What" is wary, but also enables a quick entry into the reason for the call. On his part, the caller introduces the reason for the call in his first turn, sometimes combined with a greeting, in all cases where the called has shown recognition.

In two of the cases where the callee did not display recognition in his first turn, the caller launched the reason for the call in his first turn anyway:

```
(Daniel/S144)
2000 → Ru: hallo
2001        Ps:      (0.5)
2002 → Da: hallo Ru:ne: could you bring e:h (.) some money
2003        Ps:      (0.6)
2004        Ru:      we already left
[. . .]
```

This means that in fourteen of twenty cases, the reason for the call was introduced by the caller's first turn. In four of the remaining six cases, the callee anticipated the reason for the call in his second turn:

108    *Ditte Laursen*

```
(Katrine/S54)
((summons))
2030        Ka:    halLO?
2031        Ps:    (0.7)
2032        Maj:   hi?
2033        Ps:    (0.2)
2034 → Ka: hi we're on our way
[. . .]
```

In S54, Katrine anticipated Maja's potential reason for the call: that she had arrived at the station where she was to be picked up by Katrine (as apparent in the previous call). This means that in eighteen of the twenty calls, the reason for the call was introduced by the callee's second turn.

The fact that the two parties in eighteen out of twenty calls skip a step-by-step identification and recognition indicates a strong orientation toward a continuing conversation. The parties thereby cooperate in treating the call as one that relates to the previous conversation, despite the fact that no plan for further communication was made in that earlier call. This orientation is confirmed in the launch/pre-anticipation of the reason for the call, which in an implicit way refers back to the topic of the previous conversation, e.g,. >*where are you*< *now* (S136), *could you bring e:h (.) some money* (S144), *we're on our way* (S54).

In addition, the reason for the call indicates an orientation toward changed circumstances in relation to the earlier call. This is most obvious in cases where the parties are on their way to meet. The high degree of orientation toward one another, and toward the purpose of the call, that the parties mutually display can thus be seen as bound up with the overall objective that the parties are engaged in, namely to meet up. Until they actually meet, the conversation can, in principle, be reopened, and when it is resumed, the call is treated as part of a continuous interaction. For example, >*where are you*< *now* (S136) oriented Daniel's present whereabouts in relation to where he was the last time the two friends talked. In the same way, the callee Katrine's pre-anticipation of the caller Maja's reason for the call, *we're on our way* (S54), presupposed that Maja had arrived at the station where the two of them in the earlier call agreed to meet. In her presumption, Katrine drew on information in the previous call, but she also showed that in her mind, she had followed Maja on her train trip. Thus, in the orientation toward changed circumstances, the parties display 'my mind is with you', e.g., that they have been following the other party's activities or movements in their mind, in the period in which they did not speak together.

The remaining two cases were deviating. In those cases, the reason for the call implicitly referred back to a topic in the previous call, but the reason for the call was not introduced by the caller's first turn, and the callee did not anticipate it in his following turn. Only after step-by-step identification and recognition was the reason for the call introduced:

(Daniel/S116)
((summons))
546 Da:     it's Daniel?
547 Ps:     (0.2)
548 Ru:     it's Rune?
549 Ps:     (0.5)
550 Da:     hi::?
551 Ps:     (1.0)
552 →       Ru:      >listen up< now they have obtained
553 some extra tickets for tonight right
554 Ps:     (.)
555 Da:     THEY HAVE
[. . .]

In his reason for call, Daniel implicitly referred back to a previous call, but only after a step-by-step identification and recognition and a pre-beginning (>*listen up*<). Also, the reason for the call was treated as news by both parties in the two deviating cases. With the news delivery, one might say that the reason for the call displays an orientation toward changed circumstances, as in the other cases. However, since the change is treated as news, it is treated as an inconceivable change, outside the range of possible courses of action that could have been imagined after the topic was closed in the previous call. In addition, the two deviating cases are not related to an imminent face-to-face meeting.

## CLOSED MOBILE PHONE CALLS FOLLOWED BY A TEXT MESSAGE: THE "RESUMPTION MESSAGE" AND THE "EPILOGUE MESSAGE"

In the data set, calls and text messages were very often linked to other text messages and calls in continuing, interconnected communication sequences. In twenty-four cases, a call was followed by a text message in a continuous communication sequence. For example, two parties could agree in a call to continue their conversation via text message. In this section, I will focus on the data sets' nine cases where a text message followed "closed" calls, i.e., calls where the conversation initiates no further communication. After a closed call in a continuous communication sequence, two different types of text messages may follow. I will call the two types the "resumption message" and the "epilogue message".

The resumption message reopens an otherwise closed topic in the earlier call. Either party can send the message, and the message is sent within an hour after the call was closed.[21] Figure 7.1 depicts examples of "resumption" messages via text messaging.[22]

Even though the conversation in the previous call was closed, no interactional work is devoted to reopening the conversation in the following text message. There is no "hi", "hello" or "by the way". Also, the sender of the text message implicitly creates the link back to the topic in the previous conversation, presupposing that the topic persists in the recipients' mind. For example, when Daniel wrote *I might come by later* and Malene wrote

(Katrine/S3-T9-T10)

| | [ ... ] | [ ... ] | [ ... ] |
|---|---|---|---|
| → | | Monday 3:28 pm | *Rune calls Katrine [call ends 3:29 pm]* |
| → | Rune | Monday 3:39 pm | Where are you now... |
| | Katrine | Monday 3:40 pm | Take it easy we see the bus will be there in 5 min.! |
| | [ ... ] | [ ... ] | [ ... ] |

(Daniel/S119-T63)

| | [ ... ] | [ ... ] | [ ... ] |
|---|---|---|---|
| → | | Wednesday 4:23 pm | *Daniel calls Rune [call ends 4:24 pm]* |
| → | Daniel | Wednesday 5:14 pm | Nobody answers at felix's house! If you see/meet him then get him to call... If not have a nice concert... |
| | [ ... ] | [ ... ] | [ ... ] |

(Daniel/S148-T102-T103)

| | → | | |
|---|---|---|---|
| → | | Saturday 2:20 pm | *Katrine calls Daniel [call ends 2:21 pm]* |
| → | Daniel | Saturday 2:43 pm | I might come by later! We have to buy groceries and then we will probably leave. |
| | Katrine | Saturday 2:44 pm | Okai dokai....! I Love you.... |
| | [ ... ] | [ ... ] | [ ... ] |

(Malene/S247-T417-T418)

| | → | | |
|---|---|---|---|
| → | | Friday 6:12 pm | *Malene calls Dorte [call ends 6:14 pm]* |
| → | Malene | Friday 6:35 pm | Now there's no time to get wasted :( |
| | Dorte | Friday 6:35 pm | Why not? |
| | [ ... ] | [ ... ] | [ ... ] |

(Malene/S249-T423-T424)

| | → | | |
|---|---|---|---|
| → | | Friday 6:30 pm | *Malene calls Sara [call ends 6:32 pm]* |
| → | Malene | Friday 7:04 pm | What's going on? Did you succeed? |
| | Sara | Friday 7:06 pm | You only got bows! You will get destroyed! Need to get some swords! |
| | [ ... ] | [ ... ] | [ ... ] |

(Malene/S258-T434-T435)

| | [ ... ] | [ ... ] | [ ... ] |
|---|---|---|---|
| → | | Friday 11:27 pm | *Sara calls Malene [call ends 11:28 pm]* |
| → | Malene | Friday 11:35 pm | Who are there? |
| | Sara | Friday 11:37 pm | Hmm.... No one special! It's kind of boring! people are watching tv! Uh I'm sorry but he said you could come! |

*Figure 7.1*   Examples of 'resumption' messages via text messaging

*who are there*, they presuppose that their recipient knows what place they are referring to. Thus, the previous conversation is treated as immediately available for the recipient, thereby presupposing and claiming a close relationship. On his part, the recipient responds without delay and shows a high orientation toward the two parties continuing business, thereby confirming a close relationship. In that way, both parties display that the topic and their friend is present in their mind.

In contrast to the resumption message that continues an otherwise closed topic from the earlier call, the epilogue message refers back to the earlier call as a whole. Either party can send the message, and the messages are sent within an hour after the call was closed. Figure 7.2 depicts examples of the "epilogue" message via text messaging.

In contrast to the resumption message, the epilogue message is based more loosely on the previous conversation. The message adds a new perspective in which the sender shows how he chooses to understand certain elements of the conversation and how he reacts emotionally to them: *FUCK YOU! YOU'RE REALLY A WEIRD DUDE!* (T27), *Nice to know that you don't want to take us to the party!! I think you r stupid! And Mean!! But have a nice time.. We will try. . . ..* (T139) oh *I just want you to know that I am VERY much in love with YOU!I hope it is reciprocated as much..* (T144).

The new perspective is evaluative and meta-communicative, and the messages are so broad and detached from the previous conversation that the reference back is difficult to specify precisely. For example, what precisely

(Katrine/S32-T27)

| → | | Wednesday 12:03 pm | *Rune calls Katrine [call ends 12:03 pm]* |
|---|---|---|---|
| → | Katrine | Wednesday 12:14 pm | FUCK YOU! YOU'RE REALLY A WEIRD DUDE! I'll see you at Joshi's at 1.00.01 pm |
| | [ ... ] | [ ... ] | [ ... ] |

(Michael/S169-T139)

| | [ ... ] | [ ... ] | [ ... ] |
|---|---|---|---|
| → | | Friday 7:52 pm | *Michael calls Susanne [call ends 7:59 pm]* |
| → | Susanne | Friday 8:11 pm | Nice to know that you don't want to take us to the party!! I think you r stupid! And Mean!! But have a nice time.. We will try..... *From the 2 Angry and Disappointed Girls* |
| | [ ... ] | [ ... ] | [ ... ] |

(Michael/S183-T144)

| → | | Saturday 9:26 pm | *Susanne calls Michael (call ends 9:29 pm]* |
|---|---|---|---|
| → | Susanne | Saturday 10:27pm | I just want you to know that I am VERY much in love with YOU!! hope it is reciprocated as much.. Have a nice night Honey! Say hi if there r some people that I know! Susanne* |

*Figure 7.2*   Examples of 'epilogue' messages via text messaging

in the previous conversation made Rune a *weird dude*? As the epilogue message did not clearly refer to specifics in the earlier call, it detaches itself from a stepwise transition and refers back to the earlier call as a whole. Since it also contains an evaluation, it can be understood as a "summary assessment".[23] A summary assessment is often implicative of closure for a topic,[24] and indeed the evaluative and meta-communicative perspective in the messages seems closing implicative. The terminal greetings in the messages supported this: *I'll see you at Joshi's at 1.00.01 pm* (T27), *\*From the 2 Angry and Disappointed Girls\** (T139) and *Have a nice night Honey! Say hi if there r some people that I know! Susanne\** (T144). Although the messages can be responded to, they do not make a response conditionally relevant and they seem almost dismissive of feedback. A text message can close an interaction in this way,[25] while the closing of a call is a common concern, which takes place over several turns from both parties.[26] Thus, the epilogue message can be understood as an attempt to ensure one's own perspective and to get the last word.

## CONCLUSION

This study shows how the young people in the data set use their mobile phones to engage in, over time, ongoing, interconnected communication sequences in a remote state of continuous talk in which closed interaction (by call) is followed by interaction (by text message or call) that is constructed as continued interaction. Even though the interaction after the closed interaction could be constructed as new interaction, the findings show that the participants do no interactional work to reopen the communication. In the mobile phone openings, the participants do minimal identification and recognition, demonstrating in various ways that they are fully aware of their previous communication and of what they are doing now, often even before the first topic or reason for the call has been given. In addition, the callee will regularly anticipate the caller's reason for the call. In the text messages, the interaction is constructed as continued through temporal proximity to the previous communication and various forms of "tying techniques".[27]

The way in which talk is engaged in the mobile phone openings in this study is somewhat similar to Schegloff's call-back call, in that, in the previous call, no plan for further communication was made. In this study, the young people's communication was also somewhat similar to a continuing state of incipient talk, known from the talk-in-interaction of co-present parties.[28] In a continuing state of incipient talk, turn-by-turn talk occurs; then lapses, then occurs again. Speakers in an incipient state of talk, for example travelers seated next to each other on an airplane, do not use greeting to initiate talk, nor do they issue good-byes prior to a lapse in talk. In the data set, however, the young people closed their conversation, issuing goodbyes, but the previously concluded communication could at any time be resumed without opening formalities.

According to the sociologist and conversation analyst Harvey Sacks, two parties in a telephone conversation can show each other in various ways that "my mind is with you": "Now, in the middle of a conversation, we know well, in some ways, who it is we're talking to. And there are enormously elaborated ways in which we bring off that 'my mind is with you' [. . .] And the question is, at the beginning of a conversation, how rapidly can parties achieve that sort of a thing?".[29] Sacks shows how, for example, that posing the question "How's your mother?" very early on, as the first topic in the conversation, can show the other party that "my mind is with you". In the data set, the young users were even quicker to show one another that they were completely au fait with what the other had been up to recently. The mobile communication via calls and text messages was constructed as an ongoing dialogue that could, of course, be put on standby, but then could be resumed as if there had been no pause in communication. In the mobile phone calls, the parties succeeded, even before the first topic was presented, in showing a high degree of orientation toward each other and the purpose of the call. Through the minimal use of opening formalities, a demand for and an expectation of availability was reflected. By mutually displaying such a high degree of presence, the young mobile users demonstrated and (re)created a close relationship with one another.

# NOTES

1. Harvey Sacks, *Lectures on Conversation*, 2 vols. (Oxford, UK: Blackwell, 1992).
2. Ibid., 167.
3. Ylva Hård af Segerstad, "Language in SMS—A socio-Linguistic View", in *The Inside Text: Social, Cultural and Design Perspectives on SMS*, ed. Richard Harper, Leysia Ann Palen and Alex Taylor (Dordrecht: Springer, 2005), 33–51; Dafydd Gibbon and Malgotzata Kul, "Economy Strategies in Restricted Communication Channels. A Study of Polish Short Text Messages", in *Vallah, Gurkensalat 4U & Me! Current Perspectives in the Study of Youth Language*, ed. Normann J. Jørgensen (Frankfurt am Main: Peter Lang, 2010), 75–98; Carmen Frehner, *Email, SMS, MMS: The Linguistic Creativity of Asynchronous Discourse in the New Media Age*, Linguistic Insights (Bern; New York: Peter Lang, 2008), 1424–8689; Rich Ling and Naomi S. Baron, "Text Messaging and IM: Linguistic Comparison of American College Data", *Journal of Language and Social Psychology* 26, no. 3 (2007), 291–298; Caroline Tagg, *The Discourse of Text Messaging: Analysis of Text Message Communication*, Continuum Discourse (New York: Continuum, 2011); David Crystal, *Txtng: The Gr8 Db8* (New York: Oxford University Press, 2008); Crispin Thurlow, "Generation Txt? The Sociolinguistics of Young People's Text-Messaging", *Discourse Analysis Online* 1, no. 1 (2003), accessed: February 23, 2013, http://extra.shu.ac.uk/daol/articles/v1/n1/a3/thurlow2002003-paper.html.
4. Ditte Laursen, "Please Reply! The Replying Norm in Adolescent SMS Communication", in *The Inside Text: Social, Cultural and Design Perspectives on SMS*, ed. Richard Harper, Leysia Ann Palen and Alex Taylor, *Kluwer International Series on Computer Supported Cooperative Work* 4 (Dordrecht: Springer, 2005), 53–73; Ian Hutchby and Vanita Tanna, "Aspects of Sequential

Organization in Text Message Exchange", *Discourse & Communication* 2, no. 2 (2008), 143–164; Anna Spagnolli and Luciano Gamberini, "Interacting via SMS: Practices of Social Closeness and Reciprocation", *British Journal of Social Psychology* 46, no. 2 (2007), 343–364.

5. Ian Hutchby and Simone Barnett, "Aspects of the Sequential Organization of Mobile Phone Conversation", *Discourse Studies* 7, no. 2 (2005), 147–171; Ilkka Arminen and Minna Leinonen, "Mobile Phone Call Openings: Tailoring Answers to Personalized Summonses", *Discourse Studies* 8, no. 3 (2006), 339–368.

6. Ditte Laursen, "Sequential Organization of Text Messages and Mobile Phone Calls in Interconnected Communication Sequences", *Discourse & Communication* 6, no. 1 (2012), 83–99.

7. Emmanuel A. Schegloff, "Sequencing in Conversational Openings", *American Anthropologist* 70, no. 6 (1968), 1075–1095; Emmanuel A. Schegloff, "The Routine as Achievement", *Human Studies* 9, nos. 2–3 (1986), 111–151; Emmanuel A. Schegloff, "Identification and Recognition in Telephone Conversation Openings", in *Everyday Language: Studies in Ethnomethodology*, ed. George Psathas (NY: Irvington Publishers, 1979), 23–78.

8. Emmanuel A. Schegloff, Sound data for: "Reflections on Studying Prosody in Talk-In-Interaction", accessed October 10, 2012, http://www.sscnet.ucla.edu/soc/faculty/schegloff/prosody/.

9. Anna Lindstrom, "Identification and Recognition in Swedish Telephone Conversation Openings", *Language in Society* 23, no. 2 (1994), 231–252; Hanneke Houtkoop-Steenstra, "Opening Sequences in Dutch Telephone Conversations", in *Talk and Social Structure: Studies in Ethnomethodology and Conversation analysis*, ed. Deidre Boden and Don H. Zimmerman (Oxford: Polity, 1991), 232–250; Gitte Rasmussen, *Zur Bedeutung kultureller Unterschiede in interlingualen interkulturellen Gesprächen: eine Mikroanalyse deutschsprachiger Interaktionen zwischen Franzosen und Dänen und zwischen Deutschen und Dänen*, Reihe interkulturelle Kommunikation (Iudicium, 2000).

10. Arminen and Leinonen, "Mobile Phone Call Openings"; Hutchby and Barnett, "Aspects of the Sequential Organization".

11. Emmanuel A. Schegloff, "Answering the Phone", in *Conversation Analysis: Studies from the First Generation*, ed. Gene H. Lerner (Amsterdam: John Benjamins, 2004 [1970]), 73.

12. Ibid.

13. Graham Button, "Conversation-in-a-Series", in *Talk and Social Structure: Studies in Ethnomethodology and Conversation Analysis*, ed. Deirdre Boden and Don H. Zimmerman (Oxford: Polity, 1991), 251–277; Graham Button, "Moving Out of Closings", in *Talk and Social Organisation*, ed. Graham Button and John R. E. Lee (1987), 101–151; Graham Button, "On Varieties of Closings", in *Interactional competence: Theory and research*, ed. George Psathas (Washington, DC: University Press of America, 1990), 93–147.

14. Button, "Conversation-in-a-Series", 269.

15. Ibid., 272–73.

16. Christian Licoppe, "Recognizing Mutual 'Proximity' at a Distance: Weaving Together Mobility, Sociality and Technology", *Journal of Pragmatics* 41, no. 10 (2009), 1924–1937.

17. Jenny S. Mandelbaum, "Interactive Methods of Constructing Relationships", in *Studies in Language and Social Interaction: In Honour of Robert Hopper*, ed. Robert Hopper et al. (Mahwah, NJ: Lawrence Erlbaum, 2003), 207–219; Anita Pomerantz and B. J. Fehr, "Conversation Analysis: An Approach to the Study of Social Action as Sense Making Practices", in *Discourse as Social Interaction: Discourse Studies 2—A Multidisciplinary Introduction*, ed. Teun A. van

Dijk (London: Sage, 1998), 64–91; Anita Pomerantz and Jenny Mandelbaum, "A Conversation Analytic Approach to Relationships: Their Relevance for Interactional Conduct", in *Handbook of Language and Social Interaction*, ed. Kristine L. Fitch and Robert E. Sanders (Mahwah, NJ: Lawrence Erlbaum, 2005), 149–171.

18. Marjorie Harness Goodwin, *He-Said-She-Said: Talk as Social Organization Among Black Children*, 2nd ed., Midland book (Bloomington: Indiana University Press, 1992), 618.

19. The transcription conventions are Jefferson's as described in J. Maxwell Atkinson and John Heritage, *Structures of Social Action: Studies in Conversation Analysis*, Studies in Emotion and Social Interaction (Cambridge, UK: Cambridge University Press, 1984).

20. Schegloff, "Answering the Phone", 70.

21. Typing and spelling errors, abbreviations, and fluctuation in the use of capitals and lowercase lettering have been reproduced in the translation from Danish.

22. S3-T9-T10=Call3–Text9–Text10

23. Gail Jefferson, "On Stepwise Transition from Talk About Trouble to Inappropriately Next-Positioned Matters", in *Structures of Social Action: Studies in Conversation Analysis*, ed. J. Maxwell Atkinson and John Heritage (Cambridge, UK: Cambridge University Press, 1984), 191–222.

24. Ibid., 211.

25. Ditte Laursen, "Did He Make the Bus? Continuous Communication Among Young People via Mobile Telephone", in *Vallah, Gurkensalat 4U & Me! Current Perspectives in the Study of Youth Language*, ed. J.N. Jørgensen (Frankfurt am Main: Peter Lang, 2010), 25–42.

26. E.A. Schegloff and H. Sacks, "Opening Up Closings", *Semiotica* 8, no. 4 (1973), 289–327.

27. Sacks, *Lectures on Conversation*.

28. Schegloff and Sacks, "Opening up Closings"; Margaret H. Szymanski et al., "Organizing a Remote State of Incipient Talk: Push-to-Talk Mobile Radio Interaction", *Language in Society* 35, no. 3 (2006), 393–418.

29. Sacks, *Lectures on Conversation*, 166–67.

# 8 Wandering Between Self-Expression and Recognition

## A Case Study of the Mobile Microblogging Practices of Young Chinese Women in Hong Kong

*Meng Di*

## INTRODUCTION

The diffusion of mobile media devices has exploded on a global basis in recent years, even as the gadget itself has been transformed as a convergent technology that includes a mobile phone, a digital camera and an mp3 player, and provides an Internet portal. One reason for the commercial success of the latest generations of mobile devices is the inclusion of an imaging tool—for most users, camera phones are no longer the poor cousin of stand-alone cameras. Through the capacity of the camera to capture, edit and share everyday experiences, we are seeing the development of new forms of visual culture that foreground user agency, and through user-created content (UCC) traditional consumers have been transformed into "prosumers". This term, coined by Toffler in *The Third Wave*, suggests the fusion of producer and consumer enabled by new technologies.[1]

As described more recently by Ito, mobile technology has been seen as "located in specific social, cultural, and historical contexts, rather than as a cross-culturally universal solution (as Internet protocols are often portrayed)".[2] On the other hand, conventions of local culture and social relationships have been affected by widespread mobile adoption. In China, playing with the mobile handset (*Shouji*) to access the Sina microblog (a dominant mobile social networking site) has become a popular urban youth culture phenomenon. The resulting visual presentations of the self, as well as the surrounding material and social environment, through mobile microblogs may shed light on everyday city life in contemporary China.

China is standing at the crossroads of industrialization, technological development and modernity.[3] In order to understand contemporary Chinese society, a study of emerging socio-technologies in everyday urban life should not be underestimated. China has rapidly become the biggest market for mobile technology and one of the world's leading nations in the production of information and communication technologies. Previous qualitative research has demonstrated that the use of mobile devices has influenced social structures and interpersonal relationships in China. Meanwhile, mobile usage patterns differ significantly in relation of criteria including gender, age, education level and economic status.[4] In this situation, my exploration of mobile media use is conducted through an ethnographic approach, concentrating on a demographically similar group of subjects.

China's modernization is both the result of and a trigger for urbanization and population migration. With the relaxing of the residential system of the Mao era, which forced the rural and small-town residents to stay on the land or pursue a subsistence existence, millions of people have migrated to work and live in large coastal cities, especially metropolises like Beijing, Shanghai and Shenzhen. Previous research on the social effects of mobile adoption have focused on migrant workers from the countryside, who have the lowest incomes and occupy the lowest social stratum in the cities. Although it is important to explore mobile communication of "the information have-less working class",[5] we should not overlook the fact that the most forward-thinking avatars of mobile media culture are the young people of China's new middle class, who have grown up with and adapted easily to new media technologies. As many members of this group have themselves migrated to large cities for educational or employment opportunities, new media technologies have provided them an ideal platform for self-expression and social networking, especially during the early stages of cultural adaptation. Although there is a small body of existing research on China's mobile youth culture, it is limited in scope and often rendered obsolete by the rapid transformation of mobile platforms. To partly fill this gap, my study focuses on visual presentations of the self and microblog social interactions on the part of young, migrant, middle class women in Hong Kong, a significant subset of "Hong Kong's professional immigrants from mainland China".[6]

In response to a need for local economic restructuring and the development of innovative industries, the Hong Kong government has launched various magnet programs designed to attract mainland professionals to work in Hong Kong. Given the city's colonial background and postcolonial status, the cultural, social and economic differences between the average mainland immigrant's home city and Hong Kong are larger than those of other Chinese metropolises. Consequently, a study of "Hong Kong's professional immigrants" does not capture all aspects of the contemporary Chinese transient experience within China, but such an investigation nonetheless may highlight relevant issues, some of which are unique to a Hong Kong–based experience, and some of which may well apply to the rest of China. In any case, previous research suggests significant gender-based differences in mobile technology adoption in China, and that young women are more aggressive than young men in adopting and using the new multimedia functions of the mobile phone. Partly for this reason, this study is developed around sixteen in-depth interviews of active young female users, and through an analysis of their online microblog activities over a period of thirteen months (from October 2010 through October 2011).

## A BRIEF LITERATURE REVIEW

With the development of mobile technologies and the steady decrease in the cost to consumers of mobile communication, affective exchanges through mobile technologies have increased. As mobile Internet access has become more widespread, ambient virtual co-presence has become a newly identifiable social modality.[7] Due to the increasing number of phones with built-in cameras, heightened forms of visual intimacy have been realized through mobile communication. Furthermore, following integration with the mobile Internet, virtual visual co-presence has been enabled not only through mobile emailing and mobile texting, but also through online mobile publishing.[8]

Mobile visual culture has become an increasingly attractive area of exploration for scholars from diverse perspectives. As often-diary-like examples of UCC in the age of Web 2.0, mobile phone snapshots present the users' "personal experiences and impressions of the world", and record "the ephemeral moments from the users' subjective gazes".[9] In Lee's opinion, women, and especially young women, are active users of new media technologies for purposes of articulating and maintaining relationships, and to empower themselves and produce their own culture.[10] Considering modes of circulation, Villi discussed the sharing of camera phone photos separately from photo messaging, with the latter understood as a "push" mode of interpersonal communication, and photo self-publishing as a "pull" modality that developed with the introduction of mobile social networking services.[11]

Moreover, scholars have provided insights into mobile visual culture by contextualizing the sociocultural specificities of local communities. For instance, in an account of the unique and uneven development of mobile technologies in the Asia-Pacific, Hjorth's very useful work concentrates on female consumption of mobile media in the region through case studies of Tokyo, Seoul, Hong Kong and Melbourne.[12] Through an ethnographic approach, Japanese scholars have demonstrated the importance of the three 'S's—sharing, storing and saving—in camera phone practices.[13] For Korean researcher Minhee Son, "a culture of ambivalence" manifests in Korean urban youth culture through three 'D' features: delay, deference and detachment.[14] Through an investigation of the use of camera phone and Cyworld's minihompy in 2007 and 2008, Son has analyzed the "ambivalence culture" resulting from personal experience with and the technological characteristics of camera phones at that time—the low quality of pictures and the small screen prevented details from being presented and generated user ambivalence concerning the experience.

In recent years, the amount of qualitative research of information and communication technologies (ICTs) in China has increased and established a solid empirical basis for further studies.[15] Although demographic analyses have appeared in China in recent years, more attention has been paid to socially vulnerable groups like migrant workers, inquiring about how they achieve better-paid jobs[16] and develop intimate relationships with their loved ones[17] facilitated by working-class ICTs.[18] Using a cultural studies approach, Wallis has examined new media practices in contemporary China, and deemed new media technologies "constitutive of complex processes of social changes in China".[19]

In the context of mobile diffusion and technological convergence, native scholars have begun to explore urban dwellers' self-construction and processes of social reflectivity by studying their camera phone practices in the context of contemporary China's sociocultural transformations.[20] But the demographic diversity of this literature is still limited, and theory-based new media cultural studies must be updated to account for developments following the adoption and diffusion of 3G mobile Internet.

This research attempts to explore strategies of visual presentation and self-expression by a particular demographic slice of young Chinese women who are heavy users of their camera phones and the mobile Internet, and who live within the context of commercialization and consumerism. This study *investigates these women's self-identification through concrete case studies of their mobile microblogging in Hong Kong*, and analyzes women's self-construction and social networking processes through their performances through the "online stage"—they present and express themselves for their imagined audiences, while at the same time, they recognize and revise their self-identities in response to diffused media images and audience responses characteristic of the Web 2.0 age.

## METHODOLOGY

An analysis of the visual self-representation of sixteen mobile microbloggers was undertaken to investigate the questions following questions: First, what are *their favorite* content and subjects on the Sina mobile microblog? Second, what are the users' experiences and usage patterns? Third, how do they visually present their online images? How do they use mobile devices as extensions of their bodies to facilitate the expression and construction of their identities? Finally, as new arrivals in Hong Kong, what strategies do they use to manage their social networks in this somewhat unfamiliar setting? In order to better answer the questions, textual analysis was combined with in-depth interviews.

## ETHNOGRAPHIC APPROACH

Data for the study was collected in Hong Kong, which is now a special administrative region of China, and was previously a British colony until the "return to sovereignty" in 1997. As a cross-cultural city with a population that is 95% Chinese, of whom the substantial majorities are first- and second-generation arrivals, Hong Kong is an ideal and attractive place for mainland immigrants to study and/or pursue a career. Also, Hong Kong people historically have been early and heavy adopters of new media technologies. As of July 2011, the mobile subscriber penetration rate in Hong Kong has reached 200.6% (the city's population is a little over seven million). The number of mobile subscriptions is 14,256,416 (i.e., about two for every person in Hong Kong), among which the number of 2.5G and 3G subscribers is 7,458,803.[21]

In keeping with broader cultural differences between Hong Kong and the mainland, the media experiences of people in each locale are also different. The microblog phenomenon, which is approximately a Chinese version of Twitter, exploded in 2010 on the mainland, but the platform has not achieved a similar level of popularity in Hong Kong. In this situation, the China-centered Sina microblog works as a medium through which mainlanders in Hong Kong can maintain contact with friends and family, and provide them a platform to document their experiences in and impressions in of Hong Kong.

The target group of *mainland immigrant women in Hong Kong* was selected based on certain shared characteristics. First, these women are in their twenties or early thirties. Experienced at and proficient in new media technologies, all of them are active users of mobile devices and online social networks. Second, this group of "talented immigrants" is well educated and equipped with professional knowledge and qualifications. They are "outstanding individuals seeking a competitive edge from mainland and are looking for a chance to settle in Hong Kong".[22] Third, they are experiencing a transitional phase in their lives, as early career professionals faced also with the dilemma of adapting to a new social and cultural environment. These characteristics distinguish these women from the "new mainland immigrants" in Hong Kong, who are mainly of lower economic status, seeking a family reunion or a more purely pragmatic improvement in income. Also this group of women shares common features with other internally transient citizens as part of what has been described as China's "brain circulation".

## TEXTUAL ANALYSIS

Based on my own experience as a microblog practitioner and observer (as well as a member of the demographic group under investigation), the practices of twenty-five active female microbloggers, all of whom are mainland immigrants in Hong Kong, drew my attention. An analysis of microblog content during the period of observation showed the following shared features: First, all use nicknames and self-identifier tags and provide a self-introduction and profile page. Second, the content uploaded through mobile devices (the Sina microblog can provide the source of an upload) includes pictures, video, and comments. Since there is a140-character limit, and entries are often made on the fly, in the midst of other activity, mobile microbloggers tend to post only a few words followed by a picture or short video. This snapshot style of writing and imaging is a dominant feature of mobile microblogging.

## IN-DEPTH INTERVIEW

Among the twenty-five selected mobile microbloggers, sixteen accepted my request for in-depth interviews. All were interviewed face-to-face for more than one hour. The interviews were conducted in Chinese, recorded and translated into English by the author. The informants were asked first for general information concerning age, marital status, occupation, education, income, and basic elements of their mobile phone and mobile Internet use. For details, please refer to Table 8.1. Second, mobile microblog usage conventions and patterns were explored in more detail, including when they usually access microblogs by mobile phone, under what circumstances this use occurs, as well as the frequency and duration. Third, the women were asked to provide background and contextual information on selected camera phone picture postings, as well as their expectations of participating in this form of UCC and the nature of feedback they have received.

In the next step, in order to explore the connection between online and offline social relationships, participants were invited to discuss the overlap (or lack thereof) of microblogs friendships and "real world" relationships. It was also important to pay attention to the interactive discursive framework of microblogger comments and the responses from readers/viewers. Finally, I invited the women to make an open-ended personal statement by asking them to describe their own self-identity as well as their ideal self-image and their understanding of the social relationships in which they were currently participating. To avoid overly guiding the informants' responses, semistructured interviews were conducted. When one of my prepared questions was answered, further questions were asked based on the nature of response, leading to a more open-ended conversation.

## ANALYSIS

### Creativity and Sensibility

Using a mobile device to participate in microblogging activities is a popular leisure activity among Chinese youth. This entertainment aspect is reflected in the descriptions by informants' of their activity as "playing with the mobile microblog". Besides the instrumentality of the three 'S's of camera phone imaging practices,[23] mobile microblogging also reflects "imaginative" and "recreative" processes.

Compared with the live broadcasting practices of "webcam girls" (e.g., Annacam and Jennicam) in the late 1990s, visual presentations on the mobile Internet today are more casual and spontaneous. On the one hand it is a more widely adopted activity in part because the technological interface is much more convenient to use; on the other hand the practice includes more obvious and calculated artifice, as image editing applications are also very user-friendly. One of my informants, 24-year-old Tina, holds a master of

*Table 8.1* Demographics of participants

| Informant | Sex/Age | Marital Status | Occupation | Education | Monthly Income (HKDollar) | Mobile Phone | Mobile Internet |
|---|---|---|---|---|---|---|---|
| Emma | F/27 | Single | Banking officer | Master's | >10,000 | Blackberry 9230 | Peoples 98 |
| Rain | F/24 | Single | Administrative Assistant | Master's | Unknown | Nokia N70 | Free Wifi |
| Tina | F/24 | Single | Manager Assistant | Master's | >10,000 | Nokia N72 | Free Wifi |
| Eva | F/22 | Single | Administrative Assistant | Bachelor's | >10,000 | Nokia 6610 | Smart tone |
| Miffy | F/24 | Single | Online shop owner | Bachelor's | Unknown | I-phone 4 | Three 158 |
| Lisa | F/26 | Single | Banking officer | Master's | >10,000 | I-phone 4 | Peoples 98 |
| Judy | F/26 | Single | Junior Clerk | Master's | 10,000 | Nokia 5800 | Free Wifi |
| Goldie | F/25 | Single | Primary school teacher | Master's | 10,000 | HTC Desire | Three 98 |
| Anna | F/27 | Engaged | Research Assistant | PHD | 14,000 | HTC wildfire | Peoples 98 |
| Piggy | F/28 | Married | Research Associate | PHD | 19,000 | Sony Ericson Vivas | Peoples 98 |
| Vivian | F/25 | Single | NGO | Master's | 13,000 | I-phone 4 | Peoples 98 |
| Belinda | F/28 | Single | Photography Designer | Master's | >20,000 | I-phone 4 | Peoples 158 |
| Estellabing | F/33 | Married | Instructor | PHD | 30,000 | I-phone 4 | Peoples 98 |
| Bear | F/29 | Married | Coordinator in Air Company | Bachelor's | >10,000 | Samsung Galaxy-S | Peoples 98 |
| Vivienne | F/30 | Single | Magazine Editor | Master's | >20,000 | I-phone 4 | Three 98 |
| Sinnyc | F/26 | Single | Financial Journalist | Master's | 13,000 | I-phone 3 | Peoples 98 |

arts degree earned in Hong Kong and is now a managerial assistant in a law office. Though the job is not a logical outgrowth of her academic studies, she enjoys Hong Kong and also works part-time jobs in art galleries. "That's my dream, to do anything related [to] art", said Tina. "The longer you live in Hong Kong, the more difficulties you'll have when you go back to the mainland". One of Tina's mobile images was taken at an art exhibition, which she then mashed up with a cartoon character (Figure 8.1).

"At that time, I was playing with 'Smurf" [a mobile phone application]. It was interesting to DIY my image into the cartoon character, so I posted it on my microblog at once". DIY image manipulation was a recurrent motif on Tina's microblog. Another, titled "my brightest eyes" (Figure 8.2), was taken at a bar. Tina said "I edited it by mobile phone the following day to mark my experience being drunk".

These examples (and others) suggest that young Chinese women are not only confident of their ability to manipulate the imaging capabilities of new media technology, but also *creative and humorous* in visualizing their life experiences. The social myth that "technological ability is a masculine characteristic and technical inability is a feminine characteristic" is contradicted here.[24] The argument that "soft technology belonging to women's domain has not often been considered real technology" is also a cliché, and should

*Figure 8.1*   Tina's microblog image

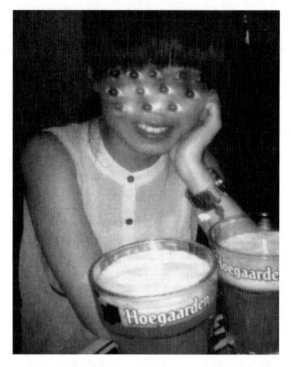

*Figure 8.2*    Tina's microblog image

be replaced by an acknowledgment that different and more complex usage patterns are built in relation to interwoven elements of personality, life experience, education, age, etc.

In another case, 27-year-old Emma, who works as a bank officer and lives with her boyfriend in Hong Kong, is satisfied with her work and relationship. In a picture taken by Emma on Friday after work from a moving bus (Figure 8.3), she used a mobile phone app to retouch a series of images and bond them into a new work. Emma described her relaxed mood looking out on the sky and sea, and looked forward to enjoying the coming weekend. "We were planning to visit Lantau Island tomorrow . . . and we'd normally take a professional camera on that kind of outing". When I asked whether the camera phone snapshots made her interested in pursuing professional training in photography, Emma said, "I always like images, beautiful images, whatever a camera is, or whatever a software could do, that's the same thing, I am a 'visual animal' ".

Although a stand-alone camera can achieve high quality images, a portable device is good at catching fleeting moments and documenting everyday routines. Each of the above examples, whether manipulating self-portrait images or building a mini-collage from scenic snapshots, vividly expresses a personal mood and demonstrates both a measure of technical fluency

*Figure 8.3*   Emma's microblog image

as well as an ability to use that technology imaginatively in the service of self-expression.

## Consumerism and Narcissism

Hjorth has explored mobile media culture in Japan and introduced the concept of "kawaii (cute) domestication" to describe the nation's "cultural capital" and embodied "habitus".[25] In my study, young Chinese women share an interest in decorating their portable media devices in diverse styles, depending on the owners' personality, taste, age, occupation and so on. Some informants changed their portable devices' protective "skins" from time to time. For instance, 26-year-old Lisa, who described herself as interested in accessories, shared a photo of her collection of nine mobile phone protective shells on her microblog and kidded, "I will continue to collect them and run a shop". Beyond embellishing their portable devices for their own pleasure, some informants also like to share images of these enhanced phones with friends, partners and lovers.

In another example, Bear, whose husband works in Beijing, posted a picture of a pair of mobile phones wearing "his-and-hers outfits", and explained, "My husband's and my phones are decorated like a real couple". Another informant, Belinda, shared an image of three Rilakkuma protective shells in different colors on her microblog to ask her girlfriends to pick a favorite as a souvenir. Through decorating portable devices, these women find a means to express their personal taste and manage relationships. Figure 8.4 depicts examples of these images. The appearance of portable devices not only presents a sense of style, but also works as a signifier of personal relationships.

*Figure 8.4*   Examples of microblog images

As a world-class trading center, Hong Kong itself is often seen by many residents as a giant shopping mall that people live in. Insofar as shopping centers are integrated with the surrounding geographic and social land-scapes, this is in a sense true: practices of business, leisure and shopping converge. The "universalist model" of consumption encourages, as part of the process through which new arrivals are socialized within the community habitus of Hong Kong, to get used to perpetual opportunities for shopping.

The process of commodification turns objects, events and services into things for sale, while at the same time working to construct individuals as consumers, for whom a central life-interest lies in the consumption of com-modities.[26] This is not a recent observation, of course; in Debord's words, "Contemporary society makes the world into spectacle because it is orga-nized by capitalism, which has commodified everything and has thereby colonized everyday life".[27] The processes of consumer colonization points to "a massive internal extension of the capitalist market- the invasion and restructuring of whole areas of free time, private life, leisure, and personal expression".[28] People living in Hong Kong are accustomed to wandering in the shopping malls to shop for or celebrate something specific, or simply to pass the time, often regardless of targeted marketing enticements. Shopping becomes a mundane routine, internalized as a lifestyle.

Among my case studies, 28-year-old photographic designer Belinda fea-tured a series of posts on the "outfit of the day" (Figure 8.5). She posted these thematic self-portrait images every few days, followed by descriptions of the brands, styles or accessorizing ideas. In her mind, "I share them not because they are a famous brand or expensive, but rather I'm pleased with matching them to get different feelings. *I need to satisfy others at work, but please myself in life.* I will go with different outfits, according to my mood or my schedule on that day. The photo collection on my microblog is actu-ally a record of my life status".

Abercrombie and Longhurst observe that everyday life is aestheticized in the contemporary world, and the cultivation of style is a dominant charac-teristic of modern society. As Ewen writes, "style was definitely more than a question of fashions in clothing or in literary expression. It was a general sensibility that touched on countless arenas of everyday life, yet was limited

*Figure 8.5*   Belinda's microblog image

by none of them. It was something intangible yet important, everywhere and nowhere, inchoate". In modern societies like Hong Kong, this consumerist aesthetic concern is predominant especially among young women. Among my case studies, it is not necessary for Belinda to buy so many clothes, nor does Lisa need to change her mobile phone protective shells so frequently, but both of them live within the culture of consumerism and enjoy this aspect of it.

Consumerism does not simply involve purchasing goods and services, but also can be understood in relation to the gaze of commodities on us, and how we return that look. Abercrombie and Longhurst describe "the possessive gaze" as a key part of the process of internalizing particular ideas about the nature and scope of commodities in a consumer society. From this perspective, people gaze at the world as if it can be owned, at least potentially. Immigrants to Hong Kong from China often wander in shopping malls to window shop the new season designs, but rarely to buy them. Tina, for example, told me that she is keen about trying out different styles, "Although I will not buy all of them, as I don't need to, and I don't have enough money to afford it all . . . I like to take pictures [of items I like], and sometimes I share them with friends [on my microblog]". Tina photographs herself looking into the mirror, capturing her image as she tries on different outfits, while at the same time, her audiences on the microblog are also possessively gazing at these images.

Street snap(shots) are one of the most popular subjects in Sina microblogs, through which users record and pass on the fashion decisions of other people in an ongoing, improvised chronicle of contemporary style. The microblogged street snap is a fragmented and personalized variation on the conventional fashion magazine. Street snaps are not selling only, or primarily, the idealized (and often impossible) self marketed through magazines, but also they contain a documentary, street-style edge that may be easier for many women to connect with. It is well established that representations of fashion conveyed through the mass media communicate to women that the adoption of a certain style or appearance expresses what kind of person you are. These representations naturalize the idea that clothed bodies are tools for managing identity. In a broad sense, this is true enough; the process of constructing personal identity includes a systematic ordering of the body's shape through diet and a fitness regime (or the lack thereof).

In addition, the adornment of the body has meaning in all cultures—but how one dresses in a consumer society becomes a marker of taste, personality and socioeconomic status. As a result, dedicated effort to rituals of making up, dressing up and accessorizing are considered necessary for an adequate self-performance. People in public spaces are presenting themselves to others and, in doing so, imagining how others will see them. In Abercrombie and Longhurst's words, they are performing for an imagined audience. This argument of everyday life as performance is, of course, not an original observation; decades ago, Goffman employed analogies from the theater to argue that many forms of social interaction are similar to performances on the dramatic stage. He proposed that, if there is a stage for performance of a public self to a public audience, there must be a "backstage" where individuals cease performing, where one's true self is revealed, since there is no audience.[29]

Belinda posted a picture on her microblog in which she is looking into a mirror, with an accompanying commentary asking, "Is that you in the mirror? Who are you? Get rid of the elegant cosmetics, magnificent clothes, and fussy ornaments, who are you? Could you ever find you? I guess I have lost myself." This monologue, as intimate as it seems, is of course in this context not backstage behavior—paradoxically, this performance of the private self is calculated for and made a part of the individual's public persona. This can be understood as part of a motivated self-identification process, through which the subject/object asserts control over the self even as she claims to have lost that control—although the author knows the image and the words will be seen by others, the aim is to look for the inner self, and for at least the reassurance that the *image* of that self can be controlled. This wandering process of self-expression and identification is common among Chinese women immigrating from mainland to Hong Kong.

My informant Piggy, who is teaching and working as a research associate at a university, posted a series of hand-drawn self-portraits. Among these a work named "Double me" was tagged with the comment, "I do have an ego, though you cannot see it". Some of these practices may be characterized as narcissistic, but in Abercrombie and Longhurst's words, "narcissism should be more seen as a cultural condition, diffused widely, rather than a personality disorder".

The same authors propose further that, in a narcissist's world, the self is the central focus of the real and imagined audience, and a situation in which the boundary between the self and the outside world is blurred. For the narcissist, all the people and things that stand outside the self are merely a reflection, as in a mirror, of the self. This concept of narcissism is closely related to the idea of the reflexive projection of the self—individuals understand themselves, construct their self-identity, by working and reworking their interpretations of their own biography in the form of narrative or story.[30] In my case studies, the women's presentation of self-portrait images through mobile microblogging functions similarly as self-narrative. By means of self-presentation and interactions with the online audience, the women continuously examine and revise their activities in the light of incoming information, and in an endlessly circulating routine of character recognition, construction and modification.

My informant Vivian once won a television competition in her hometown designating her as "the most beautiful middle school student". She majored in media studies as an undergraduate and now works as a magazine editor. With a history of external validation as an attractive person, she is enthusiastic about sharing her self-portrait images through her microblog. She posted 143 pictures on the subject of herself over the study's thirteen months. This practice received additional confirmation when Vivian posted a statement reading, "I was despised as a narcissist by someone, but my narcissism has nothing to do with you, nor does my self-confidence and optimism", accompanied by another self-portrait featuring a big smile and a V gesture. The response was nine universally supportive comments encouraging her to keep posting beautiful self-portrait pictures and to disregard her critic. In discussing her blogging practices with me, although Vivian said she didn't care about others' criticism, she acknowledged, "I always go through all the comments and reply to the interesting ones, if I have time. The followers' comments and support encourage me to share my images".

## Sociability: Private or Public?

Sharing images of gatherings with friends is one of the favorite subjects on the targeted microblogs. Twenty-seven-year old Anna, who works as a research assistant at a university, shared a celebratory picture on her microblog with the caption, "Happy ladies' day my dearest girl friends!" (Figure 8.6). She explained, "I post it at the moment I take it with the camera phone. If I look at the picture later, many shortcomings will be noticed, the canted camera position, the dark lighting, the blurred images . . . any way it is imperfect, but otherwise there will be no pictures and relevant records on my microblog. But that is the nature of everyday life, like what has been written in a conventional diary".

The mobile microblog provides a platform for documenting daily life with fewer constraints of time and space. As flawless images and resonant prose are not generally a goal of the microbloggers, meaning is discovered instead in building an ongoing chronicle of certain subjective and fleeting moments from everyday life and collating them as a life journal—a storehouse of memories that later can be recalled with friends. In recording a fragment of personal experience, the mobile microblogger certifies her presence at that

*Figure 8.6*    Anna's microblog image

moment and that place, and attempts to set personal experience within a particular context.[31]

Beyond assembling collective memories that are primarily of interest to a core group of friends, this form of microblogging can also provide a template of form and content for other people with similar backgrounds or interests who may be interested in constructing their own online communication circle. Occasionally, participants in this online virtual community will get together in the physical world. I once joined a group called "mainlanders working in Hong Kong" on Sina microblog and witnessed its transformation over time. In the first stage, members shared mainly practical, instrumental information within the virtual group, having to do with "the procedures for extending a work visa" and where to find a useful "transportation map".

In the second stage, topics like "How long do you plan to stay in Hong Kong?" were discussed—this was relevant as all the group members were raised in China. The shared educational and cultural background made it easier for them to construct an emotional support group. During this time, some contributors became online friends through the ongoing process of sharing and exchanging.

During the third stage, some members began to initiate offline gatherings involving other participants, including a meal of Sichuan food. New discoveries about the relationships were made at this point: learning that an online friend worked in the same building (Hong Kong has many high-rise office towers), or that another person studied in the same city. These offline gatherings, that is, began to transform virtual images into embodied individuals. At the end of the Sichuan dinner, the initiator announced that it was her birthday and shared a birthday cake. When the candles were lit, ten mobile phone camera flashes were going off at the same time. Several participants immediately uploaded images to live-broadcast "the event" on the microblog that brought the group together in the first place. Within a few minutes, the birthday cake pictures on the microblog were followed by a rush of comments from absent (co-present) members sending their best wishes. In this situation, the virtual community and the embodied community were interwoven; on the one hand, "intimate visual co-presence" could be realized through a camera phone integrated with the mobile Internet. Mobile microbloggers in separate physical locations shared a virtual co-presence.[32] On the other hand, even in a situation in which the group members are sitting around the same table, several women spent a good deal of time "away" from the gathering by simultaneously communicating through mobile devices.

Through the lens of mobile microblogging, two dominant tendencies of social connection were observed among young Chinese women in Hong Kong. First, small circles and private spaces were developed. Case study participant Goldie said, "I don't want Sina microblog to expand its business to the Hong Kong market. Because now my microblog followers are all mainlanders, my old friends, so I can complain about my work in Hong Kong without fear, but if one day my colleagues and even my boss have an account, I will definitely quit it".

Another informant, Tina, said, "Sometimes I play with my mobile phone by putting it on my desktop keyboard, since my supervisor checks what we are doing through the back window, so I pretend to type on the keyboard". That is, mobile microblogs provide these mainland new arrivals a protective space in Hong Kong in which they feel free to express themselves and escape from the pressure of work. At the same time, an opposite tendency suggesting a sense of loneliness and alienation is also manifested through the microblogs, an anxiety of invisibility in a large, impersonal urban space.

One of the more significant observations resulting from the development of webcam culture in the late 1990s was that this online space provided women with new opportunities to achieve a certain amount of self-directed public visibility, and even fame (Jennifer Ringley's Jennicam being the most well-known example here). While the Internet can be used as an additional platform for traditional forms of celebrity, it also has spawned the phenomenon of the "microcelebrity," defined as individuals whose popularity is generated only through their online presence. As Senft notes in her discussion of camgirls, celebrity and capital are inextricably linked in the modern age, and furthermore, the former exists to prop up the latter.[33]

Similarly, some women are exploring ways to monetize their microblog experiences. One of my participants, Miffy, runs an online shop through her microblog, featuring women's clothing and accessories, modeled by herself. At the same time, Miffy also chronicles her daily life through her mobile device. Through this managed visual presentation accompanied by written descriptions and stories, Miffy manages her image as a beautiful, fashionable young woman with lots of friends and living in Hong Kong. This has won her an audience of admirers and fans, especially young women from the mainland. She has developed her self-image as a popular brand. As a microcelebrity, the ongoing, diary-like process of "intimate visual co-presence" earns trust in both her aesthetic taste and her persona.

CONCLUSION

The convergence of mobile devices and Web 2.0 has provided a platform for people to chronicle the routines of their everyday lives. Through the lens of mobile microblogging, this study investigates young women's visual presentation and personal expression, as well as their strategies of social relationship management. From the textual analysis and in-depth interviews of sixteen active users—all of whom are immigrant women from mainland China in Hong Kong—three interesting phenomena emerge. First, this young generation of Chinese women has been empowered to an extent through their use and fluency with new media technologies, which have provided them a venue for expressing their creativity, sensibility and sense of humor.

As has been the case with other art and media forms, when women gain access to the tools of expression and creativity, the conventional role of woman as the object of the gaze becomes transformed as she becomes the subject—and in the case of mobile microblogging, this access also has the effect of helping to transform the stereotyped image of Chinese women as meek and passive. Second, as new arrivals in Hong Kong, these young women are immersed in a capitalist consumer culture. Through decorating portable devices and building a photographic diary of themselves, they express their personal taste and personalities through mobile representations. Although some of them experience identity confusion as they learn their way around a new social and cultural environment, the microblog's ongoing online self-performance and audience feedback helps them in the larger process of understanding and constructing a sense of personal identity.

Within the anxieties of everyday life and the pressures of work, different social networking strategies are developed. Some combine online and offline social relationships and operate within the private/public spaces created through a mobile microblog. These women use this online space as a medium of self-expression, self-exploration and community building. But there are other women in this consumerist context who, through the practice of microblogging, link the entrepreneurial opportunities of capitalism with these other pursuits, and who market themselves as "microcelebrities" and merge their self-image with a postmodern brand identity.

NOTES

1. Alvin Toffler, *The Third Wave* (London: Pan Books, 1984).
2. Mizuko Ito, "Introduction: Personal, Portable, Pedestrian", in *Personal, Portable, Pedestrian: Mobile Phones in Japanese Life*, ed. Mizuko Ito et al. (Cambridge, MA: MIT Press, 2005), 1–18.
3. Leopoldina Fortunati et al., "The 'Mobile' Face of Contemporary China", in *New Connectivities in China*, ed. Pui-lam Law (New York: Springer, 2012), 53–65.
4. Ibid.
5. Jack L. Qiu, *Working-Class Network Society: Communication Technology*

and the *Information Have-Less in Urban China* (Cambridge, MA: MIT Press, 2009).

6. Kwok-bun Chan, "Hong Kong's Professional Immigrants from Mainland China and Their Strategies of Adaptation", *Report to Central Policy Unit, Government of the Hong Kong SAR*, June 2008, http://www.google.com/url?sa=t&rct =j&q=&esrc=s&source=web&cd=8&ved=0CGAQFjAH&url=http%3A%2 F%2Fwww.cpu.gov.hk%2Fdoc%2Ftc%2Fresearch_reports%2F20080601% 2520HK%2527s%2520Professional%2520Immigrants%2520from%2520 Mainland%2520China%2520and%2520their%2520Strategies%2520of% 2520Adaptation.pdf&ei=h5kpUcX_MuSq0AG7t4CgAg&usg=AFQjCNEp Ws_-PRyB2AUlPL6kp_rYTfsgxw&bvm=bv.42768644,d.dmQ, accessed: February 23, 2013.

7. Mizuko Ito and Daisuke Okabe, "Technosocial Situations: Emergent Structuring of Mobile E-Mail Use", in *Personal, Portable, Pedestrian: Mobile Phones in Japanese Life*, ed. Mizuko Ito et al. (Cambridge, MA: MIT Press, 2005), 257–276.

8. Mikko Villi, "Publishing and Messaging Camera Phone Photographs: Patterns of Visual Mobile Communication On the Internet" (paper presented at the 61st Annual ICA Conference, Boston, MA, May 2011).

9. Dong-Hoo Lee, "Mobile Snapshots and Private/Public Boundaries", *Knowledge, Technology, and Policy* 22 (2009): 161–171.

10. Dong-Hoo Lee, "Women's Making of Camera Phone Culture", *The Fibreculture Journal*, December 10, 2005, accessed May 1, 2011, http://six. fibreculturejournal.org.

11. Villi, op. cit.

12. Larissa Hjorth, *Mobile Media in the Asia Pacific: Gender and the Art of Being Mobile*, (London: Routledge, 2009).

13. Ito and Okabe, 2005.

14. Minhee Son, "Cultures of Ambivalence: An Investigation of College Students' Uses of the Camera Phone and Cyworld's Mini-Hompy", *Knowledge, Technology, and Policy* 22 (2009): 173–184.

15. Fortunati et al, op. cit.

16. Raymond Ngan and Stephen Ma, "The Relationship of Mobile Telephony to Job Mobility in China's Pearl River Delta", *Knowledge, Technology and Policy* 21 (2008): 55–63.

17. Angel Lin and Avin Tong, "Mobile Cultures of Migrant Workers in Southern China: Informal Literacies in the Negotiation of (New) Social Relations of the New Working Women", *Knowledge, Technology and Policy* 21(2008): 73–81.

18. Qiu, op. cit.

19. Cara Wallis, "New Media Practices in China: Youth Patterns, Processes, and Politics", *International Journal of Communication* 5 (2011): 406–436.

20. Bo Gai, "A World through the Camera Phone Lens: A Case Study of Beijing Camera Phone Use", *Knowledge, Technology, and Policy* 22 (2009): 195–204.

21. "Data from Office of Telecommunication Authority, the Government of HK SAR." Accessed February 1, 2012, http://www.ofta.gov.hk/en/datastat/key_stat.html

22. Chan, op. cit.

23. Ito and Okabe, op. cit.

24. Lee, 2005.

25. Hjorth, op. cit.

26. Nicholas Abercrombie and Brian Longhurst, *Audiences: A Sociological Theory of Performance and Imagination*, (London: Sage, 1998), 66–77.

27. Guy Debord, *The Society of the Spectacle*, (New York: Zone books, 1994), 25.

28. Abercrombie and Longhurst, op. cit.

29. Erving Goffman (1959) *The Presentation of Self in Everyday life*, (N.Y.: Doubleday, 1959), 3–12.

30. Abercrombie and Longhurst, op. cit.
31. Lee, 2009.
32. Ito, 2005.
33. Theresa M. Senft, *Camgirls: Celebrity and Community in the Age of Social Networks*, (New York: Peter Lang 2008), 97–99.

# 9 The Networked Familiar Stranger
## An Aspect of Online and Offline Urban Anonymity

*Raz Schwartz*

## INTRODUCTION

It was high noon when I walked into the local bakery situated just a few blocks away from my apartment. As I opened the door and stepped inside I immediately recognized him, my nemesis. He was standing in line, much taller than I thought he was, wearing a black suit that confirmed my inkling that he was a lawyer in the nearby office building. Although I had seen only one photo of him, I knew he was the guy that I had been battling for the last month of my life.

That was the first time I saw him in the flesh. And still, although we both didn't say a word, our knowing looks said it all. It was obvious that our battle was far from over. Only one of us could be the Foursquare mayor of the bakery and neither of us would give up the fight.

I am not the only one having these kinds of confrontations on a daily basis. In recent years, the online sphere has been transforming into a less anonymous and a more accurate depiction of our daily life.[1] With social network sites that display only "real identities", search algorithms that provide the most precise "personalized results"—based on search history and browsing activity—and location-based services that pinpoint other users' whereabouts, we are witnessing a growing crossover of social interactions between the physical and the virtual sphere.

The emergence of smartphones with GPS capabilities, for example, paved the way for the development of online services that utilize users' physical locations and enable them to interact with others in their close proximity in new ways that did not exist before.[2] Popular mobile social networks such as Foursquare, SCVNGR and Instagram, along with mobile versions of websites like Facebook and Yelp, encourage users to "check in" to places they visit, leave tips and see who else is in their surroundings.

This study sets to examine social interactions in location-based social networks and their implications for the users' daily lives. The hypothesis for this research is that these interactions portray distinct characteristics due to their existence in "Net Locality", a hybrid space that carries influences from both the local physical place and the virtual sphere.[3] This space is generated by a ubiquitous networked information condition that combines both digital information flows and daily practices of everyday life.

## Foursquare

I chose to study these interactions through Foursquare, a service that is mostly used to broadcast and receive location updates among groups of friends, while at the same time offering recommendations for places in the immediate surroundings. Foursquare—a location-based service application for smartphones with GPS capabilities—was launched in March 2009 and has over ten million users worldwide (according to company data from August 2011), making it one of the biggest location-based services in the world.[4]

The service provides its users a way to share their location with friends and explore places in their local surroundings. Users may leave tips, bookmark information about places and retrieve suggestions for recommended places nearby. By using a "curated social graph"[5] method, the application prioritizes venues in close proximity and recommends places that match the users' personal preferences.

After downloading and installing the free application, the user registers and creates a Foursquare profile. The profile can be based on a user's email address or Facebook account credentials. When the user launches the application, Foursquare generates a list of nearby places based on GPS information (See Figure 9.1).

The list shown by the application is based on places submitted by its own users.[6] For example, one list could display a restaurant, a coffee shop and a place called "the bench on the corner of Butler and 35th", all user-submitted places. A user can select to check in at any of these places or add her own place to the list. In this way, the venue's database is constantly updated with user-generated places that may be accurate or completely made up (there are venues called "hell" or "the love shack" that I have encountered in numerous locations).

Then, the user checks in and selects if she would like to stay "off the grid" or share this information with friends who use Foursquare, Facebook or Twitter (See Figure 9.2). If the user selects to broadcast the information, the application sends a notification to the user's friends stating her current location. The manual check-in option mitigates privacy concerns users might have and allows for social performance.[7]

In addition to sharing the location of the user, the service also uses game mechanics to motivate its users to compete with each other and earn virtual titles and badges. These accomplishments rarely have any real-life benefits, and they are mostly earned only for the inherent gaming aspect. For example, if a user takes ten trips to the gym in thirty days, she will receive the "Gym Rat" badge. If a user checks in at twenty different pizza places, she will be rewarded with the "Pizzaiolo" badge.

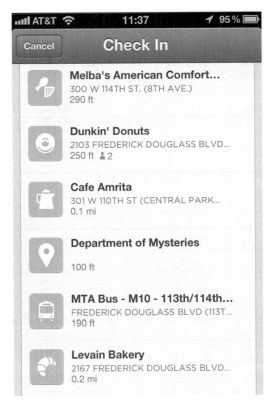

*Figure 9.1* List of nearby places based on GPS data (© 2012, Foursquare Labs, Inc., reprinted with permission)

In this game, users can become the "mayor" of a place if they visit it often. A "mayorship" is awarded to the person who checked in to a specific venue the most times in a certain period. Consequently, people become competitive and try to win the title. Retaining one's mayorship often proves to be a hard task since it requires the mayor to keep visiting the place in order to prevent the possibility of anyone else stealing the title.

When a certain mayorship changes, the old mayor receives a notification with the new mayor's information saying that the mayorship "was just stolen". In this way, although the mayorship is handed over from one user to another, there is no direct interaction between the users themselves. The game mechanics embedded in the service often lead to "mayorship battles" between avid users.[8]

Due to privacy concerns, the application developers made these battles one of the only interactions Foursquare users may have with people outside of their circle of friends. When a user signs up to the service, she is prompted to connect her Facebook, Twitter and Gmail accounts, so the application will find friends who also use the service and connect with them. The user can

*Figure 9.2*   Check-in screen (© 2012, Foursquare
Labs, Inc., reprinted with permission)

then send friend requests to other users, which, once approved, will enable
both parties to receive location notifications from each other's check-ins.

Other than battling for a mayorship title, Foursquare users can also interact with strangers over the application when they check in to a venue or
when they read tips left by others at the places they visit. After completing the
check-in action, the application displays the current mayor of the venue together with a list of users who are also publicly checked in to the same place
in the same relative timeframe (not "off the grid"). Using this display, users
can go through other users' profile pages and pictures, see who else is checked
in there and even view their profile pages on other social networks such as
Facebook and Twitter, if they were connected to their Foursquare profile.

## METHODOLOGY

This work is based on a six-month study conducted from September 2010 to
February 2011 using participant observation, user observation and in-depth

interviews. Twenty-five in-depth interviews were conducted with Foursquare users from three cities in the United States. The participation requirement for interviewees was to have used Foursquare in a specific area for a period of at least three months and with an ongoing activity of at least three days a week. These criteria ensured that the participants had a reasonable chance to interact with friends, explore places and come across other users in their daily routine.

The users were recruited by sending out Twitter messages to my follow- ers asking them to retweet the message to their own followers. The message linked to a Web page inviting people to participate in a study that focuses on "how people use Foursquare". These Twitter messages were retweeted by several people to an audience of approximately 2,000 people. I received mes- sages from twenty-seven people expressing their willingness to participate, finally resulting in thirteen users who met my participation requirement.

In addition, I used Foursquare's website to identify fervent users by the number of mayorships and titles they held. I contacted these users through their Twitter and Facebook accounts with a request to participate in my study. Out of the twenty people I contacted, twelve agreed to take part and share their experiences. I conducted my fieldwork in Pittsburgh, New York City and San Francisco; the demographics of this study consist of twenty-five Four- square users (thirteen men and twelve women) ranging in age from 24 to 35, living in Pittsburgh ($n$ = 8), San Francisco ($n$ = 7) and New York City ($n$ = 10). The users I interviewed had a friends network ranging from twelve to 117 friends. All interviewees received $10 compensation for their participation.

The interview protocol was structured from open-ended questions inves- tigating the nature of the social interactions people experience when using Foursquare. More specifically, the interviewees were asked about various topics such as their check-in practice (type of place, hours of the day, etc.), motivations, interactions with friends and strangers, place attachment, pri- vacy concerns and more.

All interviews were conducted and recorded face-to-face and later tran- scribed. Following grounded theory method,[9] after the interviews were tran- scribed and coded I noticed several themes that repeatedly emerged from the results. One of these themes was the idea of recognizing familiar faces of strangers through the use of the application. Consequently, this coding led me to examine these interactions in light of the "familiar stranger" notion, a prevailing offline term used to describe the nature of this kind of urban ephemeral relations.

## RELATED WORK

### The Familiar Stranger

In his 1972 paper "The Familiar Stranger: An Aspect of Urban Anonymity", social psychologist Stanley Milgram coined the term "familiar stranger" to depict a common social phenomenon—a relationship between two strangers who recognize one another through their daily encounters in public places (such as the subway, gym, etc.) but choose not to interact.[10] Milgram claims that although these two people never communicate, their relationship is real and it is based on both sides agreeing to ignore each other. Consequently, if one of the two is missing from the frequent encounters, the other will notice her disappearance. This notion aligns with Simmel's idea regarding the nature of strangers where he sees strangers as an important part of the individual's life and the community rather than distant and disconnected.[11]

Familiar strangers are part of the physical environment, a fixture of the local milieu. Milgram claims that one of the main characteristics of urban life is the fact that people often gain familiarity with the faces of people around them, yet they never interact. He sees these people as part of the urban environment, rather than actual persons with whom people interact. In this way, familiar strangers are as important to the perception of the local surroundings as street signs, public park benches and other local landmarks. All of these in turn support the feeling of local identity and belonging. Without them, the local living environment becomes unfamiliar and lonely.

In 1972, a group of Milgram's students at the City University of New York performed a short experiment among commuters in New York City. In the early morning hours, they went out and photographed large clusters of people waiting for the trains. Then, they gave a unique number to each figure in the photographs and a week later returned to the same stations and handed out the photographs to the commuters together with a cover letter and a questionnaire. The results showed that 89.5% of the people reported at least one familiar stranger. The average commuter identified four individuals whom she recognized but never spoke to, compared with a mean of 1.5 individuals with whom she conversed.

Milgram claimed that the status of familiar stranger does not reflect an absence of a relationship, but a different form of interpersonal relationship that has properties and consequences of its own and that is created due to the gap that exists between people's intentions and actions.[12] He noted that when familiar strangers see each other in places other than the site of their routine encounters, they would be more likely to interact with one another.

## The Familiar Stranger in Online Research

Since the study of location-based services is a relatively new research field, there are few earlier references or studies that noticed the connection between this emerging technology and the familiar stranger.[13] Even the social study of online social network websites assigned limited attention to this phenomenon. Baym, for example, describes how online interaction of music fans could translate to local physical relationships such as familiar strangers, while boyd examines this term in an online social networks context when she studies the use of Friendster.[14]

Following Milgram's idea, boyd claims that the virtual sphere within which Friendster operated provided the additional context needed for familiar strangers to approach each other when they are both outside of their regular environment. According to boyd, by browsing the site, users found the profiles of people who they saw when they were out with their friends. Based on the additional details they acquired from a user profile on Friendster, they had enough information to message that person on Friendster or approach her in real life. Since her study refers only to online social networks, this conclusion should be reexamined in the light of location-based services.[15]

From a different lens, several projects in the field of human–computer interaction have dealt with the phenomenon of the familiar stranger. Paulos and Goodman created studies such as "The Familiar Stranger Project" and "Jabberwocky" that examined the ways technology can affect users' connection to their physical surroundings.[16] These projects tried to extend the familiar stranger relationship through sensors and Bluetooth technology so they could be used in two scenarios: when someone is new to a city and wants to feel more familiar with the place and the people around her, and when someone is too familiar with the place and people around her and wants to go to an area to visit new places and see new people.

## The Networked Familiar Stranger

Based on the interviews findings, I offer to revisit the *familiar stranger* term and depict the *networked familiar stranger* that both complies with Milgram's original ideas but at the same time merges with the influence of the virtual sphere. This updated term therefore is a direct result of both the local and virtual interactions in the hybrid space created by location-based social networks. Since the original term is strongly rooted in the local physical place, I ask to embody the connectivity that is provided by the virtual sphere by adding the "networked" element to it.

The term does not refer only to users we see first on our mobile phone and then in real life, but it spans across interactions both in the virtual and the physical world. For example, noting the current mayor on Foursquare each time we visit the local bakery and then seeing the mayor in person is equally as significant as spotting someone first in real life and then identifying her profile on the mobile service. Although these two narratives of interactions differ, I suggest that they both conform to the added characteristics of the networked familiar stranger. These characteristics include the *shared stranger, enhanced storytelling* and the *virtual filtering*. The *shared stranger* refers to the possibility of different users having the same familiar strangers and sharing them among themselves even though they do not attend the same places at the same times. By *enhanced storytelling,* I refer to users using the additional details provided by other user profiles to create a more elaborate imagined narrative for their familiar strangers. Lastly, *virtual filtering* is the process of singling out the familiar strangers out of an urban or virtual crowd through the application.

## Shared Stranger

It is easier to share our relationship with networked familiar strangers among our friends, as the virtual sphere does not confine the interaction to a specific time. For example, although my friend Brian goes to the university library in the mornings and I go in the afternoons, we discovered that we both recognized the library's mayor when we saw him at a local bar. Although he was out of context, we both identified him as the library's mayor.

Since the application promotes its users to add their Gmail and Yahoo contacts together with Facebook and Twitter friends, the likelihood that several close friends will have the same networked familiar stranger is high. For example, Josh, an informant from New York City, described how he and his friends recognize and share people from the application in real life:

> It's just about the curiosity and being connected to people, even strangers. It's fun to see how many people are on the app and who checks in where . . . when I'm out with friends who are also on, we play the game of trying to spot the people we have seen on the app. It's only connecting virtually to people through sight and adding as friends to Foursquare. I never met anyone new in person from Foursquare. Seeing people you recognize from the app is interesting in a fun way, I've never approached someone to say "hey I just saw you checked in." I'm always curious to see if people look like their pictures.

As we can see, Josh enjoys sharing the experience of identifying a familiar face with his friends. In a way, the game Josh and his friends play allows them to share personal experiences with their familiar stranger among themselves and by doing so expand the number of shared networked familiar strangers. Throughout the interviews I noted that sixteen out of the twenty-five users had at least one instance in which they shared a networked familiar stranger with their friends.

This practice might also lead to a situation in which two friends share the same networked familiar stranger, but she will be associated for each one of them to a different physical place. Thus, in addition to the physical venues, the social space[17] created by the application becomes the "place" from which users identify their networked familiar strangers. Sharing the networked familiar stranger therefore can be considered as a way for users to strengthen their ties with their close friends. In other words, when we discuss with friends the experiences of identifying the same familiar faces around us, our interpersonal connection with them grows stronger since we now have even more joint interests.

The shared stranger is a specific characteristic to location-based services due to the built-in sharing tools provided by the virtual sphere. These tools create sharing opportunities that might not have been realized in the physical place. For instance, two friends who took different trains into Grand

Central each day might have found themselves commenting about the pretzel salesman near Track 8. But the fact that their visits to the train station are documented and shared through the application contributes to the possibility of a shared stranger.

## Enhanced Storytelling

We know more about our networked familiar strangers. As Milgram notes, many people often think about the familiar strangers around them and try to imagine their lives, jobs, etc. These details contribute to the imagined relationship with our familiar strangers.

In this way, people build a background story for their familiar strangers and by that differentiate them from all other strangers. I argue that location-based social networks enhance and expand these imagined narratives due to the personal information people post to their profile pages in addition to other details that are presented by the services. For example, by browsing a user's profile on Foursquare, one can learn the user's first name and the initial of her last name and the user's home town; one can also browse her other Foursquare friends, see the number and kinds of badges she obtained, and view the places where she holds a mayorship together with tips she might have left in other places. In addition, if the user connects her Facebook and Twitter to her Foursquare profile, other users can also browse through them. The sum of these details can greatly help in the storytelling process of the networked familiar stranger.

Twenty informants out of the twenty-five I interviewed confirmed that after they check in to a place they use the application to look up the mayor. From the mayor's profile page they sometimes also see which other mayorships this mayor holds and by that learn more about the places where she is considered to be a regular. For example, Lisa, one of my informants from New York City, told her Foursquare fairytale story about how she virtually met her dream guy, although she never really did meet or talk to him:

> The mayor of my favorite coffee place is this guy I've seen there several times and have been keeping an eye on for some time now. It all started when I saw he was the mayor of my local sushi place and since then I noticed that he is also the mayor of several other places I really like. I'm pretty sure he is an architect because he is the mayor of an architect's office and the Bronx Department of Buildings. We've never talked and I think we never will but he is dreamy.

Lisa's depiction of her dream guy is a common way users utilize the information shared on the service to learn more and become familiar with the people around them. Although even before location-based social networks people imagined what their familiar stranger's life is like based on clothes, behavior, and the hours and places where she was seen, the use of this service provides additional information that is otherwise not easily available. This information can include the frequency of visits to certain places (browsing the mayorships a user obtained), personal preferences and opinions (reading tips the user left) and social circles (going through her list of Foursquare friends).

In other words, users build their impression of their networked familiar strangers based on the information shared on this platform. Twenty of the informants said they feel these details have more credibility than online dating or Facebook profiles due to the fact that people cannot forge their actual location or their check-in history.

## Virtual Filtering

The way we single out the networked familiar stranger from the crowd now takes place also in the virtual sphere. The overwhelming amount of people and possible interpersonal connections from the urban surroundings together with the online sphere must be reduced and filtered. Since the networked familiar stranger is a direct result of that, we are now filtering out the masses not only based on their visual appearance but also through the use of location-based technology.

Some familiar strangers in Milgram's study turned out to be "socio-metric stars" in that they were recognized by a large group of people. One of these stars was a woman who waited for the train in a miniskirt every day, even on cold winter days. As a result, many of the commuters recognized her in the study pictures.

If the familiar strangers stood out of the crowed based on their visual appearance, I suggest that the networked familiar strangers stand out for additional reasons. Eighteen out of the twenty-five informants said that unless they had used Foursquare they would not have noticed the networked familiar strangers in their daily life. Patrick, one of the informants from New York City said:

> It's New York so people are everywhere. Especially when you are at a particularly crowded venue like a bar or at a concert. If you aren't looking for someone specifically, you likely won't see them.

For Patrick, Foursquare is another filter for the masses. It seems that although the city overload is making users filter out their surroundings, the addition of location-based services to the equation seems to actually promote users to be more aware of those around them. The virtual sphere expands our perception of strangers in our local surroundings. It works in both ways; people who we see on the mobile service and get familiarized with in the virtual sphere are then identified in the physical place we visit. But also, people we first see in real life and to whom we pay no attention can suddenly become networked familiar strangers after we see their profile picture in the virtual sphere.

The information overload of the virtual sphere adds to the urban overload and together they form the networked familiar strangers. Based on my interviews, I argue that networked familiar strangers would not have been noticed otherwise in the daily life setting. In several cases, it was the actions in the virtual world such as being the mayor of a place, that introduced them and made them familiar. Such a situation happened to Justin, a Foursquare user from Pittsburgh:

> There was a guy at my gym that was the mayor for a while before I stole it from him. I kept seeing his picture but I thought it was strange to me that he did not look familiar to me. Someone I would see often at the gym. I eventually recognized him in person but strangely enough it took a while for me to cross paths with him. I have still never spoken to him though. It felt bizarre. You just have this one picture representing him on Foursquare and that's all you have to go by in terms of information. I would definitely not notice him otherwise. He just would have blended in with the rest of the regulars. I doubt he would have caught my eye.

As we can see from his story, Justin's networked familiar stranger was not someone he would notice unless he had used Foursquare. In this case, the use of the application made Justin pay closer attention and actively look for his networked familiar stranger. The application serves as an additional filtering platform that promotes us to identify the networked familiar strangers not only based on their visual appearance but also based on other characteristics, such as their visit frequency to a specific place or the tips left there.

## DISCUSSION

The overlap between the vast amount of digital information and the urban city overload creates the terms for the emergence of the networked familiar stranger. This social interaction takes place in a Net Locality space, which represents the need of people to contextualize themselves within a massively growing network of information. Consequently, interactions that are produced in this condition share characteristics of both the local physical world as well as of the online sphere. Viewing this type of interaction as one that aligns with previous ideas about the ordering mechanisms of strangers in urban settings[18], I argue that the networked familiar stranger, therefore, is an ordered way to acknowledge and handle the different aspects of offline and online urban anonymity.

Gaining a networked familiar stranger is the result of a social process, which takes time, like any interpersonal interaction. In this regard, my informants indeed noticed that their connection to the networked familiar stranger had to be built over time and through daily use of the applications mainly in third places such as coffee shops, bars, gyms etc.[19] The process of obtaining and maintaining a networked familiar stranger may include some kind of online interaction in the virtual sphere, but these interactions do not necessarily affect the users' local interactions. In other words, users can interact over the service (compete for mayorships, follow each other on Twitter, etc.) but could still ignore each other in real life.

Throughout the interviews, my informants described their networked familiar strangers as people they would not have noticed otherwise, much less be interested in knowing their background. I argue that the networked familiar strangers are added to our already established familiar strangers. The use of location-based social networks filters the networked familiar strangers based not only on physical encounters but also on their own visits to a specific place. In other words, if a user frequents a place and becomes its mayor, although we never met her, she might become our networked familiar stranger.

The real-life barriers that build up between familiar strangers are very different from the virtual ones. As boyd noticed, users feel much more comfortable approaching other users online than in real life. It seems that the fact that the users are in a different realm, with the application acting as a unifying point of interest and play, encourages users to get to know others both directly through virtual interaction or indirectly through virtual stalking.[20] This practice promotes a stronger connection to familiar strangers in our local surroundings. Users recognize more faces and therefore feel more "at home" as the use of the application contributes to the feeling of familiarity in local communities. For example, Kyle, an informant from Pittsburgh, noticed that whenever he used the application in a place he felt had many strangers, having a prior connection to someone through Foursquare instantly transformed his connection to them and "made the place more welcoming."

And it might indeed feel that way for Kyle, since the networked familiar strangers are rarely different from him. The familiar faces users recognized through Foursquare were of people who visited the same places as they did and shared the same interests. Just like in Milgram's familiar strangers, the service promotes segregation among users with the same cultural capital, distinguishing themselves based on cultural and financial factor.[21] This could lead to overfiltering, which results in encountering the same people in the same places.[22] For example, if a certain user frequents a pricey restaurant or a posh sports club, she will encounter other users who visit the same places and contribute to the formation of an area that carries a distinct character.[23]

Humphreys suggests that location-based services can change the way users experience urban public space and rearrange social and spatial practices.[24] In this way, spotting familiar faces from the application in the busy urban streets, browsing through profile pages of users who are also checked in at the same place and time, and sharing these experiences with friends can create a social setting that contributes to the users' perception of their local area.

Sutko and de Souza e Silva have challenged the idea that location-based services increase social interactions and help users meet new people in public space.[25] They claim that location-based services only support already established social norms of interactions, despite challenging traditional sociability practices. These findings both differ and align with the results of this study. As we have seen from the results of this study, Foursquare interactions do reinforce already existing familiar stranger relationships, but at the same time they also create new relationships with networked familiar strangers that did not exist before.

## LIMITATIONS

This study has several limitations. First, one must keep in mind that despite the fast spread of location-based technology, it is still in an early phase of development and distribution. The users I interviewed can be generally described as early adopters of technology, and therefore their use might shape the future ways in which the general public uses them.[26] In addition, the application I chose to study does not represent all location-based services. There are several services that compete with Foursquare for the same audience. These services may offer different user interaction possibilities for their subscribers and therefore might lead to other usage patterns.

Moreover, the information gathered during this research represents only the interactions during the study's timeframe and might change due to ongoing developments and iterations in the services software. Since I conducted the interviews, Foursquare has issued several updated versions of the services that add new functions. Having said that, although the services might add or change the options they offer their users, the basic representation of nearby strangers is at its core.

## CONCLUSION AND FUTURE WORK

This study describes the emergence of the networked familiar stranger, a novel social phenomenon that is derived from the merging of the virtual and local physical spheres.

My findings show that the use of Foursquare has direct implications to our experience of familiar strangers in our surroundings and promotes the discovery of networked familiar strangers. Moreover, the additional information brought by location-based social networks contributes to strengthening connections with existing familiar strangers as well as helps users identify networked familiar strangers, share them with friends and enhance their imagined life narrative.

Future research should explore whether the relationships between networked familiar strangers affect the already-existing familiar strangers. Another issue that should be researched deals with the difference in the strength of ties with familiar strangers versus networked familiar strangers. The use of location-based services in rural areas should also be addressed in further research due to the difference it proposes to the users' local nearby social setting. Moreover, the ease of creating a crossover from a networked familiar stranger's status to an actual friendship is another aspect that should be examined.

Since location-based social networks such as Foursquare are still in their early stages, it is not yet clear which one of them, if any, will find their way to the mass use of the general public. It is clear though that the technological development of location-based services in the next years will provide researchers with exciting new subjects of inquiry to the study of local social interactions.

## NOTES

1. Bernie Hogan and Barry Wellman, "The Immanent Internet Redux", in *Digital Religion, Social Media and Culture: Perspectives, Practices and Futures*, ed. Pauline Hope Cheong et al. (Bern, Switzerland: Peter Lang, 2011), 43–62.
2. James E. Katz and Mark Aakhus, eds., *Perpetual Contact: Mobile Communication, Private Talk, Public Performance* (New York: Cambridge University Press, 2002); Janne Lindqvist et al., "I'm the Mayor of My House: Examining Why People Use Foursquare: A Social Driven Location Sharing Application", *Proceedings of the ACM CHI Conference on Human Factors in Computing Systems* (Vancouver, Canada: May 7–11, 2011), 10 pgs.
3. Eric Gordon and Adriana de Souza e Silva, *Net Locality: Why Location Matters in a Networked World* (Chichester, UK: Wiley-Blackwell, 2011).
4. *About foursquare*, accessed September, 5, 2011, https://foursquare.com/about.
5. The Curated Social Graph method, developed specifically for the service by Foursquare, is an algorithm that considers friends' check-ins, the user check-in history and other factors to produce a list of recommended places in the nearby area. Social Graph algorithms are commonly used by online social networks such as Facebook, Google+, etc. to provide a more personalized experience by using the information gathered about users relationships and interests.
6. As the Foursquare team notes on their blog (March 14, 2011, accessed September, 5, 2011, http://blog.Foursquare.com/2011/03/14/1up-the-importance-of-platforms-and-how-we%E2%80%99re-extending-ours/), one of the problems in the beginning of Foursquare was creating a venues database. The company decided to utilize their users to solve that problem and enabled user-generated venues. Two years later, the database had more than fifteen million user-submitted venues.
7. Henriette Cramer, Mattias Rost and Lars Erik Holmquist, "Performing a Check-In: Emerging Practices, Norms and 'Conflicts' in Location-Sharing Using Foursquare", *Proceedings of the 13th International Conference on Human Computer Interaction with Mobile Devices and Services (MobileHCI '11)* (ACM, New York: 2011), 57–66.
8. Simone Oliver, "Who Elected Me Mayor? I Did". *New York Times*, August 19, 2010, accessed September, 5, 2011, http://www.nytimes.com/2010/08/19/fashion/19Foursquare.html.
9. Barney Glaser and Anselm Strauss, *The Discovery of Grounded Theory: Strategies for Qualitative Research* (New York: Aldine de Gruyter, 1967).
10. Stanley Milgram, "The Familiar Stranger: An Aspect of Urban Anonymity", in *The Individual in a Social World: Essays and Experiments*, ed. John Sabini and Maury Silver (New York: McGraw-Hill, 1992), 51–53.

11. Georg Simmel, "The Stranger", *The Sociology of Georg Simmel*, ed. Kurt H. Wolff (Glencoe, IL: Free Press, 1950), 402–408.

12. Thomas Blass, *The Man Who Shocked The World* (New York: Basic Books, 2004), 163–196.

13. Lee Humphreys, "Mobile Social Networks and Social Practice: A Case Study of Dodgeball", *Journal of Computer Mediated Communication* 13 (2008): 341–360; Adriana de Souza e Silva and Jordan Frith, "Locative Mobile Social Networks: Mapping Communication and Location in Urban Spaces", *Mobilities* 5, no. 4 (2010): 485–506.

14. danah boyd, "Friendster and Publicly Articulated Social Networks." *Conference on Human Factors and Computing Systems (CHI 2004)*. Vienna: ACM, April 24-29, 2004), 5 pgs.; Nancy Baym, "The New Shape of Online Community: The Example of Swedish Independent Music Fandom", *First Monday* 12, no. 8 (2007), accessed February 23, 2013, http://firstmonday.org/htbin/cgiwrap/bin/ojs/index.php/fm/article/view/1978/1853.

15. Online social networks and dating websites differ from location-based social networks due to the added technological factor of location. In location-based social networks, the user's location is the only information detail the user cannot control. A user cannot pretend to be in another city or state, since the system is programmed to recognize attempts to check-in at places that are not actually in the users' proximity and does not award points, titles, etc. This is a key difference between online social networks websites such as Facebook, MySpace etc. and location based services.

16. Eric Paulos and Elizabeth Goodman, "The Familiar Stranger: Anxiety, Comfort, and Play in Public Spaces", in *Proceedings of the ACM CHI Conference on Human Factors in Computing Systems* (Vienna: ACM Press, 2004), 223–230.

17. Henri Lefebvre, *The Production of Space* (Oxford: Blackwell Publishers, 1991).

18. Lyn H. Lofland, *A World of Strangers* (New York: Basic Books, 1973).

19. Ray Oldenburg, *The Great Good Place: Cafes, Coffee Shops, Community Centers, Beauty Parlors, General Stores, Bars, Hangouts, and How They Get You Through the Day* (New York: Paragon, 1991)

20. Adam N. Joinson, "'Looking at', 'Looking Up' or 'Keeping Up with' People? Motives and Uses of Facebook", in *Proceedings of the ACM CHI Conference* (New York: ACM Press, 2008), 1027–1036.

21. Pierre Bourdieu and Jean-Claude Passeron, "Cultural Reproduction and Social Reproduction", in *Knowledge, Education and Cultural Change*, ed. Richard K. Brown (London: Tavistock, 1973).

22. Cass Sunstein, *Infotopia: How Many Minds Produce Knowledge*. (Oxford: Oxford University Press, 2006).

23. Justin Cranshaw et al., "The Livehoods Project: Utilizing Social Media to Understand the Dynamics of a City" (paper presented at International AAAI Conference on Weblogs and Social Media, Dublin, Ireland, May 2012).

24. Lee Humphreys, "Mobile Social Networks and Urban Public Space", *New Media & Society* 12, no. 5 (2010): 763–778.

25. Daniel M. Sutko and Adriana de Souza e Silva, "Location-Aware Mobile Media and Urban Sociability", *New Media & Society* 13, no. 5 (2011): 807–823.

26. Wiebe E. Bijker, Thomas P. Hughes and Trevor J. Pinch, eds., *The Social Construction of Technological Systems: New Directions in the Sociology and History of Technology* (Cambridge, MA: MIT Press, 1987); Howard Rheingold, *Smart Mobs: The Next Social Revolution* (Cambridge, MA: Perseus, 2002).

# 10 Checking In or Checking Out?

## Self-Presentation and Privacy Considerations of Foursquare Users

*Kelli S. Burns*

We are building a Web where the default is social.

Mark Zuckerberg[1]

## INTRODUCTION

This view of the Web by Facebook founder Mark Zuckerberg provides insight into how questions of presentation and privacy will be answered. Today, a user's online presentation must be consistent with his or her offline self, because Web platforms make it difficult to operate in anonymity and maintain a separate life. Furthermore, privacy concerns are set aside as sharing in social networks is embraced by users and rewarded by marketers.

This study involves observations of check-ins and privacy settings and then interviews with twelve Foursquare users to discover how users draw a line between their online and offline selves or whether these two selves have become seamless. In doing so, considerations of self-presentation and privacy concerns of Foursquare users are explored. It is presumed that self-presentation and privacy cannot be studied separately because users who wish to present an ideal self to the public may require a certain amount of privacy. The presentation and privacy issues that pervade computer-mediated communication may be in some ways more exaggerated in mobile-mediated communication. With a direct link to social networking sites at their fingertips, users can easily communicate in real time their offline activities to their online followers, which is a practice that should raise concerns about the privacy of that information and the presentation of self the user makes with that information.

### History of Foursquare

Created in 2009 by Dennis Crowley and Naveen Selvadurai, Foursquare is a mobile location-based social networking service. A predecessor of Foursquare was Crowley's Dodgeball, a mobile service that used texting to communicate locations. The Foursquare app, which can be downloaded to a smartphone with a GPS receiver, provides an interface for users to view all nearby locations and then select their current location for a check-in.

The growth of Foursquare has been astonishing. In September 2012, the company hit a milestone of twenty-five million registered users.[2] Part of the appeal of Foursquare is the game element of unlocking badges for certain types of check-ins. Users can also become mayors, who are users with the most check-ins to a venue in the past sixty days. Foursquare also allows merchants to communicate special offers to Foursquare users for checking in or becoming the mayor. It is this combination of special offers and gaming that encourages frequent check-ins among users.

## Privacy Issues

Like with other social networks, Foursquare users also have friends, a feature that allows users to view at any time the last place their friends checked in and vice versa. Check-ins are shared only with friends unless the user participates in the mayorship program, where anyone who checks in to a venue can see the mayor's profile photo and first name/last initial. Check-ins may also be shared with strangers if the user allows other people at a particular venue to see that the user has also checked in there. Further compromising privacy is the ability of the user to push check-ins to Twitter and Facebook with the click of a button, which links more personal data to the user's location. Despite the risks, many Foursquare users publish their locations on Twitter, which is more problematic than Facebook because many Twitter users are followed by strangers.[3]

Foursquare users can also allow their user name to be included in friends' status updates to Twitter or Facebook. By allowing this, when a user and a Foursquare friend both check in to a venue (even at different times in the day) and the Foursquare friend pushes that check-in to Twitter or Facebook, not only will the status update on Twitter or Facebook reveal that the friend is there, but it will also include the user's name in that post. Therefore, the user's location will be broadcast to the network of the Foursquare friend. Users also have the option to allow local businesses to see the profiles of mayors and top customers.

Even when Foursquare users attempt to protect their profiles, several techniques make it possible to discover their identities. When users participate in mayorships or allow people at venues to see that they are in a certain location, their profiles photos and first name/last initial are revealed. A Google search of that first name/last initial, the city, and Foursquare will likely produce results that link to that user's profile. Many users include their last name on their profile. Foursquare users can include their mobile number and e-mail address on their profile, as well as links to their Facebook and Twitter accounts. Although not currently in operation, the site PleaseRobMe.com listed real-time updates from Foursquare users who broadcasted this information on Twitter to demonstrate how easy it is to know when people are away from home.[4]

At the same time, users can still exert a great deal of control over their Foursquare privacy settings. In the most extreme case, users can keep check-ins private and not make them visible to even their friends. Users can also choose not to participate in the mayorship program, be revealed in the "who's here" at different venues, include their name with friends' status updates in Twitter or Facebook, or allow local businesses to see that they have checked in. Users may also wish to omit their e-mail addresses, cell phone numbers, and Twitter and Facebook accounts on their Foursquare profile. Users should be wary of pushing check-ins to Twitter or Facebook and checking in at home.

## LITERATURE REVIEW

### Self-Presentation

Previous studies have explored Goffman's[5] theory of self-presentation in personal Web spaces,[6] in an online dating environment,[7] or on MySpace.[8] In an earlier study of presentation of self within a geolocation service, Humphreys explored the function of messages among Dodgeball users.[9] Her research found that not only do users coordinate meetings through the service, but that they also check in to link their identity to the brand image of a particular location, a practice that might demonstrate social elitism. Furthermore, some Dodgeball users also send check-in messages to create a social diary of their travels. Although self-presentation motivations were revealed in Humphreys' results, her main purpose was to explore how linking social networks to physical locations could strengthen the experience of urban public spaces. In addition, because Dodgeball operated as a text-based system, messages to friends were somewhat ephemeral and not stored on a profile within a social network that created a presentation of self for friends.

Goh et al.'s study of mobile photo sharing grouped motivations into categories.[10] In their study, eighteen participants maintained a diary in which they recorded their motivations for capturing and sharing photos and the emotions experienced at the time. Sharing photos for the creation or maintenance of social relationships, the most frequent motivation, appearing in 52.8% of entries, usually occurred when the person receiving the image was part of the activity captured. The second most common motivation was to use sharing as a way to remind the user of experiences, followed by self-presentation and then task performance, such as reminders of tasks and as a substitute for writing. Finally, self-expression, the least frequently occurring motivation, explains how participants used photos to share their view of the world, whether environmental, social or news reporting.

Lindqvist et al. found self-representation to play a role in determining whether to check in to a particular venue on Foursquare.[11] Through interviews, they found that many users were not interested in checking in to fast food places and to some extent, doctor's offices, banks, or "boring" places. Although self-presentation was explored in Lindqvist et al.'s study, it was neither elaborated upon nor emphasized.

These self-presentation studies raise questions about the motivations of location-based service users and how self-presentation factors into their motivations for sharing locations. The following research question is proposed:

> RQ1: What role does self-presentation play in Foursquare users' motivations for using the service?

## Privacy

Much work in the area of social media privacy has emerged from the computer science field. A study by Gross and Acquisti of 4,540 Facebook users at Carnegie Mellon in the early days of Facebook found that students revealed a great deal of information about themselves through the site, including a profile image (90.8%), birthdate (87.8%), AIM screen name (77.7%), current residence (50.8%) and phone number (39.9%).[12] Almost 99% of those who listed a birthday included the day, month and year as opposed to just the month and day. Most users (89%) also included their full names, which means that all this personal data is linked to their actual names. In terms of privacy settings, only 1.2% had changed the default setting so that their information was not searchable by all Facebook users, but only Carnegie Mellon University users, and only .06% had changed the setting to restrict profile visibility to only CMU users.

More recent studies on social media privacy have focused on location-based services. Li and Chen explored the proportion of protected updates for the location-based service Brightkite from a worldwide sample of over 74,000 users.[13] They found that women are more privacy conscious than men and that older people are more privacy conscious than younger ones. Almost 23% of users did not reveal gender and 59% did not disclose their age in their profiles. As check-ins increased, the proportion of protected updates similarly increased.

Page and Kobsa interviewed users and nonusers of Google Latitude, a real-time mobile sharing feature within Google Maps, to understand real-world adoption of and resistance to the service.[14] Users generally practiced responsible checking in, where they checked in only to their actual locations and felt the need to keep their location up to date. Others were not as comfortable with people knowing their exact locations and often gave weak ties, people with whom they have infrequent or distant contact, only partial profile access, while some ignored friend requests. Some opted for lowest-common-denominator information disclosure and made this available to all friends. Finally, participants had different notions of the social norms for using this technology as related to privacy settings.

Several others studies have explored privacy concerns of users of location-based services through field or laboratory experiments involving smartphone devices where users participated in real or simulated scenarios. Tang et al. were particularly interested in one-to-many sharing situations.[15] Nine participants carried phones equipped with location-logging software. For each location, participants were asked how to describe the place using up to eight labels and then explain which label they would share in a hypothetical purpose-driven location-sharing scenario and then a social-driven location-sharing scenario. The places were classified as either semantic or geographic. Overall, more semantic labels were provided than geographic for both purpose-driven and social-driven sharing scenarios, but significantly more were provided for social-driven sharing. Furthermore, of the semantic names, social-driven sharing was more likely to be labeled by the activity or personal name instead of functional or business names. Reasons provided for choosing such labels included privacy concerns and attracting attention. Like with studies of purpose-driven location sharing, users in social-driven location situations also use sharing to locate other users. Impression management was found to be important too, with users sharing location information as a way to enhance their self-presentation with their networks.

Ben Abdesslem, Parris and Henderson also used an experimental design that included the use of mobile phones and a Facebook application that shared locations with a network defined as either "all friends" (in the user's social network) or "everyone" (all Facebook users).[16] Six types of questions or activities were sent to the forty participants during the experiment related to their willingness to share their current location with different groups. The study found that location type impacts willingness to disclose location. Participants at leisure and academic locations were more likely to share than those at home or a library. Debriefing revealed a desire to reveal "interesting" places and an unwillingness to share locations where participants do not want to be disturbed. Participants were also hesitant to flood their friends with too much information on the Facebook feed and did not want to be disturbed by those who might join the location-sharing program.

Kelley et al. explored attitudes toward locating-sharing with advertisers in a study in which participants carried smartphones with location-tracking software.[17] For each location where participants checked in, they were asked whether they would have been comfortable sharing that location with advertisers during the time they were there. A post-study revealed strong general privacy concerns. Similarly, participants were not comfortable sharing locations with advertisers all the time, but were more comfortable sharing during specified times or specified locations. Factors impacting the decision to allow access to advertisers included the number of ads, location, type of advertiser, type of product, time of day, and brand of the advertiser. In terms of time of day, weekdays during business hours were preferred to other times, and in terms of location, the second and third most visited places were preferred over the most visited place, which for many participants was their home. In summary, Kelley et al. discovered that although users had strong privacy concerns, advanced privacy settings will increase sharing and make users more willing to share locations with advertisers.[18]

Humphreys explored how Dodgeball users think about privacy and surveillance when using the service.[19] She found that although most were not concerned about their privacy because they felt in control of their personal information, the users did present evidence of three kinds of surveillance: voluntary panopticon (i.e., voluntary submission to corporate surveillance), lateral surveillance (i.e., aymmetrical monitoring of citizens by one another) and self-surveillance (i.e., recording one's own behavior for potential replaying).

Lindqvist et al. examined privacy concerns in their study of Foursquare users.[20] In interviews with eighteen Foursquare users, the researchers found that half of the users interviewed did not have privacy concerns. Strategies for controlling access to private information included not posting personal information, only having real-life friends as Foursquare friends, not linking check-ins to Facebook or Twitter, and not sharing every check-in. Those with privacy concerns offered such reasons as the potential for stalking. In a subsequent survey, Lindqvist et al. found that most users included a recognizable photo, phone number, e-mail address, and links to Facebook and Twitter.[21] In addition, a majority of respondents had friends they had not met in person.

These privacy studies lead to the following question about Foursquare:

RQ2: What are the privacy concerns of Foursquare users?

RQ3: What strategies do Foursquare users use to allay their privacy concerns?

Although Lindqvist et al.'s qualitative study of eighteen participants addresses some of the privacy concerns and strategies of Foursquare users, their survey did not fully explore privacy concerns, but mostly reported users' privacy settings.[22] Being that geolocation services are such a new application, the topic is worthy of further exploration and more detailed analysis.


## METHODOLOGY

Consumer research can provide three types of knowledge, with everyday knowledge, as opposed to scientific or interpretive knowledge, being the most relevant here. Qualitative research is suggested as a way to tap into everyday knowledge.[23] In addition, everyday knowledge can stimulate scientific theories, and scientific theories should be grounded in everyday knowledge. The desire for rich detail[24] necessitated the use of qualitative research to explore this topic. Furthermore, qualitative research will help establish variables that could be used in a subsequent quantitative study.

The sample consisted of twelve active Foursquare users who were selected through convenience sampling from the network of the author and a research assistant. The sample consisted of five women and seven men ranging in age from 21 to 42. Five of the twelve participants were young adults in the age range of 21–25, four were 26–30, and the remaining three were 35, 37 and 42 years old. One participant is married with children, one is single with children and one is married with no children. The remaining participants are single with no children. Ten participants live in Tampa, Florida, and the remaining two live in Texas and Kentucky. The author and her research assistant shared the responsibility of interviews, which were conducted in person, recorded and transcribed during April 2011. The semistructured interview guide included approximately twenty-four questions with many follow-up prompts. The resulting data were then coded, patterns in the data were discovered, and these patterns were analyzed to produce an explanation. The author served as the primary data analyst. In some cases, names were changed to protect identities.

## RESULTS

### Self-Presentation

Some Foursquare users consider the impression a venue checked in to might make on followers. Many participants were worried about presenting a negative image of themselves, rather than a positive one. When check-ins or mayorships are broadcasted on Twitter or Facebook, an impression is created not just among the user's Foursquare followers, but within their Twitter and Facebook networks as well, which further spreads the location information:

> When I earn a mayorship or earn a badge, a tweet is sent from my Twitter account announcing it. I checked in to my town's Coldstone and became the mayor after two visits so it announced it to all my followers. I was embarrassed that my followers probably think I'm a fatty. (Diana)
>
> I got a speeding ticket and had to go to the courthouse. I checked in there and became the mayor. It showed up on Twitter, and I thought, "should I be proud of that?" (Katie)

Kris, who checks in often when at school, noted that "the concern is in the back of my head and it may seem like I don't have a life". Others are less troubled about what their check-ins communicate about themselves to others. Some of these participants are those who limit their Foursquare followers to real friends and do not push check-ins to broader networks on Facebook or Twitter:

> I'm not one to care what people think about what I do or where I go. The only people on my Foursquare are my friends so they have a good idea of what I do and what type of person I am. No one else matters. (Alexa)
>
> From what I look at, it shows that I usually check in at restaurants and bars. I don't think about what this says about me to others because I know the places I go don't define me. (Tom)

Another attitude was expressed by Bill, who felt that his check-ins were a representation of himself that he was interested in communicating to other people:

> Many of my check-ins are revealing in that they showcase one activity, barhopping and restaurant patronage, to be highly prevalent. I do tend to check in when I'm out and about and for social purposes because I am very social and I apparently feel a need to communicate that to others. (Bill)

Adding another layer to self-presentation on Foursquare is the ability of users to earn points and collect badges for check-ins. The gaming element of Foursquare is attractive to some users, who aspire to collect a lot of unusual badges to impress their friends:

> The accumulation of badges is like my show off. My trophy case is bigger and better than yours thing. For example, I have "Panel Nerd" from SXSW. A lot of people don't have this badge. Also, I have the "New Year's Eve" badge. I think you can get this for any New Year's Eve party check-in, but I was in Times Square. (Pat)

Others, like Katie, do not care as much about badges and described them as "lame, but cool". When she checked in somewhere and earned the "Fashionista" badge, she said that although it was "cool to get the badge, it doesn't mean anything". The purpose of Foursquare is not solely to create and manage a presentation of oneself, as established in the above discussion. Another motivation for using Foursquare is to connect to other people.

> I don't check in all the time but will if I think my friends may be out so they know where I am and can join me. (Dennis)
>
> I check in to a location when I enter so my friends can stop by if they are in the area. (Rhonda)

In the community where most of this study's participants reside, Foursquare is not used as extensively as in other cities. As Foursquare grows, these users should see more friends signing up for the service, which increases this benefit. Participation in Foursquare is more than just presenting a certain impression to followers. For some, the check-ins represent a diary of their travels or adventures.

> I've found it to be nice to be able to see what I did on a daily basis and remember the exact dates where I did special things. It's almost like a diary that's kept without much effort. (Diana)

These findings are consistent with Humphreys' study of Dodgeball users who use the service to connect with others for in-person meetings, to manage self-presentation by linking personal identity to a brand image of a certain venue, and for social or spatial cataloguing.[25] This study does, however, extend Humphreys' study by highlighting the negative impact of checking in on self-presentation and how the gaming aspect of Foursquare can be used to further build an online identity.

## Privacy

In general, content shared by users in social media tends to be low-risk, such as funny incidents or random thoughts. Some users are differentiating between networks, sharing some content on certain sites and other content on others.

> The kind of information I share depends on the social media platform. Since my Facebook is only for friends, I don't mind sharing more personal content. Now that I have acquired so many Twitter followers, I'm more hesitant to share as much personal information. (Diana)

Most participants have developed a stance on privacy through their experiences with other social media sites that is reflected in how they use Foursquare.

> I don't really have privacy concerns because all of this information can be found online without including Foursquare. For example, before I checked in to my daughter's school, I had a small concern over someone knowing where she went to school. Then I realized that the information was already out there because of photos that have been posted online with her in her school shirts. (Jesse)

**Friends as followers.** Most participants in this study only accept Foursquare follower requests from friends, yet some will consider requests from people they meet when they are out or people they do not know well but feel they can trust.

I stick to accepting only friends because of the trust factor. I do not want some random person knowing where I am. I have accepted a request from people at the same location, after I have met them and have seen them out at the same places I've been frequenting. (Amanda)

Others, however, do not have issues with strangers following them. Jesse will accept most follower requests as a way to meet new people, unless they seem "too shady" based on their photo. Bill will accept strangers given certain circumstances.

I get a sense of prestige or flattery in knowing that someone I don't know has expressed some sort of interest in whatever it is I may be doing. Obviously, there is a need for precaution in accepting strangers into your world. However, I feel that I am a relatively security-conscious individual and often set my Web settings as to prevent misuse. (Bill)

These results are consistent with Ellison et al., who described Facebook as a way to maintain existing social networks instead of creating new connections.[26]

**Checking in at home.** Any scan through Foursquare venues will reveal home locations that users have created to check in to. One strategy of some of the participants in this study who wish to check in at home is to create a pseudonym for its location.

I check in at home but it's not the name of my apartment complex because I made up a place for home. I don't have any privacy issues with this because I don't accept stranger's friend requests. (Rhonda)

Kris checks in to his neighborhood as opposed to his home address, but usually it is when he is leaving. He added that, "I don't feel Foursquare was meant for that [checking in at home]". Others do not check in at home under any circumstances. As Katie noted, "If you check in at home, I think you are asking for trouble". Ryan and Amanda also had privacy concerns:

I think people need to be very careful because they are telling everyone that follows them on Foursquare exactly where their home is and when they're there. Even if the settings are very private, there has to be a database of it somewhere. (Ryan)

I absolutely do not want people to know where I live unless I bring you to my place personally or by invitation. Being a female, you have to be very mindful of these scenarios so when I see more and more people checking in to their homes, I just don't understand that. (Amanda)

Others, like Jesse, check in at home to get the easy mayorship and will check in at other people's houses if already listed as a venue on Foursquare. Alexa will also check in at home if she is bored.

*Checking in away from home.* In addition to the issue of checking in at home, users are also concerned when they check in away from home. Some of their hesitation is related to the possibility that someone who knows this information might try to rob their home.

> If I happen to check in at a venue twenty miles away from home, I am very obviously not at home and the potential for robbery, etc. is there. However, I am consoled by the fact that I happen to know that only a small handful of individuals happen to know where I live, having just recently moved. For this reason, I am readily willing to use Foursquare on a regular basis. (Bill)

Others have more general concerns about people knowing where they are.

> Some places are just too personal and private. I only check in at places that I am at with friends or that I know friends are at. I don't want people to know where I am all the time. (Alexa)

*Checking in off the grid.* Foursquare users have the option to check in "off the grid" and not have their location published to their feed that is visible to friends. Ryan noted, "I used to check in off the grid at my apartment complex because I was close to becoming mayor, but it wasn't happening so I gave it up". Jesse checks in off the grid when he wants privacy and does not want people to know he is in town. Diana checks in this way when in personal locations like other people's houses if they are not already listed on Foursquare. Others do not see a good reason to check in off the grid.

> I never check in off the grid because if I don't want people to know where I am, I just don't check in. (Rhonda)

*Privacy settings.* Foursquare profiles can include a name of the user's choosing, phone number, e-mail address, and links to Twitter or Facebook. In addition, users can also adjust whether they participate in mayorships (where anyone who checks in to a venue can see the profile photo and first name/last initial of the mayor) or allow their profile photo and name to be included in a list of "who's here" for anyone who checks in to the same venue to view. Users also specify whether they want their name included if a friend broadcasts a check-in to Twitter or Facebook and the user has also checked in to that venue. Finally, users can opt to include their profile in the metrics data for participating merchants if they among the top or most recent visitors.

The participants in this study had different combinations of personal information available in their Foursquare profile. Pat has just his first name on his profile with his cell phone number and links to Twitter and Facebook. Kris has his full name and e-mail address. He does not connect his Foursquare account to other social media sites because he does not want to clutter the other sites with his Foursquare check-ins. Some participants include their full name, e-mail, phone number, and links to other social media sites. As Jesse noted, "There is no point in hiding my information because it is very easy for people to find this online elsewhere". Others do not include contact information, but do include social media account links.

Anyone at a particular venue will be able to view the mayor and the people who are currently checked in there, assuming that the people checked in allow Foursquare to share this information. Most participants have no problems with strangers being able to see that they are the mayor of a location or with being listed in the "who's here?" at a particular venue. As Dennis said, "It might be a cool way to meet new people". Bill has no concerns about the mayor program, adding that it's "fun and that's why I play". As far as strangers being able to see he has checked in to the same venue, he responded, "it's always nice to make new friends". Diana described the benefits that go along with being the mayor:

> There are many venues with deals for mayors and if I didn't have it checked, I wouldn't be able to take advantage of them. (Diana)

Some users have concerns about sharing location information on Facebook and Twitter. Kris finds it annoying when he gets checked in to Facebook Places by other users because then he loses control over who knows his location. Others do not mind. Dennis, for example, believes "the more, the merrier". Rhonda has her Foursquare account linked to Twitter and Facebook so that "I don't have to update each one individually". She added, "I have no privacy concerns because I keep my personal information private and I only accept friend requests from people that I actually know". Amanda said that she thinks about where she is before determining whether to post her check-in to other social media sites. Others do not like to broadcast check-ins to Twitter or Facebook.

> I keep my accounts separate so that I know what information I'm putting in, one place at a time. Broadcasting my information to more people concerns me so I don't want to link them. (Tom)

When users have a certain box checked on their privacy settings, their check-in will be noted along with a friend's if that friend pushes a check-in to Twitter or Facebook. For some, this practice could be a privacy concern. Katie said that that "happens sometimes in the mass comm building, but it's different if it's a smaller place" and was "not too concerned".

Foursquare users are learning privacy strategies as they gain experience with the service. Privacy settings are sometimes a surprise to users. Pat changed his profile during the interview so that it did not show his cell phone number. Also during the interview, when he noted that the box was checked to include his name when his followers pushed their check-ins to Twitter or Facebook if he was also checked in at the same location, he said, "I didn't know that was there" and was reconsidering this setting. Bill also dislikes this feature of Foursquare "because you may not have actually been with this person". Diana said that she was "reconsidering it [allowing others to see she is at a venue] now that I think about it as it may be a privacy concern". When Katie saw that her phone number was on her profile, she asked to "mark that off". Users are also learning lessons about check-ins. As Rhonda said, "The first time I checked in at home, it showed the name of my apartment complex with detailed directions to my house, so I had to delete that because I didn't feel comfortable".

*Advertisers.* Foursquare users are rewarded with special offers at certain merchants and most participants are willing to give up some personal information in order to acquire these deals.

> I have concerns about brands being able to see the other places I check in to but if it gets them to treat me better or offer me deals because I'm a fan or frequent their stores, I might be inclined to let them know more often. (Tom)

Diana was the only participant who expressed real concern with this practice.

> I have some concerns in them [advertisers] being able to see the other places I've checked in. I wonder who the person behind the account is. Some brands like Bravo and Ellen are so large that I don't think my personal location is relevant, but other brands are much smaller and it concerns me. (Diana)

These findings related to Foursquare are consistent with Humphreys' study of Dodgeball user privacy.[27] Many Foursquare users were initially confident in their privacy settings and therefore did not have many concerns about privacy. Foursquare facilitated voluntary panopticon when users allowed advertisers access to their locations and personal information in exchange for special offers; lateral surveillance when users expressed concerns about being monitored by other users; and self-surveillance when users checked in off the grid for future reference. In addition, many of the privacy strategies used by the participants are similar to those reported in the study by Lindqvist et al.[28]

## DISCUSSION

The present study juxtaposes an analysis of self-presentation and privacy on Foursquare, recognizing that the two constructs cannot be studied in isolation. Foursquare is still a growing platform and is not as integrated into the lives of as many people as Twitter or Facebook. For this reason, users may not be as concerned about the image they are projecting on this network because it is only being broadcast to a limited number of people, generally close friends. In addition, privacy issues related to Foursquare have not received the same kind of mainstream press coverage of those of Facebook, and users may not be as aware of the implications of their privacy setting decisions. The participants in this study were sometimes surprised about their settings and opted to make changes during the interview.

Self-presentation is a slight concern for users, but mainly in terms of whether check-ins are creating a negative impression. Because most participants are connected to their friends through Foursquare and their friends know and accept them for who they are, presenting a certain image is not important. Some users strive to get a lot of check-ins to unlock badges. For these users, the badges are used to impress others or for their own sense of accomplishment. Others do not aspire to unlock badges, but merely use Foursquare to connect with friends or to save a record of their travels and adventures.

For the most part, participants seem savvy about their knowledge of different social networks and the information they are willing to broadcast on each. Most are accepting only friends as followers on Foursquare and not checking in at home. Some choose to check in off the grid to protect their location, but still earn points and rewards. Participants had different combinations of information included in their profiles. Not one participant mentioned any concerns about the mayorship program or the "who's here" feature, although it is fairly easy to identify the real name of a user through the limited information available. These features contribute to users' self-presentation. Furthermore, many participants publish check-ins to Twitter or Facebook and allow friends to include their names in their check-ins when they publish check-ins to these sites. Again, this practice should raise privacy concerns among users because their location is being linked to more personal data, but it did not seem to be of concern to most participants in this study, possibly because they enjoy being linked in this way to friends. Participants are also willing to trade personal data for special offers from advertisers.

Because many users limit their followers to friends, they are not as concerned about managing their self-presentation in front of this group. Furthermore, they feel that they tightly control their social networks and are not as concerned about privacy, while others feel that the information is already out there so extra privacy measures on Foursquare are not helpful. On the whole, users appear to be presenting a seamless online and offline identity.

## LIMITATIONS

The primary limitation of this study is the sample size. Although the sample size is small, this study provides a framework for future studies in this area. In addition, the sample included more men than women, more single people than married, more younger people than older, and many people from the same geographic region. According to a 2011 report by Ignite Social Media, Tampa is not one of the top U.S. cities for Foursquare use, 60% of Foursquare users are women, and the most popular age is 35–44 followed by 25–34.[29] Finally, exploratory research raises questions of internal and external validity.[30] Internal validity will affect the interpretation of the findings if the researcher makes inferences about that which cannot be directly observed. External validity was compromised by the small sample size and the inability to generalize the results to a larger population. However, among this group of participants, findings were generally consistent, suggesting that results could be generalized to a larger population of similar people, but not necessarily to the general population.

## IMPLICATIONS

As Barnes described in a study of social networks, "Many people may not be aware of the fact that their privacy has already been jeopardized and they are not taking steps to protect their personal information from being used by others".[31] Similarly, it is possible that Foursquare users are using the service without being fully aware of possible dangers. Experience and mainstream media stories of privacy breaches will help users of Foursquare and other location-based services understand how to protect their privacy. The platform should also consider user privacy concerns in future development.

## NOTES

1. Erick Schonfeld, "Zuckerberg: 'We Are Building a Web Where the Default Is Social'", *Techcrunch*, April 21, 2010, accessed October 25, 2012, http://techcrunch.com/2010/04/21/zuckerbergs-buildin-web-default-social/.
2. Foursquare, "About Foursquare", accessed October 25, 2012, https://foursquare.com/about/.
3. Frederic Lardinois, "PleaseRobMe and the Dangers of Location-Based Social Networks", *ReadWriteWeb*, February 2010, accessed October 25, 2012, http://www.readwriteweb.com/archives/pleaserobme_and_the_dangers_of_location-aware_social_networks.php.
4. Ibid.
5. Erving Goffman, *The Presentation of Self in Everyday Life* (New York: Doubleday, 1959).
6. Hope Jensen Schau and Mary C. Gilly, "We Are What We Post? Self-Presentation in Personal Web Space", *Journal of Consumer Research* 30, no. 3 (2003): 385–404.
7. Nicole B. Ellison, Rebecca Heino and Jennifer Gibbs, "Managing Impressions Online: Self-Presentation in the Online Dating Environment", *Journal of Computer-Mediated Communication* 11, no. 2 (2006): article 2, accessed October 25, 2012, http://jcmc.indiana.edu/vol11/issue2/ellison.html.
8. Heather Perretta, "Presentation of Self in MySpace.com, an Online Social Networking Site" (master's thesis, State University of New York Institute of Technology, 2007).
9. Lee Humphreys, "Mobile Social Networks and Social Practice: A Case Study of Dodgeball", *Journal of Computer-Mediated Communication* 13, no. 1 (2007): article 17, accessed October 25, 2012, http://jcmc.indiana.edu/vol13/issue1/humphreys.html.

10. Dion Hoe-Lian Goh et al., "Why We Share: A Study of Motivations for Mobile Media Sharing", in *Active Media Technology, 5th International Conference Proceedings of AMT*, ed. Jiming Liu et al. (Heidelberg: Springer, 2009), 195–206.

11. Janne Lindqvist et al., "I'm the Mayor of My House: Examining Why People Use Foursquare—a Social-Driven Location Sharing Application" (paper presented at the CHI Conference on Human Factors in Computing Systems, Vancouver, BC, Canada, May 7–12, 2011).

12. Ralph Gross and Alessandro Acquisti, "Information Revelation and Privacy in Online Social Networks", in *Proceedings of the 2005 ACM Workshop on Privacy in the Electronic Society* (New York: ACM, 2005), 71–80.

13. Nan Li and Guanling Chen, "Sharing Location in Online Social Networks", *IEEE Network* 24, no. 5 (2010): 20–25.

14. Xinru Page and Alfred Kobsa, "Navigating the Social Terrain with Google Latitude", in *Proceedings of the 2010 iConference*, ed. Maeve Reilly (2010, Urbana-Champaign, Illinois): 174–178, accessed October 25, 2012, http://nora.lis.uiuc.edu/images/iConferences/2010papers2_Page-Zhang.pdf.

15. Karen P. Tang et al., "Rethinking Location Sharing: Exploring the Implications of Social-Driven vs. Purpose-Driven Location Sharing", in *Proceedings of the 12th ACM International Conference on Ubiquitous Computing* (New York: ACM, 2010), 85–94.

16. Fehmi Ben Abdesslem, Iain Parris and Tristan Henderson, "Mobile Experience Sampling: Reaching the Parts of Facebook Other Methods Cannot Reach", in *Proceedings of the Privacy and Usability Methods Pow-Wow (PUMP)*, Dundee, UK,(British Computer Society, September, 2010), 1–8, accessed October 25, 2012, http://scone.cs.st-andrews.ac.uk/pump2010/papers/benabdesslem.pdf.

17. Patrick G. Kelley et al., "When Are Users Comfortable Sharing Locations with Advertisers?" *CMU Technical Report* CMU-ISR-10-126, 2010, accessed October 25, 2012, http://www.cs.cmu.edu/~mbenisch/publications/CMU-ISR-10-126.pdf.

18. Ibid.

19. Lee Humphreys, "Who's Watching Whom? A Study of Interactive Technology and Surveillance", *Journal of Communication* 61, no. 4 (2011): 575–595.

20. Lindqvist et al., "I'm the Mayor of My House".

21. Ibid.

22. Ibid.

23. Bobby J. Calder and Alice M. Tybout, "What Consumer Research Is . . .", *Journal of Consumer Research* 14, no. 1 (1987), 136–140.

24. Ibid.

25. Humphreys, "Who's Watching Whom?", 575–595.

26. Nicole B. Ellison, Charles Steinfield and Cliff Lampe, "The Benefits of Facebook "Friends: Social Capital and College Students' Use of Online Social Network Sites", *Journal of Computer-Mediated Communication* 12, no. 4 (2007): article 1, accessed October 25, 2012, http://jcmc.indiana.edu/vol12/issue4/ellison.html.

27. Humphreys, "Who's Watching Whom?", 575–595.

28. Lindqvist et al., "I'm the Mayor of My House".

29. Ignite Social Media, "2011 Social Network Analysis", 2011, accessed October 25, 2012, https://s3.amazonaws.com/ignitesma/ignitewebsite/2011-social-network-analysis.pdf.

30. Robert K. Yin, *Case Study Research*, 4th ed. (Thousand Oaks, CA: Sage, 2009).

31. Susan B. Barnes, "A Privacy Paradox: Social Networking in the United States", *First Monday* 11, no. 9 (2006), accessed October 25, 2012, http://firstmonday.org/htbin/cgiwrap/bin/ojs/index.php/fm/article/view/1394/1312.

# Section III

# Mobile Media

## Reading Between the Seams
## of Expression & Sharing

# 11 MobileTV @ the Crossroads? Broadcasting vs. IP-based services in Germany and Austria

*Veronika Karnowski and Claudia Riesmeyer*

## INTRODUCTION

MobileTV, sometimes considered an eternal failure in mobile communications, finds itself at another crossroads in the face of mobile IP-based services. There were initially high expectations for MobileTV: the combination of two well-established media innovations—TV and the mobile phone—was considered bound to succeed;[1] however, expectations regarding broadcasting to mobile devices have never been realized.[2] Furthermore, IP-based mobile services, including those with audiovisual content, are gaining momentum,[3] and MobileTV has to adjust to these ongoing changes before even becoming established itself. Comparing Germany (which has a history of several Digital Video Broadcasting–Handheld [DVB–H] failures and currently has no DVB–H service) with Austria (which has a largely successful DVB–H service), we evaluated the future of MobileTV from various viewpoints.

### Status Quo: Unmet Expectations

Gerard Goggin[4] called it "the paradox of mobile TV: namely, it looks exciting, but the results so far are uninspiring": initially the prospect of adding TV to the so-called "Swiss army knife of new media"[5] was considered bound to succeed. These high expectations included both the vision of new usage situations for TV (commuting, mobile@home, etc.[6]) and a playground for new forms of content.[7] However, reality proved different.

On the usage side, in most of the trials, MobileTV could hardly find its niche in the users' media mix.[8] On the content side, new forms of content like mobisodes proved too costly to produce[9] and viewers were highly reluctant to adopt these new formats, rather sticking to well-established media brands.[10] Obviously, this led to a lack of sustainable business models.[11] Exceptions are the more-or-less successful broadcast-based MobileTV services operating in Korea[12] and Austria.[13]

From a technical side, bringing content to this 'third screen' in the users' media mix[14] is based on various solutions that have been discussed for more than a decade. In terms of broadcasting, MobileTV is currently realized via various competing broadcast-based technologies that permit an unlimited number of users to receive mobile television without an adverse effect on quality. The most widely used standard is DVB–H, which is primarily used in Europe,[15] while Digital Terrestrial Multimedia Diffusion is an alternative technology that is well established in South Korea. This latter approach uses digital radio as a base, but can provide only approximately six channels,[16] whereas DVB–H allows access to more than thirty channels.[17] Despite these technological advantages, the rollout of DVB–H has been beset by repeated failures. Introduction of the service has been continually postponed, as in the case of France and Belgium,[18] unexpectedly slow, as in the case of the United States, or even—as was the case in Germany—withdrawn after a substantial loss incurred by the provider.[19] In contrast, IP-based mobile services[20]—including audiovisual services[21]—are rapidly gaining momentum. Worldwide, there is far greater coverage by 3G-based MobileTV services than by broadcast-based MobileTV services.[22]

The regulation of MobileTV, namely via broadcasting, has seen a lot of discussion during the past years, too. First, there is an ongoing discussion on the regulation of MobileTV: Who is responsible? Which guidelines are to be applied?[23] Second, MobileTV got immersed in the highly controversial discussion about the digital dividend, i.e., broadcasting bandwidth available because of the digitalization of standards.[24]

In this unique situation of uncertainty and ongoing discussions mixed with high expectations, our aim is to understand the relevant actors' perceptions and ideas on these problematic fields, in order to draw conclusions regarding future development. Therefore, we refer to the analytical framework of guiding principles.

## ANALYTICAL FRAMEWORK: APPROACH OF GUIDING PRINCIPLES

The approach of guiding principles stems from media policy research. Guiding principles are one form of ideas that guide political decisions. Institutional, interest-group and idea-centric approaches[25] are established in media policy research. The idea-centric approach enables media policy to be explained in terms of the perceptions, objectives, norms and values of the policy actors.[26] Ideas may have the following consequences:

- direct the actor's perception of specific political matters to be solved, and exclude other problems;
- permeate policy making because they "not only define how political actors interpret the issues at stake but also because they alleviate uncertainties and help define acceptable courses of action";[27]

- define the ways that can be considered rational and suitable in pursuing a political goal or solving a problem; and
- shape conceptions of the impact that various policy instruments might have.[28]

Künzler developed a systematization of different types of ideas into three divisions: first, complex and general ideas (such as the idea of culture); second, guiding principles and interpretive patterns; and third, concrete ideas (such as norms).[29] Our interest lies in guiding principles. Guiding principles are defined as a fundamental value or norm to be achieved in the future, or even as a description of the instruments or measures by which the value or norm may be achieved. As ideas, guiding principles do not remain static, but change over time in an ongoing process of social construction via interaction and communication among the actors.[30] The development of ideas is shaped by existing interpretive patterns and by the general conditions that prevail in society and that are perceived and interpreted by relevant actors. General conditions could be politics, technology, economy and sociocultural aspects.[31] Guiding principles, as general and mostly firm moral concepts of the actors, can contribute to developing a co-orientation of all relevant actors and mold the future of this field.

To answer our research question and evaluate the future development of MobileTV, we drew on and adapted the aforementioned general conditions to form the following dimensions of guiding principles, according to the problematic status quo of MobileTV:

- *technology*: technological standards (device and transmission standards) and their recent development;
- *regulation*: responsible actors, existing regulating structures (e.g., federal vs. national), problems and challenges of regulation; and
- *usage/content/business model*: financing, advertising, target group, formats and their adaptation for MobileTV.

## METHOD

The decision to undertake guided interviews was based on our theoretical background. Guiding principles as ideas (norms and values, instruments or measures) are so complex that they can barely be captured using a standardized questionnaire. Guided interviews are open conversations that provide space for the interviewees to express their ideas. The aim is to understand the actors' perspectives in order to recognize parallels among actors, problem perceptions, goals, solutions and measures.

Although guided interviews feature open conversation, they require structural elements; in our case, interview guidelines were constructed based on the five dimensions of the guiding principles.[32] The following possible questions were included:

- *technology*: Which devices are used to watch MobileTV today? What is the influence of mobile network operators (MNOs) and hardware producers on the development of MobileTV? Which transmission standard is currently supported and which will be favored in the future?
- *regulation*: Do the current patterns of regulation involve MobileTV? Are there (potential) conflicts among specific actors? What are the most important challenges regarding regulation?
- *usage/content/business model*: Who belongs to your MobileTV target group? How do you analyze your MobileTV target group? Is pay-per-view relevant? Are there specific formats for MobileTV? Are special-interest proposals a possible format? Could MobileTV be a platform for user-generated content?

Relevant actors should be persons who are experts in the market and have exclusive knowledge regarding MobileTV. They are selected according to the procedure of theoretical sampling,[33] representing as many different viewpoints as possible. Following Hohlfeld and Wolf, relevant actors in the field of MobileTV are—besides regulators—public and private broadcast and press content providers and MNOs.[34] We chose to compare Germany and Austria because of the unclear situation, development and future perspectives of MobileTV in these two countries. We conducted twenty-four interviews with experts in the field of MobileTV in both countries in December 2009, as follows:

- *regulators*: three from Germany, one from Austria and one from the European Commission;
- *MNOs*: three from Germany and two from Austria; and
- *content providers*: ten from Germany and four from Austria.

All interviews were taped and transcribed. Analysis was based on our theoretical perspective. Our procedure could best be described as a 'theoretical coding', using our theoretical concept to interpret the qualitative data.[35] We followed six steps in handling the data: (1) data management, (2) close reading and marking of interview passages, (3) describing and condensing the meanings, (4) classifying by coding the statements, (5) interpreting by contextualizing the statements and (6) representing the data.[36] Each interview was analyzed by both of the present authors and subsequently discussed.[37]

## RESULTS AND FUTURE PERSPECTIVES: TWO SCENARIOS

First, we will outline the different definitions of MobileTV given by the interviewed experts. Second, we present two competing scenarios of the future development of MobileTV.[38]

## Status Quo: Definitions of MobileTV

There is no agreement on what MobileTV is. This first significant finding became especially clear when one German MNO even asked for the question to
be clarified before being able to answer—referring to IP-based vs. broadcasting
services: "Which type of MobileTV are we talking about?" (MNOGER01).

This distinction between broadcasting and 3G dominated all statements
about the definition of MobileTV. When digging deeper into the experts' statements, a connection between the experts' experiences and their definitions of
MobileTV became clear. German experts mostly defined MobileTV as IP-
based services (i.e., streaming) or even all audiovisual *content*, "transmitted
via mobile networks" (ContentGER01). Apparently their experiences with
the ongoing failures of MobileTV led to a high degree of uncertainty on
what this service actually is/should be. Nonetheless a German MNO felt
certain that MobileTV has a future, albeit dependent on technologies and
marketing strategies: "The MobileTV issue, i.e., [. . .] moving image, will
probably always exist" (MNOGER02).

Austrian actors in contrast emphasized the broadcasting component of
MobileTV, emphasizing its advantages. Nonetheless, some of them opened up
their minds to a broader definition of MobileTV including 3G services, e.g.,
"TV on a cell phone, including all different characteristics" (MNOAUT02).
This is due to the fact that some of the Austrian actors already feared the end
of MobileTV via broadcasting in Austria, both because a lack of devices and
the soon "far better coverage" (ContentAUT04) of 3G services. Based on this
opposition between broadcasting and 3G services, we extracted two possible scenarios from the interview data regarding the future of MobileTV.

## Scenario A: Broadcasting

Scenario A describes the pursuit of a broadcasting model for MobileTV
services. This scenario presents lots of difficulties and uncertainties, but
also some striking advantages. First, regulation needs consideration. The
transmission of MobileTV via broadcasting has to be regulated in the same
manner as existing broadcasting services. And there will be regulation of
MobileTV, as a German regulation expert emphasized: "Classical MobileTV [DVB–H] is subject to the regulatory authority for commercial broadcasting" (Regulation GER01).

Since there will be regulation in place, the regulation authorities, both
on the national and the European level, felt that it was unnecessary to move
first with regulatory procedures but rather it would be better to wait until
there was demand for regulation (Regulation GER01, RegulationEU01), thus
creating an atmosphere of uncertainty, which has the potential to hinder sustainable business development. Content regulation in this scenario is to be
handled along the lines of 'regular' television. Consequently the rules for
the protection of children and teenagers are to be applied to MobileTV,

too, as an Austrian content provider explained: "There is no difference. We have to abide by protection of children and teenagers in the same way" (ContentAUT03).

A third aspect of regulation includes the licensing of transmission standards and content. Licensing of transmission standards is connected with high costs for MNOs because there is a license fee for every broadcasting transmission standard. A German regulation expert saw recourse in the purchase of licenses for 'multi standards' MNOs to install chips for all standards in all of their devices, which could then be unlocked according to the country of use. This scenario would enable MNOs to be prepared for the 'world market' and to reduce costs—costs unique to scenario A. The licensing of content remains totally unclear in Scenario A, and no standard contracts exist yet. U.S. production companies, for instance, do not "license content for mobile distribution. Right now, mobile transmission is not in their focus" (MNOGER03).

Second, we consider target group and type of business model. Because a sustainable business model and an evident market for MobileTV are still lacking, marketing activities remain difficult. Experts still do not know how to refinance the expensive licenses and network infrastructure in this field. This could certainly only work in the long run, as a German regulation expert emphasized: "Making these high investments, you don't want to get a license for only four years. You need at least ten or twelve years" (RegulationGER01). One possibility of financing MobileTV in this scenario is advertising, as is done on 'classical' free TV. But the experiences in Austria are disappointing, as an Austrian expert had to admit: "The advertising market does not as yet allow for any advertising via MobileTV only" (ContentAUT02).

Moreover, the experts still have no clear conception of their target group. This lack of direction complicates the development of an advertising model and refinancing plans.

The economic problems of DVB–H are closely connected with a third factor: the use of provided content. According to our experts, users attribute certain features to MobileTV; however, the experts' opinions on these crucial features were varied. Some content providers believe in exclusive made-for-mobile content, while others assert that the letters 'TV' refer to the classical programming scheme. Thus with regard to the users' perceived conceptions of MobileTV we have to add another dimension that remains unclear in the conception of MobileTV: content. An Austrian MNO illustrated this dilemma between new content for new services and sticking to traditional TV brands this way: "MobileTV is on the one hand an expansion of linear TV to a third screen. On the other hand, MobileTV offers the possibility to watch TV in a complete different way" (MNOAUT01).

Nonetheless, all of the experts agreed that content has to be adapted to the mobile use situation—no one wants to watch a Hollywood blockbuster on a cell phone. Thus, adaptation of length is most important. But there are some more content-related rules for adaptation: "You have to reduce motion sequences. Rapid panning is unwatchable on such small screens".

(ContentGER09). Instead, the content must catch the users' attention by different effects, because "The usage situation is quite different using this small screen, and generally the user is much more distracted" (ContentGER09).

The experts agree that the most important genres for MobileTV are sports events (such as the FIFA World Cup and boxing matches), news (such as news programs delivered in a brief slot of 100-second duration) and entertainment formats (such as comedy and cartoons). These formats have already proved attractive to the providers of 3G MobileTV services. Another point relevant to the use of MobileTV is usability. This clearly needs to be improved before MobileTV via DVB–H can be a success. Battery power must be extended, the display must be improved, and menus should be easier to use. In addition, the built-in speakers do not yet meet the users' expectations. Nearly all of the experts made reference to the iPhone on this point. In their eyes, this end device opened up a whole new category regarding usability, and all devices must now meet the standards set by the iPhone, which they described as "a devilish evolution" (RegulationGER01), "showing the direction for future development" (ContentGER04) and having "positively influenced the whole industry" (MNOAUT02).

Summing up these thoroughly negative characteristics of Scenario A (regulation both of transmission and content, unclear business model but investments in licensing of transmission standards needed, unclear licensing of content . . .), Scenario A seems not to be worth considering at all, but this scenario does have one prominent advantage as compared to streaming: the unlimited number of users that can be accommodated because of the broadcasting technology.

## Scenario B: Streaming (3G)

This leads us to Scenario B, 'Streaming (3G)', subsuming MobileTV under the much broader field of online activities: "MobileTV, for us it's a subtopic of the online sector" (ContentGER10). The convenience of IP-based services regarding regulation issues is obvious. To date, the transmission side of IP-based audiovisual services has not been regulated following the norms for broadcasting, thereby providing a wider scope of action for providers; however, the regulation side of IP-based audiovisual services remains unclear, as a German content provider pointed out (ContentGER08).

In addition, regulation does not apply to the content of IP-based audiovisual services—except for legal norms, such as the protection of minors—which is another advantage of IP-based services over broadcast standards. The licensing of content for streaming services is also easier compared with broadcasting. Normally, content providers just sell the content to MNOs, as for any other online service. A German content provider described this process: "For our MobileTV-products, well . . . the MNOs just buy these channels from us. And they offer those channels to their customers for a certain service fee. . . ." (ContentGER07).

Summing up, from a licensing and regulation perspective, Scenario B is far easier to handle for both content providers and MNOs; consequently, both actors prefer this scenario. As in Scenario A, the marketing of MobileTV is difficult for IP-based services. First, both the content providers and the MNOs are not sure of the target audience for MobileTV, and there are no clear definitions. At the utmost the actors referred to the somewhat stereotypical attributes of 'First Movers', e.g. this German content provider: "The First Movers in this area are probably very mobile, and heavy TV-viewers. But this does not have to be the case in the medium term" (ContentGER07).

Despite having a rather unclear target group, the MNOs are highly interested in making MobileTV via IP a success. Worldwide, MNOs have paid large amounts for UMTS licenses (for an overview, see www.umtsworld.com). They now need to refinance these investments through all available services: "We paid lots of money for it, that is GMS and UMTS licenses. Our main interest is now to refinance the licenses. So, we don't want to invest in new technologies like WLAN or DVB–H" (MNOGER02). To refinance the services, the MNOs rely on typical models; i.e., paid content and commercials: "Quite conventional, we try to earn money with paid content, commercials, banners, logos, pre roll and post roll—well, on different levels" (ContentGER08).

Scenarios A and B are also similar with regard to content. Sports, news and entertainment are considered the most relevant content genres, but the specifics of streaming described above also allow additional services in this field. Our experts made particular reference to the possibility of made-for-mobile special-interest programming via streaming.

Regarding technical issues related to 3G MobileTV, our experts saw both benefits and risks for Scenario B. One advantage is the superior choice of end devices—there are no additional technical requirements besides being 3G-enabled. And there is no need for the MNOs or content providers to establish an additional and expensive network infrastructure.

But there remains one prominent technical drawback of Scenario B. As more and more users begin to use this service, network performance will diminish, leading to a loss in the quality and reliability of the service, as a German MNO described: "And then the infrastructure will collapse. [. . .] is experiencing this right now. They say, oh f\*\*\*, demand is growing; the devices become cooler, bigger devices, faster, better screens. The demand is driven by the users, and my network infrastructure is crashing. And therefore they start considering DVB-H again. . . ." (MNOGER02).

## THE USERS' VIEWPOINT—BLURRING BOUNDARIES BETWEEN SCENARIO A AND B

After more than a decade of discussion on the topic, MobileTV remains an imprecise term, leading us to a variety of conceptions. The approach of guiding principles helped us to analyze this situation and to systematize the actors' various ideas and conceptions. In doing so, we extracted two possible scenarios for the future development of MobileTV services. Scenario A comprises a broadcasting service (e.g., DVB–H) and Scenario B a 3G-based streaming service. The content providers and MNOs mainly preferred Scenario B because it has advantages in terms of regulation, the licensing of content and the cost of providing the service. In addition, Scenario B puts MNOs in a position to offer additional services in order to refinance their UMTS licenses. One prominent drawback of Scenario B remains. As these services start to gain in popularity, the network infrastructure is subjected to increasing stress, leading in the worst case to an infrastructure failure.

But does MobileTV necessarily have to be one specific service? Or is there the possibility of a slowly evolving, seamless integrated patchwork service, step-by-step making its way into our mobile devices, as suggested by Goggin?[39] From the users' viewpoint there are no differences between Scenarios A and B, as noted by a German regulator: "The user, well, the technology inside, who cares? The user doesn't want to know about the technology inside" (RegulationGER01).

## NOTES

1. Shani Orgad, "MobileTV: Old and New in the Construction of an Emergent Technology", *Convergence: The International Journal of Research Into New Media Technologies* 15, no. 2 (2009): 197–214, doi:10.1177/1354856508101583.
2. Kim Tong-hyung, "Mobile TV May Be Off Air on Subways", *Koreatimes,* February 15, 2009, accessed October 25, 2012, http://www.koreatimes.co.kr/www/news/tech/2009/02/129_39561.html.
3. The Nielsen Company, *Critical Mass. The Worldwide State of the Mobile Web* (New York: Nielsen Mobile, 2008).
4. Gerard Goggin, *Global Mobile Media* (London: Routledge, 2011), 86.
5. John Boyd, "A Cellphone Is the Only Gadget You Need", *New Scientist, 2489* (March 2005), accessed October 25, 2012, http://www.newscientist.com.
6. Caj Södergard, *Mobile Television—Technology and User Experiences. Report on the Mobile-TV Project* (Espoo: VTT Publications, 2003), accessed October 25, 2012, http://www.vtt.fi/inf/pdf/publications/2003/P506.pdf.
7. Gerard Goggin, *Cell Phone Culture. Mobile Technology in Everyday Life* (London: Routledge, 2006).
8. Harry Bouwman et al., "Reconsidering the Actual and Future Use of Mobile Services." *Information Systems and e-Business Management* 7, no. 3 (2009): 301–17, doi:10.1007/s10257–008–0094–0; Dimitri Schuurman et al., "Content and Context for Mobile Television: Integrating Trial, Expert and User Findings", *Telematics and Informatics* 26, no. 3 (2009): 293–305, Thilo von Pape and Veronika Karnowski, "Which Place for Mobile Television in Everyday Life? Evidence from a Panel Study", in *Images in Mobile Communication,* ed. Corinne Martin and Thilo von Pape (Wiesbaden: VS Verlag, 2011), 101–20.
9. Agnes Urban, "Mobile Television: Is It Just a Hype or a Real Consumer Need?", in *Innovating for and by Users,* ed. Jo Pierson et al. (Brussels: COST Action 298, 2008), 27–38.

10. Aurelian Bria, Patrik Kärrberg and Per Andersson, "TV in the Mobile or TV for the Mobile: Challenges and Changing Value Chains", in *Proceedings of the IEEE 18th Symposium on Personal, Indoor and Mobile Radio Communication*, (Athens, Greece: September 3–7, 2007), 5 pgs, accessed October 25, 2012, http://stuff.carstensorensen.com/mobility/PIMRC07-IEEE-MobileTV.pdf.
11. Urban, "Mobile Television".
12. Tong-hyung, "Mobile TV May Be Off Air".
13. Robert Briel, "3 Austria Claims 90,000 Mobile TV Users", *Broadband TV News*, February 16, 2009, accessed October 2005, 2012, http://www.broad bandtvnews.com/2009/02/16/3-austria-claims-90000-mobile-tv-users/.
14. Sylvia M. Chan-Olmsted, "Content Development for the Third Screen: The Business and Strategy of Mobile Content and Applications in the United States", *The International Journal on Media Management* 8, no. 2 (2006): 51–9, doi:10.1207/s14241250ijmm0802_1.
15. Christian Breunig, "Mobiles Fernsehen in Deutschland [MobileTV in Germany]", *Media Perspektiven,11,* (2006), 550–62, accessed October 25, 2012, http://www.media-perspektiven.de/uploads/tx_mppublications/11–2006_Breunig.pdf.
16. Seungwhan Lee and Dong Kyun Kwak, "TV in Your Cell Phone: The Introduction of Digital Multimedia Broadcasting (DMB) in Korea" (paper presented at the annual Telecommunications Policy Research Conference, Arlington, VA, September 24, 2005), accessed October 26, 2012, http://jongshin.org/docs/TPRC%202005_Final_DMB%20in%20Korea.pdf.
17. Amitabh Kumar, *Implementing Mobile TV: ATSC Mobile DTV, MediaFLO, DVB-H/SH, DMB,WiMAX, 3G Systems, and Rich Media Applications* (Burlington: Focal Press, 2010).
18. Tom Evens et al., "Mobile Television in Flanders: Multi-Methodical Approach for User-Centric Technology Development" (paper presented at the Audience section for the IAMCR-congress Media and Global Divides, Stockholm, Sweden, July 20–25, 2008.); Emmanuel Gabla, "Télé mobile: le CSA a édicté des règles intangibles [MobileTV: the CSA decreed intangible rules]", *Le Figaro*, March 23, 2009, accessed October 27, 2012, http://www.lefigaro.fr/medias/2009/03/21/04002–20090321ARTFIG00634-tele-mobile-le-csa-a-edicte-des-regles-intangibles-.php.
19. Robert Briel, "German Mobile 3.0 Service to Close Down", *Broadband TV News,* July 31, 2008, accessed October 27, 2012, http://www.broadbandtvnews.com/2008/07/31/german-mobile-30-service-to-close-down/.
20. comScore, *Mobile 2010. Year in Review* (Reston: comScore, 2011).
21. Kumar, *Implementing Mobile TV.*
22. InStat, *3G Mobile TV Worldwide* (Scottsdale: Instat, 2008); for further details on current technical standards and their prevalence, see Goggin, *Global Mobile Media*, 85–91.
23. Trisha Lin, "The Gordian Knot of Mobile TV Policy in Singapore", *Journal of International Commercial Law and Technology* 5, no. 1 (2010): 11–21; Viviane Reding, "Television Is Going Mobile—And Needs A Pan European Policy Approach" (speech at International CeBIT Summit, Hannover, Germany, March 8, 2006), accessed October 27, 2012, http://ec.europa.eu/information_society/newsroom/cf/itemdetail.cfm?item_id=2524.
24. David I. Crawford, "Spectrum for Mobile Multimedia Services", in *Proceedings of the IEEE Tenth International Symposium on Consumer Electronics,* (St. Petersburg, Russia: June 28–July 1, 2006), 444–447. doi:10.1109/ISCE.2006.1689481.
25. Robert Baldwin and Martin Cave, *Understanding Regulation. Theory, Strategy and Practice* (Oxford: University Press, 2002), 18, 26.

26. Herman Galperin, "Beyond Interests, Ideas, and Technology: An Institutional Approach to Communication and Information Policy", *The Information Society* 20, no. 3 (2004): 159–68; Matthias Künzler, *Die Liberalisierung von Radio und Fernsehen [The Deregulation of Radio and Television]* (Konstanz: UVK, 2009); Matthias Künzler, "Switzerland: Desire for Diversity without Regulation—A Paradoxical Case?", *International Communication Gazette* 71, no. 1–2 (2009): 67–76, doi:10.1177/1748048508097931; Otto Singer, "Policy Communities and Discourse Coalitions. The role of Policy Analysis in Economic Policy Making", *Science Communication* 11, no. 4 (1990): 428–58, doi:10.1177/107554709001100404.

27. Galperin, "Beyond Interests, Ideas, and Technology", 161.

28. Künzler, *Die Liberalisierung von Radio und Fernsehen*, 105–9.

29. Künzler, *Die Liberalisierung von Radio und Fernsehen*; Künzler, "Switzerland: Desire for Diversity without Regulation", 67–76.

30. Maria Löblich and Claudia Riesmeyer, "A Child of Media Policy? Guiding Principles for Germany's Open Channels at Present and in the Future" (paper presented at the IAMCR conference Communication and Citizenship: Rethinking Crisis and Change, Braga, Portugal, July 18–22, 2010).

31. Sandra Braman, "Where Has Media Policy Gone? Defining the Field in the Twenty-First Century", *Communication, Law and Policy* 9, no. 2 (2004): 153–82. doi:10.1207/s15326926clp0902_1; M. Puppis, *Einführung in die Medienpolitik [Introduction into Media Policy]* (Konstanz: UVK, 2007), 296.

32. Steinar Kvale and Svend Brinkmann, *Interviews. Learning the Craft of Qualitative Research Interviewing* (Thousand Oaks: Sage, 2009), 132.

33. Juliet Corbin and Anselm Strauss, "Grounded Theory Research: Procedures, Canons, and Evaluative Criteria", *Qualitative Sociology* 13, no. 1 (1990): 3–21,doi: 10.1007/BF00988593; Thomas R. Lindlof, *Qualitative Communication Research Methods* (Thousand Oaks: Sage, 1995).

34. Ralf Hohlfeld and Cornelia Wolf, "Media to go—erste Konturen eines mobilen Journalismus? [Media to Go—First Outlines of a Mobile Journalism?]", *Media Perspektiven*, 4, (2008): 205–14, accessed October 27, 2012, http://www.media-perspektiven.de/261.html?&tx_mppublications_pi1%5Bs howUid%5D=1122&cHash=31e0c0bf90,

35. Kvale and Brinkmann, *Interviews.*

36. John W. Cresswell, *Qualitative Inquiry & Research Design* (Thousand Oaks: Sage, 2007), 156–57.

37. Uwe Flick, *An Introduction to Qualitative Research* (London: Sage, 2009).

38. Because of the small MobileTV markets in Germany and Austria, all interview excerpts are presented anonymously.

39. Goggin, *Global Mobile Media.*

# 12 Mobile News Life of the Young

*Oscar Westlund and Jakob Bjur*

## INTRODUCTION

The mobile 'phone' has become deeply embedded in contemporary social life and interpersonal communication (i.e., voice calls and SMS) among approximately six or seven billion people around the world.[1] Mobile communication is a truly global phenomenon.[2] Numerous studies have demonstrated its increasing social impact on interpersonal communication around the globe. In recent years, the importance of mobile media for news has taken off in various countries and contexts.[3] The role of mobile devices is in tremendous flux, as it has also gained a foothold as a portable device that enables seamlessly integrated computer-mediated communication anytime and anywhere.

This chapter uses the term mobile 'device' to emphasize that continuous technological transformation has actually developed what was formerly conceived of as a mobile 'phone' into an increasingly powerful, ubiquitous multimedia device. Clearly, with the virtual explosion of mobile applications that enable personalized and location-sensitive services, the mobile empowers users with an increasingly user-friendly always-on Internet connection. In light of convergence, a blurring of boundaries between information and communication technologies (ICTs) has taken place. In addition, the boundaries between work, home and play have become blurred, as ICTs that were previously confined to particular locations (e.g., household or workplace) have now become omnipresent through their portable nature and integrated access to Internet on the go. The mobile device is, par excellence, personal, portable and ubiquitous. It presumably transforms our contemporary notions of what it means to be connected or not. Since 2010, an additional Internet-enabled device has emerged, namely tablets such as the Samsung Galaxy Note and Apple's iPad, blurring the boundaries even more regarding computers and what were formerly known as mobile 'phones'. This study, however, excludes tablets and focuses exclusively on versatile mobile devices.

A retrospective review of the development and uptake of Internet-based media for mobile devices in North America and Europe illustrates that it was considered relatively limited until approximately 2008/2009.[4] In the years prior to 2008, there was a significant discrepancy between the number of individuals who possessed mobile devices equipped with mobile internet functionality and the number actually making use of it. An explanation is that also prior to the diffusion of contemporary touch-screen-enabled mobile devices, the so-called feature phones available for sale were equipped with a mobile Web browser. As it had become a standard feature, the diffusion of Internet-enabled mobile devices was high. However, usage was limited, except for in certain Asian countries such as Japan. [5] Nonetheless, usage has since also dramatically increased in North America and Europe.[6] With the emancipation of mobile media, a wide array of contents and services has become appropriated into the media lives of different generations. This chapter focuses on describing and explaining the mobile news life of young.

## STUDY RATIONALE

News media producers have become increasingly engaged in developing mobile news.[7] Research on the adoption and accessing of news via mobile devices has shown that mobile news from the early days of use until now has constituted an important part of mobile media usage. Young men have predominantly undertaken accessing mobile news.[8] Research on mobile news accessing is scarce, and has either focused on those age 15/16 and older or on those age 18 and older.[9] These studies, from both the United States and Sweden, have suggested that the young and young adults are among those most inclined to access news via mobile devices. Other literature also presents the young as particularly inclined to adopt and use digital media, under headings such as X-, Y- and N-generations, generation digital and digital natives.[10] Nevertheless, these constructions of the young have been criticized for having an exaggerated emphasis on homogeneity regarding the responsiveness to digital (and mobile) media.[11] Furthermore, it is a daunting task to determine whether a particular group of the young actually compose a generation that is consistent with the sociology of generations,[12] or if specific usage patterns are better explained by life course approaches.[13] Empirical and cross-generational research covering extensive stretches of time makes it a prerequisite to do such assessments in a robust fashion. Such research is unfortunately scarce, and this cross-sectional study can obviously not provide those answers. Nevertheless, having acknowledged this complexity, this study provides an important conceptualization and careful analysis of the heterogeneous media behaviors of "tweens" (preadolescent youth) and teens.

The purpose of the chapter is to describe and explain how mobile news is realized in the lives of the young, assessing the explanatory power of the habitual use of mobile functions, other media and news. The chapter draws on a theoretical body in which news media orientation is situated in the context of everyday media life. Hence, by approaching the young from the perspective of their everyday *media life*,[14] the chapter departs from an understanding that there are generally indistinct boundaries between everyday life activities and the use of mobile devices and other ICTs. At the same time, however, this reveals an inexorable interconnectedness between various ICTs, as the use of mobile devices, Internet and news media is assumed to play a significant role in explaining the mobile news lives of the young. In other words, the theoretical framework suggests that the use of mobile news is intertwined with other ICTs and news media.

However, the use of mobile news by the young can also be explained by the role mobile devices have for individuals in their everyday media life. The chapter seeks to creatively explore new research frontiers by operationalizing grand theory into empirical analysis. It presents an explanatory model of mobile news accessing involving three key parts: *media life, mobile media profile* and *news life*. These are anticipated to correlate with, and ultimately explain, the mobile news accessing of contemporary youth. Age and gender complement the model, following their documented importance for news accessing and alignment to new technology. A survey instrument could have been designed to measure the effect of numerous other factors, such as the possession of technology (e.g., smartphone), economic factors (e.g., personal economy) and additional socio-demographic factors (e.g., social class). The survey instrument might preferably have been designed to test models such as the technology acceptance model (TAM), the theory of reasoned action (TRA) or the mobile phone appropriation model (MPA). However, rather than focusing on replicating earlier studies with a new sort of behavior and geographical context, this chapter focuses exclusively on the importance of how mobile news lives are interconnected with other ICTs and news media. Ultimately, the findings expand a set of factors worthy of consideration.

The data set explored was collected through a postal-based survey conducted in Sweden during 2010, by the Media Council of the Swedish Ministry of Culture in collaboration with the authors. The survey was sent to 2,000 youth age 9–16, generating 1,181 responses and a net response rate of 60%. The analysis of this cross-sectional data set does not try to determine generational or life course effects. The data set, statistically representative of Sweden, has wider implications, since the media, culture and society of Sweden share many characteristics with other Western countries. Nonetheless, one must still carefully examine the cross-cultural differences and similarities when interpreting how the findings of this chapter relate to those of other countries.

The (somewhat unconventional) disposition of the chapter has aimed for stringency of argumentation. The next section discusses the general framework used, which is followed by a section organized through three subsections dedicated to the respective key parts. Each of these three subsections consists of two parts; the first introduces and reflects on relevant contemporary research, whereas the second presents suitable inquiries. These inquiries are subsequently addressed and analyzed, leading to the presentation of bivariate explanatory effects. These findings are used to build the multivariate regression model presented in the fourth and final subsection. The conclusions close the chapter.

## TOWARD A FRAMEWORK FOR EXPLORING AND EXPLAINING MOBILE NEWS LIVES

Two decades ago, most citizens accessed news only via newspaper, television or radio. Japan, Switzerland and the Nordic countries were characterized by a strong orientation toward newspapers, whereas the United States and countries in southern Europe were more skewed toward television news. Although these characteristics remain, in some sense, the contemporary news media landscape has become increasingly complex, fragmentized, digitized and individualized. In this context, Castells has argued that we reside in a network society in which mass self-communication is prevalent.[15] One may speak of a general trend of spatial and temporal disembedding[16] to the ways media are used in an increasingly individualized manner.[17] Different individuals orient toward media and news through either 'old' (analog) and/ or 'new' (digital) media.

The virtual explosion of online news sites with linear producer-user logic played an important role in the early transformations of news usage patterns. Following buzzword concepts such as *convergence, interactivity* and *Web 2.0*, patterns of elevated participation and the sharing of news have since emerged.[18] Although some navigate to news sites through their homepage settings and bookmarks, much traffic is also generated through search engines, blogs, microblogs and social networking sites. With the growing diffusion of mobile media, it has furthermore become evident that more and more people access news both on the go and at home, either through mobile sites or mobile applications. The mobile device has emerged as a powerful means for accessing news. Through its pervasive and ubiquitous attributes, coupled with customized applications (i.e., apps), it has recently become deeply embedded into the daily textures of people's everyday lives. As it potentially enters the individualized news media lives of the young, it will lead to complementary or displacement effects.

This chapter draws on recent theorizing on media life, which is a notable approach to the intersecting and dissolving textures of media, humans and society. Media life draws on related theoretical concepts in social theory and media studies.[19] Deuze proposes that the ever-presence of media in our lives calls for treating individuals and media not only as people using media in their lives, but also as people living lives *in* media. As everyday life has become exceedingly mediated, media itself becomes more invisible. This may lead people to cease noting the presence of media in their lives. Deuze also argues that people's life experiences are framed by, made immediate by, and mitigated through media.[20] Media life engages with that omnipresent media, which has become increasingly invisible.[21] Media life takes an everyday life perspective on how media is appropriated, used and becomes part of an individual's media practices.[22]

To date, the media life perspective has not been conceptualized on meso and micro levels, or operationalized through empirical research. This chapter departs from an understanding of media as generally being deeply embedded into the textures of everyday life. Rather, it emphasizes that individuals develop media lives with varied characteristics. Such variations have been investigated in numerous studies on adoption, appropriation and domestication, and have often emphasized the factors related to either the medium or the individual. The aim of this chapter is to explore and explain youths' news accessing with mobile devices. The mobile news life of young people will be investigated through the lens of their *media life*, their *mobile media profile* and their *news life*.

## MOBILE NEWS LIVES OF THE YOUNG: RESEARCH INQUIRIES AND FINDINGS

As of 2010, 8% of youth had developed a mobile news life, which here is defined as those who had accessed news with their mobile device at some point. Among those mobile news users, 10% reported assessing mobile news daily, 20% did so weekly, and the residual 70% did so more seldom than weekly. The number of youth who had developed a mobile news life was consequently, at this stage in history (2010) and life (9–16 years old), still relatively limited in scope. The low initial level can partially be explained by low interest in mobile news. However, it must also be understood as a direct effect of how a mobile news life is encapsulated within the broader mobile media life built on the availability of and the ability level of mobile technology use among the young. In order to deliver a more profound delineation of mobile news life—what fuels it and delimits it—the three seminal parts are discussed in the following sections. Conclusions will be presented for each of these three subsections, extracting relevant variables for the multivariate regression model presented in the fourth subsection.

## MEDIA LIFE: OUTLINE OF INQUIRY

Media life concerns which roles different media have in the lives of the young. As a consequence, the degree of involvement of the young with particular media correlates then with their mobile news lives. Particular (new and digital) media are presumed to be linked to accessing news with the mobile, whereas other (old and analog) media are not presumed to have such a link. Individuals using various functions of their mobile device, engaging in activities such as SMS, voice calls and games, are also assumed to explore and use other types of functions. Some youth may be resistant to accessing news via their mobile device, since they are not keen on connecting to the Internet with it.

Consequently, there are assumed to be links between mobile news lives and more profound mobile usage and internet usage, resulting in an increased probability of accessing news. Although not studied here, the motives for refraining from usage may relate to a teenager's personal economy,[23] such as not owning an Internet-enabled mobile device or having limited financial resources to pay for the running costs of Internet access not enabled by WiFi.

To explore the effect of mobile life and Internet life, the chapter will draw on a conceptualization of media life, focusing on mobile, gaming, television and the Internet. The conceptualization was empirically grounded, as groups were divided into four categories on a scale based on the role the different media played in their lives. Based on self-reported survey data, an index was created that accounted for both frequency—divided into five categories: from daily (4), over several times a week (3), once a week (2), and more seldom (1), to never (0)—and length of usage—divided into four categories: from never (0), over less than an hour (1), and one to three hours (2), to three hours or more (3).[24] The Media Life Index was created based on simple interaction between frequency and reach, forming a scale 0–12 that was then recoded into the Media Life Index with a range from 0 to 8. On the one end, there are those individuals who are so deeply integrated with media that they can appropriately be described to have a *life in media (a value of 8)*, whereas the other end involved those who have a *life sans media (a value of 0)*. In the continuum between those two extremes, there are those who either have a *life with media (a value of 6–7)* or a *life around media (a value of 1–5)*. On the scale, those included in *the life in media* category used relevant media at least three hours or more every day. It was prevalent that fewer youth lived their life in television (11%) and gaming (14%), compared with the Internet (16%) and mobile (18%). Few had a life sans media regarding television and the Internet, whereas the number was significantly higher for life sans mobile, and highest for life sans gaming.[25]

In addition, there was also heterogeneity in terms of gender and age. Regarding the Internet, the media lives were similar across genders. However, the results showed that the mobile occupied a slightly more pronounced role in the media life of young girls than boys. The significance of age as a differentiating factor was even higher. Interestingly, the usage of television and gaming was significantly higher among tweens than their usage of the Internet and mobile. For younger teens, on the other hand, the role of the Internet and mobile was accentuated. Although television and gaming are typically introduced and used for entertainment in the household as devices that are domestic, fixed and possibly shared, the use of mobile devices and the Internet in the Western world is more individualized, and instead related to communication and information usage.[26] In light of this discussion, age differences form a background explanation for the analysis of how mobile and Internet lives are coupled with the accessing of news via a mobile.

## MEDIA LIFE: FINDINGS

Figure 12.1 shows the mobile and internet media lives of the young. Of primary focus is mobile media life, whereas Internet media life serves as a reference point in the assessment of the specificity and pace of mobile media life development. The four categories of media life—based on frequency and time of use—are presented as fields that change composition as age increases. Mobile media life shows how almost none of the 9-year-olds live their *life in media* (black field), whereas this state of media life dominates among 16-year-olds (51%). The weak position of the mobile among the youngest reflects, to some extent, a lack of mobile devices. This lack is mirrored by the category of *life sans media* (field on top), which correlates strongly with the ownership and availability of a personal mobile device. At the age of 11, approximately 90% have access to a personal mobile device. However, before that age, pure scarcity in availability keeps the usage down. The curves indicate that mobile media life is established in this actual age span—from 9 to 16. Even if 63% of all 9-year-olds have a mobile device of their own, the comprehensive use first increases at the age of 12. At the age of 16, nonusers have literally disappeared, and only 26% report living a *life around media* (moderate use). Furthermore, acknowledging that the majority of 16-year-olds spend three to four hours or more on daily mobile use indicates that this group lives a *life in media* that is strongly supported by mobile technology.

The parallel Internet media life of the young (to the right) extends in a similar manner to that of the mobile media life. A notable difference is that the Internet, to a higher extent, had become established among the youngest, who had comparatively better access to the Internet than access to mobile devices. This is illustrated by the smaller group living a *life sans media* (top field), which decreased with age. Interestingly, this initially higher level of use does not produce an equally high number of 16-year-olds reporting

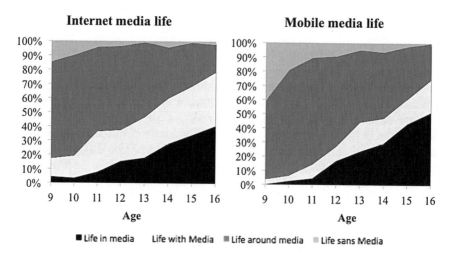

*Figure 12.1*  Mobile and Internet media lives of young—development over age (percent qualifying for different levels of media life)

leading a *life in media*. The growth of Internet use is less steep, and approximately 40 % (compared with 51% for mobile) report a *life in media* via the Internet. Consequently, affordances are tied to the mobile device—such as individualization, ubiquity, mobility and pervasiveness—that contribute to making the mobile more central than the Internet in young people's media life. Even if minor, these differences seem to indicate that the Internet is still a medium without which the young can live, and which they even stay away from occasionally. However, the mobile device by the age of 16 takes a more prominent position in young people's media life.

A prerequisite for accessing mobile news is, of course, mobile use. A reasonable assumption is that the overall probability of mobile news consumption rises with an increased amount of use. Consequently, mobile media life will be used as an explanatory factor to mobile news life later on. The demonstration of the two media lives portrayed above raises the question of whether or not Internet media life plays some part in guiding the accessing of mobile news. The plausibility of this assumption follows the notion that Internet use and mobile use rise in parallel and are relatively well correlated (.410). The frequency of Internet use may therefore indirectly fuel different mobile practices such as news usage. Based on this linkage, Internet media life should also be added to the equation, even if it is only distantly related to mobile news life. In sum, contemporary media life is increasingly a mobile media life to the young, as the gap between Internet use and mobile media use becomes blurred.


## MOBILE MEDIA PROFILE: OUTLINE OF INQUIRY

The ways in which people use particular media (mobile media and the Internet), as well as their general and specific orientation toward news accessing, are correlated to the accessing of news with mobile devices. Subsequently, the characteristics of their diverse mobile usage presumably play an important role; some only use SMS and voice communication, others make use of games and the camera, and some use it to access the Internet. Their orientation toward particular types of content and services is then assumed to be correlated to their use of news with the mobile. Consequently, this section focuses exclusively on the role played by the mobile-only world.

Rather than investigating the correlation between and effect of particular functions and services, mobile use will be conceptualized into different categories in the form of a typology. This typology of mobile usage was constructed based on the result of a recent qualitative investigation of mobile media experiences (i.e., mobile Internet and mobile search). The typology categorized users into three groups: *the traditionalists, the diversionists* and *the connected.*[27] The traditionalists are users with practices confined to using their mobile device for interpersonal communication via voice calls and SMS. They typically had no intention to use their mobile for anything but these basic communicative functions. The diversionists also used their mobile device for voice calls and SMS, but they added offline-oriented multimedia functionalities such as the camera and MP3 player.

In turn, the connected type added different practices related to accessing the Internet to the practices of the traditionalists and the diversionists. The connected involved novice users who only used mobile internet in the interstices, that is, when they cannot access the Internet by computer. In that sense, accessing the mobile Internet functions as a complement to the computer-based Internet, but is used only occasionally. Advanced connected users have media lives in which access to the mobile Internet was seamlessly integrated, rather than used only in the interstices. The advanced users had typically acquired smartphones with a touch screen and a flat-rate price plan.[28] This means that the use of Internet-based functionalities was coupled with a premium mobile device as well as a subscription to the mobile Internet. These personally oriented technological and economic preconditions postulate that the young, who are dependent on funds from their parents, are less likely to have acquired such a mobile device. Meanwhile, some have been given such devices (new or used) as they get older.

## MOBILE MEDIA PROFILE: FINDINGS

This subsection focuses on how *mobile media profile* fuels mobile news life among the young. An important explanation, in addition to mobile media life, concerns the profile orientation expressed in diverging patterns of mobile use. An initial inquiry concerns how the typology of mobile media profiles—traditionalists, diversionists and connected—plays out among the young. Mapped out in Table 12.1 are the two underlying dimensions that can be identified in the present usage patterns. Arranged in the table are widespread practices tied to mobile devices. It was determined that these practices were widespread based on how the group reported their use of mobile devices. Eighty-one percent of the group reported making voice calls and 71% reported receiving voice calls. Seventy-eight percent of the group reported using SMS, 66% reported listening to music, and 59% reported taking photos. The group also reported less common practices like gaming (43%), producing personal videos (22%), using Multimedia Messaging Services (MMS) (18%) and watching videos (8%). Only 6% of the group reported accessing the Internet through their mobile device.

When assessing the mobile orientations inherent in young people's mobile use, the three expected mobile media profiles do not emerge. Regardless if studied as correlation matrices or as above (Table 12.1) in the form of dimensional analysis,[29] the border between *traditionalist* and *diversionist* is blurred. Therefore, instead of three, two rather distinct mobile orientations emerge. The first is broad and includes traditional mobile practices such as making and receiving voice calls and SMS, together with diversionist features such as listening to music, taking photos and gaming. This mobile orientation exploits the broad potential of the mobile as a communication

*Table 12.1*   Mobile media profile assessed by means of factor analysis with varimax rotation (factor loadings and adj. $r^2$)

|  | Diversionists | Connected |
|---|---|---|
| Access the Internet |  | .652 |
| Watch videos |  | .807 |
| Produce personal videos |  | .594 |
| MMS (send) |  | .393 |
| Make voice calls | .726 |  |
| SMS | .727 |  |
| Take photos | .690 |  |
| Music listening | .649 |  |
| Receive voice calls | .694 |  |
| Gaming | .433 |  |
| R2 | *27.9* | *18.5* |

*Note:* Extraction method: principal component analysis. Varimax rotation with kaiser normalization (rotation converged in 3 iterations). Restriction: two-factor solution. Factor loadings < .300 are deleted from the table. $N = 1155$.

device and gadget for entertainment, but without making use of its Internet network capacity. The orientation has been labeled *diversionists*.

Conversely, the second mobile orientation, labeled *connected*, falls back on this specific potential to connect the device to the Internet. The mobile device is used to access the Internet, watch and produce clips and film, and send MMS. The traditionalist orientation, with an origin in the functionality of the earlier, simpler mobile 'phones' (as communication devices), is not present among the young. Their mobile media profiles are consistently characterized by a more comprehensive use of the broader functionality of today's mobile devices (as multimedia communication devices). This development is probably a composite effect, encompassing both technological leverage of the devices themselves (capacity) and leverage of the technical literacy of the users (ability). A reasonable assumption is that the mobile media profiles of the young above will contribute to explaining the accessing of news with mobile devices. Following this, both factors—diversionists and connected—will be merged into the final explanatory model. From the general media life to specific mobile orientations, the chapter will now discuss and analyze the role of news life for the young.

## NEWS LIFE: OUTLINE OF INQUIRY

The mobile news life is contextualized within a broader frame of a general news life comprising an array of different news media, in which some are presumably more coupled to the development of a mobile news life. A Danish study indicates that the mobile was generally valued as less worthwhile compared with other news media,[30] and others report that the mobile has predominantly found its niche in the interstices of everyday life.[31] Other investigations indicate that for connected advanced users, the mobile has entered the textures of numerous everyday life occurrences.[32] The adoption and use of mobile media in general,[33] and mobile news in particular, relates to both medium- and user-related factors. Many studies have stressed the medium factors such as usability (i.e., available services and content), user-friendliness (i.e., touch-screen interface) and cost (flat-rate subscription model), as well as the characteristics of user groups (i.e., age, gender, education, income).

In Sweden, the users of mobile news have typically been men age 15–49 with a personal or company-based subscription plan.[34] However, their American counterparts have been portrayed as youth or young adults with a high income and living in urban areas.[35] One factor anticipated explaining future developments regarding users' needs for news. This can be operationalized either by how interested they are in news or the ways in which people access the news through other news media. Those who are generally frequent users of news (news junkies), through one or several news media, are likely to also expose themselves to using news with other news media.[36] This relates to a functionalistic user-centric approach, accounting for users' needs and gratifications related to the complementary use of news media. A comparative pattern was also prevalent in the American Pew study, in which 51% of mobile news consumers used six or more different news and information sources or platforms every month, compared with 21% among other adults.[37]

Meanwhile, regarding today's increasingly individualized news (and media) usage patterns, some gaps have emerged. Groups have developed different news lives; some are oriented toward analog media such as printed newspapers and television, whereas others are directed toward digital and mobile media. Some studies, through the analyses of annually conducted surveys, report that the orientation of news access is very important to understanding mobile news usage. A conclusion is that the use of mobile news is particularly high among those who frequently use online news sources, much higher compared with those who frequently read print newspapers. This is partly explained by the high representation of the elderly among readers of print-quality newspapers, and that frequent news site users have developed a need for using interactive and digital news media.[38]

News usage is, in most cases, a very habitual behavior, acted out repeatedly in time and aligned to specific news platforms (e.g., reading of the newspaper at breakfast). Consequently, with the emergence of new news media, a central question regards the effect of an individual's habitual orientation toward news (their news life). Two assumptions will be investigated in light of this discussion. Firstly, do those with persistent news habits turn their attention to news from mobile devices more than others? Secondly, what characterizes the orientation of their established news lives, and how are these practices aligned with accessing news with the mobile? Frequent users of online news media (digital orientation) are expected to be the most prominent users of news with mobile devices.

## NEWS LIFE: FINDINGS

To give a preliminary answer to the two aforementioned questions, the role of TV, newspapers, the Internet and mobile for the news life of the young are mapped out. As a general background description of the news life of this group, 25% of the 9-year-olds report that they are not following any news, regardless of media. This alignment diminishes with increases in age, and is only reported by 4% by the age of 16. Figure 12.2 illustrates the prevalence of each of the four different media in the news life of the young, and also how the composite news life gradually changes with age.

The graph shows how news life expands between the age of 9 and 16. Expansion encompasses all four news media, both old (TV and newspapers) and new (Internet and mobile). These formative years are apparently the time period during which broader news consumption is established for the young, in a similar manner among both genders, contrary to general news usage. The four different media occupy different positions in young people's news life. TV (average = 81%) is the most frequently used channel for news, closely followed by newspapers (average = 77%). TV and newspapers are already relatively established news sources for the youngest (70% and 58% respectively for 9-year-olds). Online news (average = 50%), on the other hand, grows into a corresponding position with increasing age. From being used as a source of news by less than one-fifth of all 9-year-olds, online news

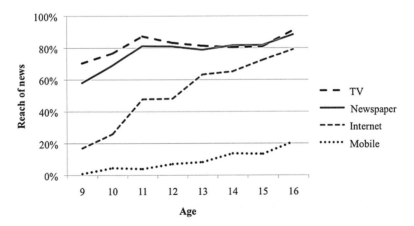

*Figure 12.2*   News life with TV, newspapers, Internet and mobile over age

usage grows toward the levels of TV and newspapers, and includes almost four-fifths of all 16-year-olds.

Young people's mobile news life is relatively limited in comparison with the news lives built around TV, newspapers and the Internet. Mobile news life (average = 8%) follows a similar growth with age, from 1% among the youngest to 21% among the oldest. In relative terms, the differences in mobile news life are massive, being more prevalent than that of online news life. However, this strong relative growth must be seen in light of the low initial level from which it increases. Two reasonable expectations are that news usage is correlated over different media, firstly by means of an underpinning news interest. Secondly, the link between online and mobile news usage is stronger than the corresponding link between mobile, TV and newspapers.

A correlation matrix of all four news lives holds both expectations to be correct. News life is correlated regardless of platform, and the probability of news usage on additional platforms is stronger if news is already in use on another platform. Underlying this pattern is a general interest in news—an articulated news habit. Although TV and newspapers are the most strongly correlated to each other (.436), mobile is much more strongly correlated to online (.305) than to TV and newspapers. The Internet emerges as an intermediate news media that is also strongly correlated to TV (.346) and newspapers (.273). Emerging among the young is a news life that is, to some extent, divided into analog/old and digital/new news media, with Internet news situated in an intermediate position. Obviously, this constitutes an important conclusion for the upcoming explanatory mission.

## MOBILE NEWS LIFE: AN EXPLANATORY MODEL

The multivariate regression model (Table 12.2) involves *mobile news life* as the dependent variable. To explain how often (divided into four steps, from daily and over weekly to more seldom and never) young access news through their mobile,[39] the model uses seven independent factors derived from news life, mobile media life and mobile media profile. The first is the background variable *gender* as a factor identified by earlier research as a guiding inclination toward news and new technology. Age is likewise an important background factor, but was excluded due to its strong correlation to other factors in the model.[40] That is, age is indirectly expressed in the model, although it is expressed through other factors. The second is *online news life*, as mobile news life is the most closely correlated part of news life. The third factor, *total news life*, embraces a general interest in news, operationalized as the amount of news media use complementary to mobile news accessing. The fourth and fifth are *mobile media life* and the closely related *Internet media life*. The sixth and seventh are the two respective mobile media profiles derived from the typology and the factor analysis (*connected* and *diversionists*). The factors have been transformed into variables and introduced in the multivariate regression.

*Table 12.2*   Explanatory model of mobile news life of young using multivariate clr (unstandardized beta, standard errors of beta, standardized beta)

|  |  | B | SE B | b |
|---|---|---|---|---|
|  | Constant | -0.003 | 0.049 |  |
|  | Gender | -0.046 | 0.025 | -.054 |
| *Media Life* |  |  |  |  |
|  | Mobile Media Life | 0.023 | 0.007 | .134*** |
|  | Internet Media Life | -0.005 | 0.004 | -.040 |
| *Mobile Media Profile* |  |  |  |  |
|  | Connected | 0.083 | 0.012 | .204*** |
|  | Diversionists | -0.022 | 0.015 | -.052 |
| *News Life* |  |  |  |  |
|  | Online news life | 0.108 | 0.019 | .237*** |
|  | Total news life | 0.009 | 0.008 | .045 |

Note: $R^2$ (adj.) = .16 N = 1155 *** p < .001

The multivariate regression analysis illustrates how three specific factors (gray rows) guide mobile news life. The factors are inherent to either news life, mobile media profile or media life. *Online news life* is the factor with the strongest effect (.237). The factor is emerging from news life, and its effect is that the more frequent the online news use, the higher the mobile news usage. Interestingly, general news interest does not suffice if not oriented toward the Internet. *Mobile media profile* (.204) is the second strongest predictor of mobile media life. The more connected are likewise more inclined to mobile news usage, in contrast to diversionists, who represent no significant effect. *Mobile media life* (.134) ranks third in terms of strength of effect.

An elaborated mobile media life is more likely to produce mobile news usage than a scarce mobile media life. It is important to note that Internet media life does not play a decisive role. A comprehensive explanatory model of mobile news consumption among young would thus be composed of *online news life*, *mobile media life* and a *mobile media profile* distinguished by being *connected*. In sum, this means that mobile news life is connected to a specific orientation toward online news and connectivity, and also sustained by an elaborated mobile media life. Rather than *general* news interest and *general* Internet use, *specific* and more detailed orientations have effects. The model explains 16% of the variance of mobile news life and makes a strong contribution to the intersecting field of research on mobile devices, news and youth.

## CONCLUSION

Seamless solutions for always-on connections are now diffusing rapidly through miniaturized mobilities such as mobile devices. Digital and mobile media have gained a pervasive omnipresence in the media lives among the young, as witnessed by the pace in which the young develop their mobile and Internet media lives as teenagers. In this regard, the chapter clearly shows how the young are embracing mobiles and the Internet into the textures of their everyday life; this empowers their possibilities for seamlessly integrating these in support of their need for both communication and information. Earlier research has shown the prevalence of using the mobile device for communication among young, whereas this study explores its role concerning how the young access news information. In contrast to mobile communications, mobile news access was still relatively limited in scope at this stage in history and life. As of 2010, only 8% of the young Swedes studied here had developed a mobile media life that involved accessing news. This result is striking, in light of previous research constructing the young as early adopters, even known as 'digital natives' and 'generation digital'. In fact, little orientation of their mobile practices conformed to other studies of so-called advanced users.[41]

This demonstrates that the young are more heterogeneous than indicated by simplistic constructions of them as digitally oriented. However, this does not mean that the young are not keen on using their mobile device at all. On the contrary, certain affordances tied to the mobile device—such as individualization, mobility and pervasiveness—make it most important to the teenagers of this study (13–16 years). Although only a limited group of the young were characterized as connected, a key finding from this factor analysis was that there were literally no traditionalists. Instead, these young were primarily diversionists. Through their adolescence, they seem to grow into more advanced usage, and then the adoption of mobile news access increases among 16–49 year olds.[42]

Another key finding is that these formative years are apparently the time period during which broader news consumption is established for the young. The produced news life tied to TV, print newspaper, the Internet and mobile media constitute an efficient blueprint of news accessing by the young. Even though media life is increasingly mobile for the young, mobile news life is not yet an internalized and natural part of mobile media life. Considering the current broader uptake of mobile news among adults, the cleavage found in 2010 between mobile news life and Internet news life is not necessarily a condition that will be replicated in the future. Rather than solely mirroring the failure of mobile news today, this cleavage should be seen as a clear-cut illustration of the future potential of mobile news.

Therefore, it would be interesting for future research to analyze how the mobile news life of the young develops in parallel to the increased diffusion of advanced mobile devices and the leveraged capacity of mobile networks.

The multivariate regression model, which explains 16% of the variance in the mobile news life of the young, constitutes the chapter's most important finding. A consistent result is that the particular orientation toward one's digital and mobile habitat explains the mobile news life of the young, rather than general news orientation and general media life (mobile and Internet life). This result indicates that the young gradually move toward individualized media lives that are seamlessly integrated with digital and mobile media. With augmented digital news accessing practices, and improving conditions for mobile news accessing, the young will presumably develop their mobile news lives. It is worth noting that during the two years following the spring of 2010, there has been a remarkable uptake of mobile news accessing among the public in Sweden.[43] The young are growing up in a society in which the accessing of the internet and news through mobile devices has blossomed. Therefore, future research should further investigate how such mobile media practices are being integrated into the textures of everyday media lives, and what the positive and negative social consequences of this change might be.

## NOTES

1. International Telecommunications Union (ITU), *Measuring the Information Society* (Geneva, Switzerland: ITU, 2011).
2. Rich Ling and Jonathan Donner, *Mobile Communication* (Cambridge, UK: Polity, 2009).
3. Gerard Goggin, *Global Mobile Media* (London: Routledge, 2011); Oscar Westlund et al., "Exploring the Logic of Mobile Search", *Behaviour & Information Technology* 30, no. 5 (2011): 691–703; Oscar Westlund, "Producer-centric Versus Participation-centric: On the Shaping of Mobile Media", *Northern Lights* 10 (2012): 105–19.
4. Taezoon Park, Rashmi Shenoy and Gavriel Salvendy, "Effective Advertising on Mobile Phones: A literature Review and Presentation of Results from 53 Case Studies" *Behaviour & Information Technology* 27, no. 5 (2008): 355–373; Jason Wilson, "3G to Web 2.0? Can Mobile Telephony Become an Architecture of Participation?", *Convergence* 12, no. 2 (2006): 229–42.
5. World Association of Newspapers, *World Digital Media Trends*. Special Report. (Paris: World Association of Newspapers, 2007); Oscar Westlund, "New(s) Functions for the Mobile", *New Media and Society* 12, no. 1 (2010): 91–108; Oscar Westlund, "From Mobile Phone to Mobile Device: News Consumption on the Go", *Canadian Journal of Communication* 33, (2008): 443–463.
6. John Horrigan, *Wireless Internet Use*. (Washington: Pew Internet, 2009), accessed June 15, 2010, http://pewInternet.org/~/media//Files/Reports/2009/Wireless-Internet-Use.pdf ; Rich Ling and Pål Roe Sundsøy, *The iPhone and Mobile Access to the Internet* (paper presented at the ICA pre-conference on mobile communication, Chicago, IL, May 20–21, 2009).
7. Gerard Goggin, "The Intimate Turn of Mobile News", in *News online: Transformations and Continuities*, ed. Graham Meikle and Guy Redden (London: Macmillan, 2010); Oscar Westlund, "Mobile News: A Review and Model of Journalism in an Age of Mobile Media", *Digital Journalism* 1 (forthcoming); Westlund et al., "Exploring the Logic of Mobile Search".

8. Oscar Westlund, "Convergent Mobile News Media: Tranquility Awaiting Eruption" ("Multimedios móviles convergentes: ¿Tranquilidad en espera de erupción?"), *Palabra Clave* 13, no. 1 (2010): 99–110.
9. Tom Rosenstiel et al., *Survey: Mobile News & Paying Online*, Pew Research Center's Project for Excellence in Journalism and Pew Research Center's Internet and American Life Project, 2011, accessed: February 24, 2013, http://stateofthemedia.org/2011/mobile-survey/
10. Don Tapscott, *Growing Up Digital: The Rise of the Net Generation* (New York: McGraw-Hill, 1998); Kathryn C. Montgomery, *Generation Digital—Politics, Commerce, and Childhood in the Age of the Internet* (Cambridge, MA: MIT Press, 2009); Marc Prensky, *Don't Bother Me, Mom—I'm Learning!* (St. Paul, MN: Paragon House, 2006).
11. David Buckingham, *Youth, Identity and Digital Media* (Cambridge, MA: MIT Press, 2008).
12. Karl Mannheim, "The problem of Generations", in *Essays on the Sociology of Knowledge*, ed. Paul Kegan (London: Routledge, 1952), 276–320.
13. John W. Dimmick, Thomas A. McCain and W. Theodore Bolton, "Media Use and the Life Span: Notes on Theory and Method", *American Behavioral Scientist* 23, no. 1 (1979): 7–31.
14. Mark Deuze, "Media Life", *Media Culture & Society* 33, no. 1 (2011): 137–148; Mark Deuze, *Media Life* (London: Polity Press, 2012).
15. Manuel Castells, *Communication Power* (Oxford, UK: Oxford University Press, 2010).
16. Anthony Giddens, *The Consequences of Modernity* (Cambridge: Polity Press, 1990).
17. Jakob Bjur, *Transforming Audiences. Patterns of Individualization in Television Viewing.* JMG Book Series no. 57 (Gothenburg: University of Gothenburg, 2009), accessed December 10, 2010, https://gupea.ub.gu.se/bitstream/2077/21544/1/gupea_2077_21544_1.pdf.
18. Oscar Westlund, "Guest Editorial—Transforming Tensions: Legacy Media Towards Participation and Collaboration", *Information, Communication & Society* 15, no. 6, (2012): 789–795.
19. Deuze, "Media Life".
20. Ibid.; Mark Deuze, "Media Industries, Work and Life", *European Journal of Communication* 24, no. 4 (2009): 1–14.
21. Deuze, *Media Life*.
22. Mark Deuze, Peter Blank and Laura Speers, "Media Life", in *Media Perspectives for the 21st Century*, ed. Stylianos Papathanassopoulos (London: Routledge, 2010), 181–195.
23. Rich Ling and Birgitte Yttri, "Hyper-Coordination via Mobile Phones in Norway", in *Perpetual Contact: Mobile Communication, Private Talk, Public Performance*, ed. James Katz and Mark Aakhus (Cambridge: Cambridge University Press, 2004), 139–169.
24. Oscar Westlund and Jakob Bjur, "Media Life of Young", *Young*, 21 (London: Sage, 2013) forthcoming.
25. Ibid.
26. Ibid.
27. Westlund et al., "Exploring the Logic".
28. Ibid.
29. To achieve clarity in presentation and explanation, the performed factor analysis has been forced to produce a two-factor solution (as the exploratory factor analysis did not indicate the presence of a third group of traditionalists).

30. Kim C. Schrøder and Bent S. Larsen, "The Shifting Cross-Media News Landscape", *Journalism Studies* 11, no. 4 (2010): 524–534.
31. John W. Dimmick, John C. Feaster and Gregory J. Hoplamazian, "News in the Interstices: The Niches of Mobile Media in Space and Time", *New Media and Society* 13, no. 1 (2011): 23–39.
32. Comscore, *Comparative Report on Mobile Usage in Japan, United States and Europe*, accessed December 6, 2012, http://www.comscore.com.
33. Westlund et al., "Exploring the Logic".
34. Westlund, "Convergent Mobile News Media".
35. Rosenstiel et al., *Mobile News & Paying Online*.
36. Lennart Weibull, *Tidningsläsning i Sverige* (Stockholm: Publica, 1983).
37. Rosenstiel et al., *Mobile News & Paying Online*.
38. Westlund, "Convergent Mobile News Media".
39. That the dependent variable is not on a 'pure' interval scale and normally distributed, to some extent, violates the basic assumptions of the CLR model. Peter Kennedy, *A Guide to Econometrics*, 5th ed.(Cambridge, MA: MIT Press, 2003). To assess the consequences of these violations, the model has also been run with a dichotomous DV in binary logistic regression. As this procedure did not change the main results, CLR has been chosen for the presentation of results as a more widely experienced and heuristic statistical procedure.
40. Age is excluded in order to avoid multicollinearity. Ibid.
41. Westlund et al., "Exploring the Logic".
42. Westlund, "Convergent Mobile News Media".
43. Oscar Westlund. "The Production and Consumption of Mobile News", in *The Mobile Media Companion*, ed. Gerard Goggin and Larissa Hjorth (New York: Routledge, forthcoming).

# 13 From SMS to SNS

## The Use of the Internet on the Mobile Phone Among Young Danes

*Troels F. Bertel and Gitte Stald*

## INTRODUCTION

The landscape of mobile media is changing. Denmark is currently witnessing a rapid uptake of so-called smartphones, mobile phones with computer-like capabilities. A recent survey from Gallup Index Denmark[1] conducted with more than 3,500 respondents found that approximately 1.5 million Danes—or more than one-third—own smartphones. A similar finding is reported by Statistics Denmark,[2] which found that in 33% of families (consisting of one or more members) at least one person owns a smartphone.

With this level of smartphone adoption, practices of mobile phone use also seem to be changing. The National Danish IT and Telecom Agency recently published data showing that data traffic from mobile phones has increased by a factor of approximately eight in the 1.5 years between H1 2010 and H2 2011[3] as more and more Danes are beginning to use the mobile Internet.

Use of traditional mobile phone functionality, too, seems to be changing in a Danish context, although not as dramatically as data-related functionality. Text messaging via the SMS protocol decreased by 6.9% and voice calls increased by 10.7% between H1 2010 and H1 2011.[4] It is important to note here that the Danish history of mobile telephony is quite different from that of for instance the U.S. Texting in 1990s and early 2000s was a main driver of the adoption of the mobile phone among Nordic youth (who were early adopters of the technology) in part due to the lower cost of communicating via SMS compared with voice calls.[5] Since around the mid 2000s texting has been ubiquitous in a Danish context, particularly among youth. When we see SMS use decreasing today, we may speculate that this is in part due to mobile- and PC-based Facebook and other services taking over some texting activity—but the data in general is inconclusive. Voice calls traditionally have been relatively expensive, but, with the cost of mobile voice calls dropping approximately 75% from 2000to 2010,[6] are becoming a more attractive option from an economic standpoint. Following these changes in both the handsets that users carry and what they use them for, it is interesting and relevant to study what motivates users to begin using these new technologies.

In this chapter, we discuss the current state of the use of the Internet on convergent mobile devices—particularly smartphones—among youth in a Danish context. We ask why young people in Denmark begin using the Internet on their mobile phones—or why they do not. Further, we discuss how using the Internet on the mobile phone interacts with the use of the Internet on the personal computer.

## FROM THE MOBILE PHONE TO THE SMARTPHONE

### The Mobile Phone

When the first 'modern' mobile phones—phones which in addition to voice communication allowed for textual communication via SMS—were introduced with the GSM standard circa 1992[7] it was in many ways a development that influenced, challenged and changed existing social practices. The mobile phone made individuals directly addressable. Where users had previously called household phones, now they called or texted directly to the person they wanted to talk to.[8] Users were placed in a state of perpetual contact—always in touch with the network, everywhere.[9] Further, the mobile phone allowed users to 'microcoordinate' daily activities with friends, partners and family, for instance, calling them from the supermarket asking whether or not to get milk and texting ahead if running late for an appointment.[10] Young people, in particular, took up texting and made it their own. Recent findings suggest that while SMS texting today is used by most age groups—the elderly being a notable exception—teens are still texting much more than any other age group.[11]

### The Smartphone

A recent industry report states that the current growth in the use of the Internet on mobile phones is "largely attributable to the growth in smartphone adoption, 3G/4G device ownership and the increasing ubiquity of unlimited data plans".[12] Since use of the Internet on mobile phones is strongly related to smartphone adoption, a pertinent question to further frame the discussion is 'what is a smartphone?' A precise definition of what constitutes a smartphone is not readily available. In the general public discourse the definition often seems to be something along the lines of 'phones with computerlike capabilities'. Casual observation tells us that they frequently run iOS or Android operating systems, they most often let the user install 'apps' as well as access the Internet, and many have touch screens. More comprehensive technical definitions (in the form of lists of typical features) are also sometimes employed.[13]

While a precise operationalized definition is important for measurement purposes, it is not equally important in helping us understand the potential of the smartphone for influencing adoption, use and social practices. Rather than being fixated on a given implementation of technology, our interests, like those of Katz and Aakhus,[14] are centered on social practices and "how mobile communication helps us understand them, as well as how the mobile character and richness of the technology change and initiate new social processes".[15] In what follows, we are focusing on individual and social practices surrounding convergent mobile media with smartphones currently being the clearest example of this general category. With this focus in mind, at least three macro-level characteristics of smartphones can be identified which seem to carry a special potential for influencing such practices and are of particular interest: The devices 1) have the computing power and technical platform to run applications and access Internet content, 2) have—in principle—a persistent data connection to the Internet, and 3) are typically equipped with positioning technology, often GPS. These three aspects are of course quite often interrelated and interdependent with the combination of a powerful open computer platform, Internet connectivity and sensors each adding to the whole.

## What Changes with the Smartphone?

With the smartphone mobiles have evolved into what Klaus Bruhn Jensen[16] has termed "media of the third degree"—media technologies or platforms integrating previously separate media and associated content into a single device. Smartphones now integrate media content, which previously was associated with many separate technologies and often distinct social spheres such as SMS, voice calls, Internet content, social network sites, positioning technology, radio and television, etc. This holds a great potential for changing how the individual media are used—by themselves or in concert.

Further, the persistent connection to the Internet associated with smartphones provides instant access to information regardless of the physical context of the user: office workers, for instance, can check their e-mail on the go, and mobile Google can be used to quickly settle any discussion, anywhere.

New modes of mobile sociability also become possible. The access to social network sites, for instance, changes the potential audiences associated with the mobile phone: where the sending of an SMS or MMS message used to occur between individuals in one-to-one communication, text or multimedia content posted directly to a social network site such as Facebook can be considered one-to-one, one-to-many or many-to-many communication depending on the settings of the poster's profile and the context of the communication. The addition of mobile location-aware sensor information further extends social network sites to allow for location-based social networking and games.[17]

It is yet unclear what the social and societal consequences of the appropriation of the smartphone and other convergent mobile media will be. They may, however, be less striking than those of the mobile phone and the Internet—evolutionary rather than revolutionary. The mobile phone in its day challenged and changed existing social practices, and the appropriate use of the device had to be negotiated through a process of domestication.[18]

Changes in and challenges to social situations were easy to observe because of the introduction of the new and quite noticeable medium—with its bright screen, clicking keypad noises and users speaking into the air. With the smartphone, the 'mechanics' of our interaction with the devices basically seems to remain the same: we still click keypads, tap bright screens or speak into our devices regardless of whether we are using 'old' features such as SMS, voice and music playback or more advanced Internet features. Thus the smartphone in a sense comes to us already domesticated—marrying the form of a previous medium (the mobile phone) and the content of another (the Internet). For this reason, the smartphone may not be experienced as being disruptive to the same degree as the mobile phone and the Internet were in their time—and challenges to existing social practices and dynamics may not be as obvious.

## METHOD

The data that is used to frame the discussions that follow come primarily from a survey conducted by the authors with students at the IT University of Copenhagen (ITU) in Spring 2011. We focus here on one qualitative aspect of the survey in particular, namely replies to an open-ended question prompting students, "Please describe in a few words why you started accessing the Internet with your mobile phone—or why you do not".

The survey was sent to approximately 1,400 full-time students, of which 338 completed the survey. Of these, 269 students answered the open-ended question forming the main empirical basis of the analysis. Since our aim with the survey was to study the motivations for using the Internet on the mobile phones among young Danes, all respondents above the age of 30 were excluded from the analysis. The number of respondents included in the analysis is 216. The mean age of the respondents is 25.1 with a standard deviation of 2.85. Males make up 64% ($n = 216$) of the respondents, and 36% are female—a distribution that is roughly similar to the overall distribution in the ITU population. The mobile Internet is used by 80% ($n = 216$) of the respondents—66% use it daily.

As the main part of what follows, we will be conducting an analysis inspired by grounded theory,[19] though we do not adhere strictly to all aspects of this approach. In our analysis, we have employed an iterative coding process performed using the ATLAS.ti computer aided qualitative data analysis software. In a first cycle of initial coding[20] the reasons respondents give for using or not using the Internet on the mobile phone were identified. A single coder was responsible for this initial coding, which stayed quite close to the data and primarily used descriptive coding[21] due to the condensed and often descriptive nature of the material. In a second cycle, two coders collaborated to form categories from the initial codes and identify more abstract themes through focused coding.[22] During the focused coding cycle, the initial codes were collaboratively revisited, discussed and revised as needed to ensure a common understanding of the material among the coders.

To strengthen the analysis and interpretation and to provide context and background for the qualitative material we will also draw selectively upon the quantitative aspects of the survey. Specifically, we will draw upon descriptive statistics about the uses and nonuses of the Internet on the mobile phone from the sample of the 216 respondents. The educational profile of the ITU is situated at the intersection of design, media studies, business and software development. Because of the university's overall focus on IT, the students are typically earlier adopters and heavier users of information technology than the average young Dane. The students of the ITU in this way cannot be assumed to be representative of the average Danish mobile phone user and it is important to keep in mind that we are not trying to generalize our findings to a wider context. However, because the students at the ITU are somewhat ahead of the Danish adoption curve—many being early adopters of technology—we expect that the categories and themes discovered here will have exemplary value for a range of the issues at stake in the use of convergent mobile media in a Danish context.

## ANALYSIS

We now move on to the analysis of the qualitative replies to the open-ended question, "Please describe in a few words why you started accessing the Internet with your mobile phone—or why you do not". This section is divided into three parts. The first part analyzes the replies from respondents who use the Internet on the mobile phone. The second part analyzes replies from those who do not. As will become apparent, some analytical concepts apply to both parts: it is clear for instance that handset affordances can be both enabling and constraining of Internet use on the mobile phone. To avoid analytic redundancy, any overlapping concepts will be considered in greatest detail in the first part. We round off the analysis with a discussion of the uses of the mobile Internet vis-à-vis PC-based internet. Categories and themes identified using the grounded theory approach described earlier are used as headings to structure the presentation of the analysis in the following.

## USE OF THE INTERNET ON THE MOBILE PHONE

### "BECAUSE I CAN!"

The in vivo code labeling this first category is a statement used by several respondents to describe their reasons for using the Internet on the mobile phone. For them, a main motivation to use the Internet on their phones is simply that after acquiring a new (smart) phone, they have the possibility of doing so:

Because I can when I have a smartphone. (Female, 20)

My old phone died and I got myself a smartphone. It seemed natural to me to use all features it could offer: Like weather forecast, browser etc. (Male, 22)

I broke my old phone and didn't see the point in not buying a smartphone. I didn't expect to get this dependent on Internet features. I guess you only realize how convenient it is once you've got it. (Second female, 20)

Statement such as the above exemplify that using the Internet on the mobile phone may not be something that there is a strong preexisting need for in the group. Once the opportunity arises—for instance through the purchase of a new handset—smartphone owners, however, come to appreciate the opportunities the extra connectivity provides. This finding resonates well with previous research. Ling and Sundsøy[23] conducted a longitudinal study of the data use patterns of Norwegian mobile phone users who switched to the iPhone. A main finding from this research is that after switching to a modern smartphone, data use patterns changed. Newly converted iPhone users began using the mobile Internet much more than they had prior to being iPhone users. This supports the notion above that once users get the opportunity to use the Internet on a capable mobile device they tend to do so.

## AFFORDANCES OF THE SMARTPHONE

It is apparent that the experience—good or bad—of using a mobile device influences patterns of adoption and use of the Internet on that device. Indeed, the fact that using the Internet on the mobile "is easy" is the most common motivation given in the material for using it—by far. This is often linked to certain properties or affordances of the smartphone—the possibilities, affordances and constraints associated with it[24]—which make it a viable and sometimes even preferred way to access the Internet. Indeed, our quantitative data show that of smartphone owners,[25] 89% ($n = 156$) use the mobile Internet on their mobile phones daily; by contrast 78% ($n = 45$) of non-smartphone owners never use the mobile Internet.

One important characteristic of most smartphones is the small physical size of the devices themselves. The following quote illustrates how the smaller size of the devices in some situations makes it the best option for accessing the Internet when the physical context is not well suited for using the usually significantly bigger computer:

"Because I got a phone which could access the Internet, it's always available, and it's nicer to handle if you're e.g. laying down or sitting without a lot of space around you". (Male, 26)

The above quotation exemplifies how the smaller physical frame of the mobile device affords easier handling than for instance a laptop computer in some situations: it is easier to use it while lying down, walking around outside or sitting on a crowded bus. The size and resolution of the screens on modern phones also makes the content more useable in comparison to earlier phones. A 26-year-old female respondent writes:

> Easier, always by your side. The screens became so big that you could actually see something on them. (Female, 26)

One aspect of the ease of use associated particularly with smartphones is due to the intuitive and fluent interaction a good touch interface implementation affords. Norman and Nielsen[26] in a recent report on the gestural interfaces employed on many smartphones and other convergent mobile media noted that these interfaces "can be extremely effective while also conveying a sense of fun and pleasure". The main point of the c, however, is that the lack of standards associated with the new gesture-based interfaces (as implemented by the programs and apps that use them) is resulting in poorer usability of the devices. For Norman and Nielsen the frame of comparison, however, seems mainly to be the usability and standardization of current personal computer interfaces—not the taxing interfaces of previous generations of mobile phones. Compared with these, modern smartphones arguably offer a much more fluent and easy access to Internet services. Associated with the large touch-screen displays of many newer handsets are also often full QWERTY keyboards, which afford the writing of longer messages with greater ease for some users when compared with the alphanumeric key pads found on older mobile phones.

'Apps'—small programs that can be installed after market on mobile phones[27]—also likely play an important part in the overall ease of use associated with smartphones. While the quantitative data show that our respondents download apps—69% ($n = 213$) download free apps and 44% ($n = 210$) download paid apps at least monthly—few mention them in the qualitative material. It is unclear why we see this discrepancy, but one interpretation would be that the use of apps may simply be an integrated part of the use of the mobile Internet in general and implicit in the statements that using the Internet on the mobile phone is easy and convenient.

Some features, then, make the smartphone the preferred way to access the Internet under particular circumstances. There are however increasingly also services that are mobile-only. This is, for instance the case with services such as Foursquare, a location-based social network[28] that uses the geographical position of the mobile phone to allow users to 'check in' to physical locations:

> Some things are done more easily on the phone, and some things are done only on the phone (e.g. Foursquare). (Male, 27)

Interestingly, relatively few of the respondents actually use location-based services (such as Facebook Places, Foursquare and Gowalla). Out of 207 respondents 16% use them daily, 18% weekly, 10% monthly and more than half never use them.

Overall, these affordances and properties help to make modern smart-phones and the mobile Internet easier to use, which is a main motivation for the adoption and use of the latter.

## Passing Time

Frequently, the Internet on the mobile phone is used as a means to pass time in various ways. One scenario that is recurring in the material is that it helps to pass time during downtime such as transport. This is similar to Cui and Roto's finding that the mobile Internet is often used in "the moments between planned activities",[29] time that would otherwise be idle. The use of mobile technologies to pass time has been well documented in earlier studies about the use of the mobile phone and in particular SMS[30] as well as mobile Internet use.[31]

One respondent describes how boredom during transport was the initial reason motivating him to get a phone capable of Internet access—only afterward did it become useful to him:

> I was bored when traveling from Ringsted to Copenhagen. That was the main reason for buying a phone with Internet access. Afterwards it became a useful feature besides transportation. (Male, 24)

This illustrates how the ability to use the technology to pass time is an important reason for its use and at the same time in many ways echoes the sentiments found in the category "Because I Can!" Passing time, of course, can be many things. One such thing is the use of social network sites. A female respondent writes:

> To check Facebook during transportation. And I use it to settle bets when we [friends] disagree on something while out. (Female, 24)

Using social network sites rather surprisingly is only mentioned specifically by few respondents. However, considering the widespread use of social network sites and similar social media, we expect that when respondents mention how the smartphone is used for passing time this most likely refers to the use of social network sites. Indeed, 61% ($n = 212$) of our respondents use Facebook on their mobile phones at least weekly and 50% use it daily.

Another variant of passing time mentioned by some respondents is the ability to be productive in otherwise unproductive situations. The quantitative data underscores this; e-mail for instance is a very popular application of the Internet on the mobile among the respondents—it is in fact the most popular application—with 59% (*n* = 206) using it daily. Online gaming is likely an aspect of 'passing time' as well. We did unfortunately not ask about online gaming behavior in the ITU study, and it was not mentioned as a reason for using the Internet on the mobile phones in the qualitative material.

## Staying Connected

A salient theme in the material is the importance of staying connected. This theme appears directly—through explicit statements—as well as indirectly in the material. When respondents discuss the ability to stay connected explicitly, they often mention the value of having access to information wherever they are:

> Very simple: Accessibility. I don't have to limit myself to the confines of my home, university or work but can gather information all the time, everywhere. (Male, 27)

Social mobile communication (such as access to social network sites) is also mentioned as a reason for using the mobile Internet, albeit not as frequently. As described earlier, however, we can see from the quantitative data that the respondents do use services such as Facebook—but they rarely give this as a specific reason for using the mobile Internet. Interestingly, e-mail (which is also a very popular application of the mobile Internet) is mentioned by several respondents in the qualitative material. A reason that mobile e-mail may be more important to the respondents than social media is that e-mail is often the preferred medium for university and work communication—important information that they would not want miss out on. Facebook on the other hand is likely more about social updating, relaxation and fun—undoubtedly important but perhaps less critically so.

It is clear that there are significant overlaps between this theme and the 'affordances' theme presented above—Internet connectivity, after all, is an affordance of the smartphone and what enables many of the use patterns associated with it.

## NONUSE OF THE INTERNET ON THE MOBILE PHONE

### Limitations of Handsets or Subscriptions

The most salient reason for not using the Internet on the mobile phone is by far that phones or subscriptions either full-out do not support or allow Internet access, or support it so poorly that the respondents cannot be bothered to use it. As was evident from the reasons given for using the Internet on mobile phones, ease of use—in this case the lack of it—is important:

I don't think it's even capable of it. I'd want an iPhone or something like that, in order to even bother trying to access the Internet with my phone. (Male, 30)

In many ways this quotation also belongs to the affordances category that we presented previously: users of the internet on the mobile phone praise the fact that their devices afford quick and easy access to the Internet whereas nonusers conversely lament the fact that their devices do not.

## Costs Associated with Handsets or Use

Another important reason for not using the Internet on the mobile phone is the issue of cost. Both acquiring the actual smartphone handset as well as the data subscription to go with it to use the Internet can seem costly—particularly when on a student's budget. For some, this is an obstacle to the use of the technology:

I would like to, but cannot afford a smartphone at the moment, with access to the internet. (Female, 24)
It's complicated and expensive with my cell—maybe if I had a smartphone and could go on wireless. (Female, 25)

The finding that cost is an important factor in the appropriation and use of mobile technology is in accordance with previous research, where cost has also been found to play an important role in the adoption of mobile technologies: the early mass adoption of SMS in the Nordic region was in part driven by the relative low cost of this communication form vis-à-vis voice calls.[32] The recent growth of texting in the U.S. too has been tied to the availability of cheap unlimited texting plans.[33] Also, the use of the Internet on the mobile phone has been found to depend on the associated costs.[34]

While we only see costs mentioned as a negative influencing factor in the material, it is clear that it may also work in a positive direction; the cost of mobile data subscriptions has decreased over the last years[35]—presumably further lowering the threshold for beginning to use the mobile Internet.

## Attitudes

Very few of our respondents provide general attitudes (such as reservations to being connected at all times) as the reason for not using the Internet on their mobile phones. Nonuse among the respondents seems to be mainly due to the more pragmatic concerns listed above and less due to general considerations. The fact that most of the respondents are users of the mobile Internet, however, probably also contributes to the relative absence of more general attitudes, as does the generality of the question they are responding to. More specific questioning may illicit more nuanced data on the attitudes toward convergent mobile technology among users and nonusers alike, an interesting topic for further research.

## Already Covered

Some respondents do not see the need for using the Internet on the mobile phone at all. Their needs for being online are already met by using the Internet on the computer and they do not experience a need for connectivity beyond that:

> [It is a] Waste of money when I have a laptop. I seldom have the need to check the Internet on my phone. (Male, 24)
> I use my phone for calling or texting people. If I want to go on the Internet I use a computer. I have no use for a phone with Internet. (Male, 26)

An important point in this context is that virtually all the respondents in the sample own a laptop computer (99%, $n = 215$) and use it at the ITU (98%, $n = 212$). Denmark in general also has a high penetration rate for laptop computers—78% of households in 2011 owned at least one.[36] When the respondents thus use the Internet on the mobile phone this occurs in a context where Internet services are already available to them much of the day through the laptop computer. The use of the Internet on the smartphone in this way becomes more of a supplement than a requisite for online access—something that some users see no need for.

## The Mobile Phone vs. the Personal Computer

As we described above, it is clear that much of the Internet-based functionality found on the smartphone is already available to users on the personal computer. Therefore it is hardly surprising that many of our respondents use the computer as the frame of reference when discussing the use of the Internet on the mobile phone. When approaching these discussions analytically, two distinct patterns emerge where the mobile phone appears in the role of either an *extension of* or a task-specific *substitute for* the personal computer.

For some respondents the Internet on the mobile phone is used as an extension of the computer by providing access to functionality and services typically associated with the computer in situations where this is not available:

> If I'm not close to a computer, I use my phone instead. I would use a computer at anytime over my mobile, but when I'm not in contact with a computer, the mobile will have to do. (Male, 27)

For other respondents, the mobile phone is used as a substitute for the computer—particularly for smaller and simpler tasks. In the material there are two main reasons given for this. First, the mobile phone is always with you and always at hand. For smaller tasks such as checking e-mail or Facebook it may simply be easier and more convenient to use the mobile phone rather than moving to use a (more spatially bound) computer. Second, the mobile phone is always and instantly on, whereas the computer can take much longer to start up. These aspects are both exemplified in the following quotation:

> I always have my phone with me, so it's easy and convenient. It's also always turned on, so I don't have to wait for my laptop to start up. Sometimes I am in a hurry. (Female, 20)

As mentioned previously, the Internet on the mobile phone may be particularly useful for smaller, simpler tasks. We see this exemplified in the following:

> It's easier to pick your phone out of your pocket than to take your laptop out of your bag. So usually it is used for quick Internet searches and mail reading, while the laptop is used for replying longer answers back. (Male, 25)

For this respondent, the mobile phone is preferred for small quick tasks such as e-mail reading. Conversely, the computer is preferred for longer replies. The physical size of the device—which we previously discussed in terms of its affordances—may be one factor influencing this use: the predominantly touch-based interaction of modern smartphones may be efficient for tasks that can be performed via the often specialized and limited interfaces of apps or adapted Web pages ideally suited for finger based interaction. However, more complicated interaction may be easier to perform on the computer with the more fine-grained pointing tools available there.[37] Reading an e-mail or writing a short informal e-mail may be fine, whereas writing longer more formal e-mails may be deemed too cumbersome. Likewise, navigating a full-sized Web page may require so much 'pinching' and moving about that it simply becomes annoying—despite the much-improved interfaces of modern smartphones.

In many ways, the above is a continuation of the affordances theme presented earlier; certain properties of the Internet-equipped smartphone make it a preferred medium in some situations. As Green and Haddon[38] have pointed out, however, while the technological properties of ICTs are important in shaping media uses and choices, the affordances view cannot stand on its own—particularly not when considering the context of mediated interpersonal communication. There are many contextual factors to consider as well. Regarding the communicational aspects of ICT use, Green and Haddon mention the urgency of the communication, the nature of the relationship between communication partners, the physical proximity of the communicating parties, and the communication norms as factors that—while in no way intended as an exhaustive list—are all considerations when making choices among media.[39] These contextual influences on media use and media choices are difficult to capture using a method such as the one used in this chapter. They are, however, interesting and future research could explore these in greater detail using qualitative methods producing richer contextual descriptions.

It is clear that both themes identified previously presuppose the presence and use of the personal computer: whether the respondents use the smartphone to extend the personal computer or use it instead on the computer for some (typically simpler or more specialized) tasks, the computer is—so far—still the preferred terminal for more advanced Internet use. Much like the introduction of the mobile phone allowed for microcoordination—which introduced increased flexibility in scheduling face-to-face meetings[40]—mobile access introduces flexibility in Internet use. This becomes less of a discrete event—lifted out of the (less mobile) use context of the computer—and further integrated into the mobile micro flows of everyday life.

## CONCLUSION

Many of the categories and themes we have presented from the material are in a way quite mundane: the Internet is used on the mobile phone because it is available, easy and convenient—when the mobile phone and associated subscription properly support such use. When the Internet is used on the mobile phone instead of on the computer—which offers much of the same functionality—this likely happens in situations when the mobile phone is experienced as the 'best choice'. That is, when it best fits the context or when it is simply easier to use the mobile because of quicker access to simple and specialized functionality in particular. Conversely the computer may be easier for more complex tasks and may be best choice in such situations.

The respondents who use the Internet on the mobile phone do not do so because they lack Internet access in general—they have it with them on their computers through much of the day. Using the Internet on the mobile phone for this reason may not seem like something there is a strong need for—which is also reflected in the nonuse and disinterest of some respondents. Once respondents acquire a capable handset, however, they tend to use the mobile Internet daily—which seems to suggest that for some the mobile Internet is somewhat of an 'acquired need'. Buying a mobile phone with Internet access is not a necessity in order to be able to go online frequently but rather an opportunity to expand the number of platforms and situations when one can be online. It allows users to do things that may not be particularly different from what they can do on the computer, but they can do so easily when and where they please. In this way mobile internet extends PC-based internet, and in some cases may even displace it. The empirical material indicates that the computer, however, at the present time is still the frame of reference and preferred terminal for more advanced Internet use.

When the Internet is not used on the mobile phone, the main reasons are that it is not possible due to handset or subscription limitations, too cumbersome to be practical or too expensive to be worth it. The last two points are often associated with older mobile phones. In our material very few more general attitudes (such as skepticism toward technology and use, etc.) are given as reasons for nonuse.

While many of the reasons given for using the Internet on the mobile phone are somewhat mundane, we do see indications that being able to use the Internet on the mobile phone is still something new and even exciting to many respondents. An example of this is that a few of the respondents spontaneously wrote in their replies that they were "in fact" doing the survey on their smartphones. The sense of wonder implicit in such statements underscores the fact that being able to use the Internet on the mobile phone in a relatively unhindered and easy way is still a very new and novel thing to many people at this time.

Even if mobile Internet access has been possible since the late 1990s when the WAP protocol first became available,[41] we are studying a phenomenon still in the making, its role still being negotiated and its consequences not yet clear. As the use of the mobile Internet continues to grow it is increasingly gaining a position as an obvious choice for communication, information access and entertainment. Some of the respondents from the ITU study whom we have quoted in the section about nonuse may be the next users of online services from their mobile—because a new phone, new apps, new pricing, new social opportunities or perhaps a new everyday life will make it the obvious choice for them. Besides this, the use of the mobile phone for an increasing number of services online as well as offline takes place in a continuous interaction with other digital platforms; ongoing negotiations take place regarding which platform to use in which situation for which purposes and with which results. Further, the balance between uses of the platforms is constantly changing. As these negotiations proceed over time, it is likely that the perception of the role of the mobile phone as a platform for personal communication, as a citizen tool and as a handheld mobile Internet platform is changing with them. This, however, needs to be studied further.

## NOTES

1. Gallup Index Danmark, "Gallup Index Danmark Pressemeddelelse", June 23, 2011.
2. "Nyt Fra Danmarks Statistik", Danmarks Statistik, April 2011, accessed: February 24, 2013, http://www.dst.dk/pukora/epub/Nyt/2011/NR206.pdf.
3. The Danish Business Authority, "Mobiltelefoni Og Porteringer—2. Halvår 2011", accessed: August 24, 2011, http://www.erhvervsstyrelsen.dk/file/232669/mobil_2h11_xls.xls.
4. The Danish Business Authority, "Telestatistik—Første Halvår 2011", April 2011, accessed: February 24, 2013, http://www.erhvervsstyrelsen.dk/file/232717/teles tatistik_andet_halvar_2011_pdf.pdf.
5. Nicola Green and Leslie Haddon, *Mobile Communications: An Introduction to New Media* (Oxford: Berg, 2009), 38; Rich Ling, *The Mobile Connection* (San Francisco: Morgan Kaufman, 2004), 113.
6. IT-og Telestyrelsen, "Det Digitale Samfund 2010", 2011, accessed: February 24, 2013, http://www.itst.dk/statistik/IT%20og%20Telestatistik/det-digitale-samfund/2010/Det%20digitale%20samfund%202010.pdf.
7. Jon Agar, *Constant Touch—a Global History of the Mobile Phone* (Cambridge: Icon, 2003); Friedhelm Hillebrand et al., *Short Message Service*

*(SMS)—The Creation of Personal Global Text Messaging* (West Sussex: Wiley, 2010).

8. Rich Ling and Gitte Stald, "Mobile Communities: Are We Talking About a Village, a Clan, or a Small Group?", *American Behavioral Scientist* 53, no. 8 (2010), 1133–1147; Gitte Stald, "Telefonitis. Unge Danskeres Brug Af Telefonen i IT-tidsalderen," *Mediekultur, 16,* (2000), 19 pgs.; Gitte Stald, "Mobile Identity: Youth, Identity and Mobile Communication Media," in *Youth, Identity and Digital Media,* ed. David Buckingham (Cambridge, MA: MIT Press, 2008), 143–164.

9. Mark Aakhus and James E. Katz, *Perpetual Contact* (Cambridge: Cambridge University Press, 2002).

10. Ling, *The Mobile Connection*; Stald, "Telefonitis. Unge Danskeres Brug Af Telefonen i IT-tidsalderen."

11. Rich Ling, Troels Fibæk Bertel and Pål Roe Sundsøy, "The Socio-Demographics of Texting: An Analysis of Traffic Data," *New Media & Society, 14,* no. 2, 281–298.

12. comScore, "The comScore 2010 Mobile Year in Review", accessed: May 2011, http://www.comscore.com/Press_Events/Presentations_Whitepapers/2011/2010_Mobile_Year_in_Review.

13. See for instance *PC Mag,* "Definition of: Smartphone", accessed: January 13, 2012, http://www.pcmag.com/encyclopedia_term/0,2542,t=smart+phone&i=51537,00.asp; Wikipedia, "Smartphone", accessed: January 13, 2012, http://en.wikipedia.org/wiki/Smartphone.

14. James Everett Katz and Mark Aakhus, "Conclusion: Making Meaning of Mobiles—a Theory of Apparatgeist", in *Machines That Become Us,* ed. James Everett Katz (New Jersey: Transaction, 2003), 301–318.

15. Ibid., 302.

16. Klaus Bruhn Jensen, *Media Convergence: The Three Degrees of Network, Mass, and Interpersonal Communication* (London: Routledge, 2010).

17. Eric Gordon and Adrianna de Souza e Silva, *Net Locality: Why Location Matters in a Networked World* (Oxford: Blackwell, 2011).

18. Leslie Haddon, "Domestication and Mobile Telephony", in *Machines That Become Us,* ed. James Everett Katz (New Jersey: Transaction, 2003), 43–56; Ling, *The Mobile Connection.*

19. Kathy Charmaz, *Constructing Grounded Theory: A Practical Guide Through Qualitative Analysis* (London: Sage, 2006).

20. Ibid., 47.

21. Johnny Saldaña, *The Coding Manual for Qualitative Researchers* (London: Sage, 2009), 70.

22. Charmaz, *Constructing Grounded Theory,* 57; Saldaña, *The Coding Manual for Qualitative Researchers,* 155.

23. Rich Ling and Pål Sundsøy, "The iPhone and Mobile Access to the Internet" (presented at the Mobile 2.0: Beyond Voice? pre-conference of the ICA, Chicago, Illinois, May 20–21, 2009).

24. Ian Hutchby, *Media Talk: Conversation Analysis and the Study of Broadcasting* (Berkshire: Open University Press, 2006), 166.

25. Respondents were asked about the make and model of their handset. Devices running an advanced operating system were considered smartphones. In the sample, these were represented by Android, Blackberry OS v. 5 (only one in the sample), iOS, Windows Mobile, and Symbian S60.

26. Donald A. Norman and Jakob Nielsen, "Gestural Interfaces: A Step Backward in Usability", *Interactions* 17, no. 5 (2010), 46–49.

27. Cindy Krum, *Mobile Marketing—Finding Your Customers No Matter Where They Are* (Indianapolis, IN: Pearson, 2010), 133.

28. Gordon and de Souza e Silva, *Net Locality.*

29. Yanqing Cui and Virpi Roto, "How People Use the Web on Mobile Devices", in *Proceedings of the 17th International Conference on World Wide Web*, WWW '08, ed. International World Wide Web Conference Committee (IW3C2) (New York: ACM, 2008), 905–914, http://doi.acm.org/10.1145/1367497.1367619.
30. Gitte Stald, "Mobile Monitoring: Aspects of Risk and Surveillance and Questions of Democratic Perspectives in Young People's Uses of Mobile Phones", *Young Citizens and New Media: Strategies of Learning for Democratic Engagement*, ed. Peter Dahlgren (London: Routledge, 2007); Stald, "Identity and Digital Media".
31. Cui and Roto, "How People Use the Web on Mobile Devices"; Peter Nielsen and Annita Fjuk, "The Reality Beyond the Hype: Mobile Internet Is Primarily an Extension of PC-based Internet", *Information Society* 26, no. 5 (2010), 375–382.
32. Ling, *The Mobile Connection*, 150.
33. Amanda Lenhart et al., *Teens and Mobile Phones* (Washington, DC: Pew Research Center, 2010), 23.
34. Nielsen and Fjuk, "The Reality Beyond the Hype".
35. See for instance The Danish Business Authority, "Telestatistik—Første Halvår 2011". "Nyt Fra Danmarks Statistik", Danmarks Statistik, April 2011, http://www.dst.dk/pukora/epub/Nyt/2011/NR206.pdf.
36. Statistics Denmark, "Nyt Fra Danmarks Statistik", accessed: July 20, 2012, http://www.dst.dk/pukora/epub/Nyt/2012/NR376.pdf.
37. Rich Ling and Dag Svanæs, "Browsers vs. Apps: The Role of Apps in the Mobile Internet" (presented at the opening conference for the Chinese Internet Institute at the University of Peking, Beijing, May 2011).
38. Green and Haddon, *Mobile Communications*.
39. Ibid., 40.
40. Ling, *The Mobile Connection*.
41. Gerard Goggin, *Cell Phone Culture—Mobile Technology in Everyday Life* (New York: Routledge, 2006).

# 14 Visual Mobile Communication on the Internet

## Patterns in Publishing and Messaging Camera Phone Photographs

*Mikko Villi*

## INTRODUCTION

Given that a significant number of mobile phones feature a camera, visual mobile communication is rapidly becoming more common—by publishing camera phone photographs on the Web or with mobile apps, or messaging the photographs. Visual mobile communication is altogether a new phenomenon, as mobile communication has been visual only since the turn of the millennium. The transition is evident in the screens of mobile phones, which have transformed from small black-and-white displays portraying numbers or names into big, phone-sized, colorful, high-resolution displays. This rise in the visual and multimedia dimensions of mobile communication indicates the transformation of the mobile phone into mobile media.[1]

The camera phone is part of an overall trend toward nonvoice functions in mobile communication. The camera phone is a popular image-recording instrument, but also a device that enables new forms of mobile interaction by adding the visual element to the communication process. Like words during a phone call, photographs can now function as communicative objects through which distant people engage with each other synchronously, performing "visual chitchat" or "visual small-talk".[2] As Ling observes, "the almost universal access to cameras in the form of camera phones means that snapshots of different situations have become a common part of interaction".[3] As a result of the inclusion of the camera into the mobile phone, photography has shifted from a stand-alone technology into an interoperable one.[4] Capturing and communicating photographs on a camera phone represents, thus, a new resource for both mobile and visual communication.

Mobile communication in general is manifested as mobile access to communication means and, increasingly, as perpetual connection to others. According to Castells et al.,[5] it is the permanent and ubiquitous form of connectivity that is the key feature in mobile communication, rather than motion or mobility. The mobile phone also serves increasingly as a device that connects the user to the Web and other services and platforms on the Internet. This trend in mobile communication will most probably intensify during the coming years.

Much of the traffic in photographs now circulates through digital networks and is facilitated by new platforms.[6] As Lapenta notes, "what is really changing has little to do with the increasing numbers of images taken every day and more to do with the increasingly differentiated forms of photographic image production, aggregation and distribution".[7] A user equipped with a camera phone can easily take part in these photographic processes by connecting the phone to the Internet. The integration of the Internet into mobile phones enables a perpetual photographic connection to other people; the users are 'visually online' all the time.

Moblogs[8] and Flickr have been popular in photo sharing communities.[9] Now, social media services such as Facebook and Twitter are integral in communicating photographs. In addition to the content sharing platforms on the Web, mobile photo apps are extending the diversity of photo circulation on the Internet. It is important to study photography in this "personal communication system"[10] of digital social networks and camera phones.

By connecting the camera phone to the Internet, photographs can be shared by using similar services as when using a computer. In the '90s and early '00s, before smart phones and the mobile Internet, sharing of photographs directly from the mobile phone was limited to using MMS (Multimedia Messaging Service), showing the image on the phone screen, using infrared or Bluetooth to send the photograph to a mobile phone in the close vicinity, or transferring the photograph to a computer. Even technologically agile people did not commonly upload their camera phone images to the Web.[11] This means that there was no practical manner to *publish* photographs to a larger group of people directly from the camera phone. However, as the rapid emergence of smart phones and mobile Internet services enables the publishing of camera phone photographs to a wider and possibly anonymous audience, the development of the mobile media device is then not limited to interpersonal photo sharing practices.

As a consequence of the advent of the mobile Internet, the practices for remote sharing of camera phone photographs can now be placed on a continuum between two dimensions: *publishing* and *interpersonal messaging*. Users can send the photographs in an interpersonal manner via IM (instant messaging), e-mail and MMS, or, alternatively, upload them to social media sites for wider audiences to view. In the chapter, I use this continuum between messaging and publishing as a conceptual framework. The framework is theoretically closely linked to the discussion on mobile communication,[12] photo messaging[13] and the private/public domain in mobile content sharing.[14] This chapter contributes especially to the study on mobile photo apps and the sharing of photographs via the mobile Internet,[15] which are rather new fields of study.

I am interested in camera phone photography as a social medium. The specific question the chapter addresses is, *How do the integration of the Internet into mobile phones and the emergence of mobile photo apps influence the circulation and sharing of camera phone photographs?* I argue that the dominant interpersonal and intimate attribute of mobile photo sharing[16] is replaced, to a degree, by the aspect of publishing, mostly by using designated photo sharing apps or mobile apps for services such as Facebook and Twitter. But, at the same time, mobile Internet-based messaging still provides the communicator with a photographic connection to the insular life, i.e., close friends and family members. To shed light on this continuum between messaging and publishing in mobile content sharing, I use a qualitative in-depth interview study focusing on the photo sharing practices of Finnish camera phone users.[17]

In the first part of the chapter, I discuss the interpersonal and intimate aspects of mobile communication, before shifting my focus along the continuum to the publishing of camera phone photographs on the Internet. In the latter part, I present results from the empirical study. In general, the studies on the communication of camera phone photographs that have been realized in the social sciences[18] can be characterized as interpretive: the overall aim has been to describe and understand rather than explain or predict the practices.[19] The study at hand shares the interpretive approach.[20]

## INTIMATE AND INTERPERSONAL MOBILE COMMUNICATION

The notion of publishing is new to telephone communication in general, as the conventional mode of telephone communication is interpersonal, dyadic communication. In addition, a common view is that the mobile phone is used in communities of a different type and scale than computer-based Internet communication.[21] According to Ling and Stald,[22] the social dynamics of the mobile phone are different from those of the more PC-based forms of interaction. Research shows that the mobile phone contributes to the development and maintenance of social cohesion within the closest sphere of friends and family. Rather than open us to many friends and acquaintances in a quasi-broadcast form of interaction, the mobile phone enforces the point-to-point form of interaction.[23]

The intimate and interpersonal traits of mobile communication can be well illustrated by the concept of "telecocoon", by which Habuchi[24] refers to a sphere of intimacy that is free of geographical and temporal restraints. People who form telecocoons can be characterized as being constantly attentive to their intimate ones. With mobile technology, people spend a major part of their communication time in the presence of "those who matter".[25]

However, this does not mean that mobile phones could not also be used for more broadcast-oriented forms of communication, such as is exemplified by the mobile use of Twitter or YouTube. As mobile phone and Internet communication are quite rapidly converging, it is not as straightforward anymore to distinguish 'using the mobile phone' from 'being on the Internet', nor is it easy to simply draw a line between the intimate mobile phone and the more anonymous Internet. Yet, as I argue, the intimate and selective attributes of the mobile phone[26] live on in messaging, even when using the phone to engage in Internet-based communication. Internet-based mobile messaging—such as when using IM—can enable a shared mobile space that is generally available between only a few friends.[27]

When personal photography[28] and photographic communication is added to the equation, the intimate attribute of messaging is further emphasized. Personal photography—such as family photography—resides in the intimate sphere, as the photographer usually knows the people in her/his pictures and the viewers either know or can identify the subjects of the pictures.[29] Snapshots serve the purposes of private visual communication,[30] and the intended viewers are typically the photographer's close associates.[31] The emphasis in snapshot photography is on loved ones and family members.[32] Interestingly, camera phone photographs can be even more personal than other snapshot photographs.[33] What contributes to the personal character of camera phone photography in particular, is that, instead of many members of a family sharing one camera, they can now all photograph with their individual mobile phones.

This insight about the prominence of visual intimacy can be supported by available research on photo messaging,[34] which shows that it is firmly grounded on the intimate mode of communication. Scifo[35] sees photo messaging as reasserting the mobile phone's cultural identity as a medium, which intensifies communication with proximate relations. Kato et al.[36] maintain that couples and close groups of friends have the highest volume of remote image sharing. Mediated sharing of photographs supports 'distant closeness' between friends and family members and functions to maintain and enforce social bonds.[37] Often, the connection between the communicators needs to be deep enough, intimate, for the receiver to really care about the personal and possibly mundane image and to appreciate the interpersonal contact established by the photograph.

Thus, although the online display and sharing of personal photographs is transforming personal photography from a private and intimate practice into a more public one, many of the photographs taken with a camera phone still work primarily to maintain and strengthen social micronetworks that are embedded in face-to-face relationships.[38] The emergence of Web 2.0 platforms and mobile photo apps does not *necessarily* alter radically the practices of camera phone photo sharing, as those practices are rooted in the established conventions of interpersonal mobile communication and personal photography. For instance, in another Finnish study,[39] 60% of the respondents agreed with the claim "My photographs published online are directed mostly to friends". Overall, 65% of the respondents informed that they never uploaded photographs to the Web.

## PUBLISHING CAMERA PHONE PHOTOGRAPHS ON THE INTERNET

When studying the effects of the current big shift—internetization—in mobile communication, it is necessary to distinguish the different modes of computer-mediated communication that have entered the mobile sphere. A study comparing Flickr with other Internet-based methods of sharing photographs[40] shows how "Snaprs"—members of a Flickr group—take photographs primarily to share with unfamiliar people. The Snapr photo sharing practices do not represent interpersonal communication, but rather mass communication to a large and undefined group of people. By contrast, those participants in the study representing the traditional, "Kodak Culture" photography[41] share photographs primarily within an existing social group, their preferred method of photo sharing being e-mail–based messaging. Both the persons in the photographs and the people they are shared with belong to the same intimate circle. The drive is to augment the existing relationships through photo sharing, not to supplant them. For the Kodak Culture photographers, privacy is a primary concern.[42]

The ever-growing practice of publishing camera phone photographs in social media is an example of a less selective mode of sharing personal photographs. The connection to the Internet opens up possibilities for the spreading of a Snapr culture and the growing popularity of more public forms of sharing camera phone photographs. People can be "privately public"[43] when they openly share personal photographs that convey private experiences.[44] The growing presence of photographs on the Web reveals how people move within and between the public and the private, at times being in both simultaneously.[45] Many of the social media platforms on the Web represent mass sharing of photographs—personal image broadcasting and narrowcasting. Castells[46] labels this new form of socialized communication in the converged media ecosystem as "mass self-communication".

The publishing of photographs on the Internet has moved partly from photo-only sites (such as Flickr) to less media-specific services (such as Facebook and Twitter). Facebook is nowadays an important platform for publishing photographs, as every day 250 million photographs are uploaded to Facebook,[47] which amounts to seven billion photographs a month (as a comparison, Flickr has gathered six billion photos in eight years). Facebook is not a totally open platform, as it is most often used in a quasi-broadcasting mode to a selected group of people.[48] Yet, posting a photograph for, say, 250 Facebook friends can hardly be considered interpersonal communication. Rather, it resembles the act of placing the photograph on a pedestal in a crowded room, entailing characteristics of both sharing and exhibition. The viewers may or may not view the photograph, and if they do view it, not necessarily immediately. This pull modality of image viewing differs from the push modality in messaging, where the photo messages are pushed directly to a specific recipient, and not placed in the open media space for possibly interested persons to pull them for viewing.

In addition to the content sharing platforms on the Web, a new generation of services is affecting the ways photographs are shared on the Internet, namely mobile photo apps.[49] Several mobile photo apps have received funding from well-known venture capital firms,[50] so the expectations seem to be quite high regarding their emerging popularity. Certain mobile photo apps (such as Hipstamatic) are directed at enhancing and manipulating the photographs during the actual capture of the photograph, whereas others are more focused on communicating the photographs from the mobile phone. Some apps (such as the popular Instagram) integrate these two functions by providing both means for communication and possibilities for emulating film types, filters, lenses and cameras. The additional, software-based 'modules' to the camera in the phone often reflect a nostalgic aesthetic attitude and orientation, for example by imitating the Polaroid aesthetic and even the functions of instant cameras some decades back. These apps combine the immediacy and spontaneity of snapshot photography with the connectivity and instant feedback provided by the social media.

Importantly, in relation to the context of this chapter, many of the popular mobile photo apps represent primarily the publishing aspect of photo sharing. They are oriented toward communicating with photographs to an anonymous and distant audience, embodying practices familiar from photo exhibitions or photo clubs.[51] These apps accentuate photography as a social medium by extending the variety of photo circulation and diversifying the communication structure by which photographs can be shared from a mobile phone. However, there also exist apps, such as Path, that are focused more on the limited sharing of photographs in 'micro-communities',[52] in a sense micro-communication or micro-sharing. Sharing on Path is not an act of broadcasting or self-promotion, but sharing a moment with someone who really knows you.[53] In addition, most instant messaging apps, such as iMessage, WhatsApp or Line, provide the possibility to communicate photographs to a narrow circle of people.

## ANALYSIS: PATTERNS OF VISUAL MOBILE COMMUNICATION

I will turn now to the analysis of how the subjects in the interview study described their practices of sharing camera phone photographs. Using in-depth interviews, I focused on a group of Finnish camera phone users. The sampling procedure was purposive and consisted of searching for exemplary informants—people who have actually shared photographs from their mobile phones. I interviewed eight subjects individually, and the interviews lasted on average one and half hours. The interviews were recorded and transcribed. The language used in the interviews was mainly English, because I wanted to obtain material that did not need to be translated. The interviewees had a good command of English and only one interviewee wished to do the interview in Finnish.

I used a semistructured model for the interviews and presented a set of questions to all of the interviewees. The dialogue during the interviews was staged according to a thematic, topic-centered structure.[54] The interviewees could continue their thoughts along new lines, and they were asked to elaborate on certain themes that seemed interesting and to express reflective and critical views. I was mainly interested in the perceptions and interpretations of the interviewees. In the article, I use pseudonyms when referring to the interviewees.[55]

The study proceeded from analysis and coding of parts of the data set to developing a holistic understanding of the practices and views expressed by the interviewees. By applying thematic analysis,[56] I classified the interview material under the following headings: sharing, interpersonal communication, visual communication, camera vs. phone, mediated presence, ritual, transmission, connection, immediacy, transience, intimacy, mundane, and personal communication. These thematical headings derived from the study of previous literature on mobile communication and camera phones.[57] I was also open to themes that emerged from the analysis or originated with the informants, but the analysis was predominantly theory-based. In this chapter, I use in particular findings that relate to sharing, intimacy and personal communication.

The results from the study are consistent with those views that I have presented earlier in this chapter[58] on how messaging is oriented at communicating personal contents in an intimate social circle. For instance, Kasper described sending photo messages "just to pretty close friends". When comparing sending photographs as messages and publishing them on the Web, he indicated that messaging is more closely tied to personal relationships: "To send [as a message] the picture, it's more personal". The photographs he publishes on the Web are less "inside jokes", and more motivated by an artistic ambition.

Mikael informed that he likes to post photographs on the Web, his friends forming a community that gathers at a blog. He is engaged in strictly one-to-one intimate pictorial communication only with his girlfriend. For Lotta, the group to which she communicates with mobile images is "kind of the same circle that I talk to": friends, boyfriend and family. Ulla explained that she sends photographs to people with whom she would communicate more often in other ways, as well. Joakim and Bengt, too, described sending photo messages to close friends, and not to random people. In a similar vein, in another study on microblogging and online photo sharing,[59] the informants talked about how important it was for them to have contacts that they know from their offline communities and networks. Close friends were always mentioned as the main audience for the photographs.[60]

Bengt commented that "They are more personal, those [the photographs] that you send [. . .] like this car that I saw and took a picture and sent to my son, it was just for him and no one else". The personality of the photograph was accentuated because his son had just bought the same model of car as depicted in the photograph. According to Bengt, if he had placed the same photograph of the car on a general photo sharing site on the Web, it would have been just a "photo of a car", but now that certain model had meaning in the interpersonal communication relationship between the father and the son.

Ulla had received a photo message from a friend showing the friend's two Belgian giant rabbits, familiar to Ulla, standing on their hind legs (Figure 14.1). In the message, the photograph was accompanied by the text "Is the grass really greener on the other side of the fence?" Ulla explained that she did not forward the image to some third person who would not be familiar with the rabbits. The photograph of the rabbits might have worked well on the Web just as a "general funny picture", but as an interpersonal message it would have been awkward, if sent to someone with no connection or previous knowledge of the rabbits.

Ulla proceeded by mentioning that she had received or sent photo messages only with personal contents, and that she would send photographs of "dead" things (e.g., buildings) only if it were of somebody's home. The contents of a photo message seem to need a personal connection both to the sender and the receiver in order for the photograph to be worth sending.

Kjell offered an example of the difference between publishing photographs on the Web and communicating them as interpersonal messages. He was planning on documenting the following summer with his new camera phone and publishing the photographs eventually on the Web; this Web album would cover the whole summer. In addition, he intended to share photographs of some special moments interpersonally as photo messages during the course of the summer. Thus, he would publish a visual record of the whole summer on the Web (after the summer had already gone), and in addition offer certain individual friends contemporaneous peeks—intermediate gazes—into his summer.

*Figure 14.1*    "Is the grass really greener on the other side of the fence?" (reprinted with permission)

These 'telling extracts', articulate and apt expressions representing those views that were pronouncedly expressed by the interviewees,[61] demonstrate the intimate character of messaging, both when using MMS[62] and communicating over the Internet. Interpersonal messaging represents a different kind of communality than that which can be achieved by publishing mobile photographs in the quite loosely knit photo services on the Web, such as Flickr, or even in the semi-intimate social networking communities, such as Facebook.

As the social media services can be more easily used with mobile phones, and because of the new breed of mobile photo apps, the aspects of publishing and a Snapr culture[63] can pervade the previously rather interpersonal mobile photo sharing scene. It can be assumed that a growing share of camera phone photographs is shared on the Web or with mobile apps in a one-to-many manner. The photograph acquires a range of new social functions and meanings in the contemporary mediated exchanges, and therefore it should be understood as a point of access to networked interaction.[64] In this context, I consider the framework of messaging and publishing to be valuable in studying the different modes of sharing photographs from camera phones connected to the Internet.

## CONCLUSIONS AND THE WAY FORWARD

The camera phone—because it is a telephone—entails exceptional possibilities for direct interpersonal communication. Nowadays, the camera phone can also be used for distributing photographs on the Web. Online sharing of photographs has brought a novel dimension of mass communication to personal photography, to which I have in this chapter referred as 'publishing'. Publishing is strongly connected to the social media platforms on the Web and the growing array of mobile photo apps. Publishing also indicates less distinct differences between mobile-mediated and computer-mediated communication.

In the practices of sharing camera phone photographs, there is a riptide between the previously dominant interpersonal and intimate conventions of mobile communication and the new possibilities afforded by the mobile Internet. One conceivable context for sharing camera phone photographs, somewhere between messaging and publishing, could be such micro-community platforms and apps that are directed toward communicating photographs (and also other media content) in communities that are larger than those of conventional telephone communication but smaller than most of the communities that operate on Facebook, for example. In this sense, they would be adequate for sharing most personal photographs.

One example of such a service is the Path mobile app that limits the network a user can share media contents with. The network allowed by the app is not too large and impersonal, which can benefit both the sender and the viewers: the platform is private enough for the sender, and the potential viewers do not necessarily consider the photographs to be too personal or even boring, as they have a close personal relationship with the sender. Interestingly, the 2.0 version of Path describes itself as a "journal", focusing not only on photo sharing, but life sharing—sharing videos, thoughts, the physical location and the music one is listening to.

In my view, the 'Path' genre of apps and services is the most appropriate one for communicating visually in an adequately small and intimate circle. They permit visual social networking in a close-knit community and the maintenance of a connection through images. These apps suit particularly well mobile photographic communication in "telecocoons",[65] consisting of strong ties that breed cohesion.[66] A close group of friends might prefer to maintain their community,[67] in times of absence, by constantly sharing photographs from their camera phones.

In fact, there is currently a conceivable trend toward 'semi-sharing'—such private modes of sharing that are not strictly interpersonal. This trend is demonstrated, for instance, by the Google+ Circles feature that enables the users to organize their contacts according to real-life connections. Lately, also, Facebook has introduced new settings that offer the possibility to adjust and reduce the group of contacts to whom the contents are targeted. These functions help to avoid the 'oversharing' of such contents that are too personal to be interesting enough for those in loose-tie networks consisting of mere acquaintances, peers or followers. Personal photographs are a good example of such content that is not functional or adequate in every social relationship, as was demonstrated by the qualitative study with Finnish camera phone users.

By using the continuum between messaging and publishing, it is also possible to anticipate the uses of emerging forms of mobile communication, such as video calling. Similar to photo messages, video calls from mobile phones appear to be popular between family members and other intimates, in particular during a state of extended absence, mediating their presence and establishing a connection.[68] On the other hand, mobile apps such as Bambuser provide the possibility to publish mobile video by live-streaming it to a wide range of Internet platforms. In this sense, also, video calling and mobile video sharing are characterized by the distinction between the two ends of the continuum of mobile content sharing—messaging and publishing.

## ACKNOWLEDGEMENTS

I would like to thank the interviewees and Matteo Stocchetti, who helped in realizing the empirical study. My appreciation also goes to the editors of the volume and the anonymous reviewer. Special thanks are in order to Asko Lehmuskallio for his comments.

## NOTES

1. Gerard Goggin and Larissa Hjorth, "The Question of Mobile Media", in *Mobile Technologies: From Telecommunications to Media*, ed. Gerard Goggin and Larissa Hjorth (New York: Routledge: 2009), 7.
2. Mikko Villi, "Visual Chitchat: The Use of Camera Phones in Visual Interpersonal Communication", *Interactions: Studies in Communication & Culture* 3, no. 1 (2012): 39–54.
3. Rich Ling, "Trust, Cohesion and Social Networks: The Case of Quasi-Illicit Photos in a Teen Peer Group" (paper presented at Mobile Communication and the Ethics of Social Networking, Budapest, Hungary, September 25–27, 2008), accessed October 14, 2009, http://www.richardling.com/papers/2008_Networking_ethics.pdf.
4. Barbara Scifo, "The Sociocultural Forms of Mobile Personal Photographs in a Cross-Media Ecology: Reflections Starting from the Young Italian Experience", *Knowledge, Technology & Policy* 22, no. 3 (2009): 192.
5. Manuel Castells et al., *Mobile Communication and Society: A Global Perspective* (Cambridge, MA: MIT Press, 2007), 92, 248.
6. Jonathan Dovey and Martin Lister, "Straw Men or Cyborgs?", *Interactions: Studies in Communication & Culture* 1, no. 1 (2009): 136–37.
7. Francesco Lapenta, "Locative Media and the Digital Visualisation of Space, Place and Information", *Visual Studies* 26, no. 1 (2011): 1–2.
8. Moblogging (mobile blogging) was an early stage in mobile photo publishing. Moblogs are web sites that are uploaded to and maintained from mobile devices, and consist mainly of mobile phone photographs. The main idea of moblogging is that there is no intermediate transfer step between capturing the photo and publishing it.
9. Karin Wagner, "The Everyday Seen Through a Camera Phone" (paper presented at INTER: A European Cultural Studies Conference, organized by the Advanced Cultural Studies Institute of Sweden, Norrköping, June 11–13, 2007), accessed March 11, 2009, http:// www.ep.liu.se/ecp/025/063/ecp072063.pdf ; Søren Mørk Petersen, "Common Banality: The Affective Character of Photo Sharing, Everyday Life and Produsage Cultures" (PhD dissertation, Department of Innovative Communication at the IT-University of Copenhagen, Denmark, 2008).
10. Jeffery Boase, "Personal Networks and the Personal Communication System: Using Multiple Media to Connect", *Information, Communication & Society* 11, no. 4 (2008): 490–508.
11. Ilp Koskinen, "From the Editor", *Knowledge, Technology & Policy* 22, no. 3 (2009): 155.
12. Mizuko Ito, Daisuke Okabe and Misa Matsuda, eds., *Personal, Portable, Pedestrian: Mobile Phones in Japanese Life* (Cambridge, MA: MIT Press, 2005); Gerard Goggin, *Cell Phone Culture: Mobile Technology in Everyday Life* (London: Routledge, 2006); Rich Ling, *New Tech, New Ties: How Mobile Communication is Reshaping Social Cohesion* (Cambridge, MA: MIT Press, 2008).
13. Barbara Scifo, "The Domestication of Camera-Phone and MMS Communication: The Early Experiences of Young Italians", in *A Sense of Place: The Global and the Local in Mobile Communication*, ed. Kristóf Nyíri (Vienna: Passagen Verlag, 2005), 363–374; Carole Rivière, "Mobile Camera Phones: A New Form of 'Being Together' in Daily Interpersonal Communication", in *Mobile Communications: Re-negotiation of the Social Sphere*, ed. Rich Ling and Per E. Pedersen (London: Springer Verlag, 2005), 167–186; Ilpo Koskinen, *Mobile Multimedia in Action* (New Brunswick, NJ: Transaction, 2007).

14. Sonia Livingstone, "Taking Risky Opportunities in Youthful Content Creation: Teenagers' Use of Social Networking Sites for Intimacy, Privacy and Self-Expression", *New Media & Society* 10, no. 3 (2008): 393–411; Amparo Lasén and Edgar Gómez-Cruz, "Digital Photography and Picture Sharing: Redefining the Public/Private Divide", *Knowledge, Technology & Policy* 22 (2009): 205–215; Dong-Hoo Lee, "Mobile Snapshots and Private/Public Boundaries", *Knowledge, Technology & Policy* 22 (2009): 161–71.

15. Lee, "Mobile Snapshots"; Scifo, "The Domestication of Camera-Phone and MMS Communication"

16. Mikko Villi, "Visual Mobile Communication: Camera Phone Photo Messages as Ritual Communication and Mediated Presence" (PhD dissertation, Aalto University School of Art and Design, Helsinki, 2010).

17. The study forms a part of my doctoral thesis, titled "Visual Mobile Communication: Camera Phone Photo Messages as Ritual Communication and Mediated Presence".

18. Ilpo Koskinen, Esko Kurvinen and Turo-Kimmo Lehtonen, *Mobile Image* (Helsinki: Edita, 2002); Tim Kindberg et al., "I Saw This and Thought of You: Some Social Uses of Camera Phones", in *Extended Abstracts of the Conference on Human Factors in Computing Systems, (CHI 2005)*, (New York: ACM Press, 2005), 1545–48; Scifo, "The Domestication of Camera-Phone and MMS Communication"; Virpi Oksman, "MMS and Its 'Early Adopters' in Finland", in *A Sense of Place: The Global and the Local in Mobile Communication*, ed. Kristóf Nyíri (Vienna: Passagen Verlag, 2005), 349–362; Rivière, "Mobile Camera Phones".

19. Ilpo Koskinen, "Pervasive Image Capture and Sharing: Methodological Remarks" (paper presented at Ubicomp '05, The Seventh International Conference on Ubiquitous Computing, September 11–14, 2005, Tokyo, Japan).

20. David Silverman, *Interpreting Qualitative Data: Methods for Analyzing Talk, Text, and Interaction*, 2nd ed. (London: Sage, 2001), 3–4; James A. Holstein and Jaber F. Gubrium, "Interpretive Practice and Social Action", in *The Sage Handbook of Qualitative Research*, ed. Norman K. Denzin and Yvonna Lincoln, 3rd ed. (Thousand Oaks, CA: Sage, 2005), 486.

21. Mikko Villi and Janne Matikainen, "Photo Messages as Communication in Communities", in *Images and Communities*, ed. Matteo Stocchetti and Johanna Sumiala-Seppänen (Helsinki: Gaudeamus, 2008), 105.

22. Rich Ling and Gitte Stald, "Mobile Communities: Are We Talking About a Village, a Clan, or a Small Group?", *American Behavioral Scientist* 53 (2010): 1133–43.

23. Ling and Stald, "Mobile Communities"; see also Kenneth J. Gergen, "The Challenge of Absent Presence", in *Perpetual Contact: Mobile Communication, Private Talk, Public Performance*, ed. James E. Katz and Mark Aakhus (Cambridge, UK: Cambridge University Press, 2002), 227–243; Nancy K. Baym, Yan Bing Zhang and Mei-Chen Lin, "Social Interactions Across Media", *New Media & Society* 6, no. 3 (2004): 314; Friedrich Krotz, "Mobile Communication, the Internet, and the Net of Social Relations: A Theoretical Framework", in *A Sense of Place: The Global and the Local in Mobile Communication*, ed. Kristóf Nyíri (Vienna: Passagen Verlag, 2005), 455; Kenichi Ishii, "Implications of Mobility: The Uses of Personal Communication Media in Everyday Life", *Journal of Communication* 56, no. 2 (2006): 346–365.

24. Ichiyo Habuchi, "Accelerating Reflexivity", in *Personal, Portable, Pedestrian: Mobile Phones in Japanese Life*, ed. Mizuko Ito, Daisuke Okabe and Misa Matsuda (Cambridge, MA: MIT Press, 2005), 178.

25. Gergen, "The Challenge of Absent Presence"", 238.

26. Ling and Stald, "Mobile Communities", 1133.

27. Mizuko Ito and Daisuke Okabe, "Technosocial Situations: Emergent Structuring of Mobile E-mail Use", in *Personal, Portable, Pedestrian: Mobile Phones in Japanese Life*, ed. Mizuko Ito, Daisuke Okabe and Misa Matsuda (Cambridge, MA: MIT Press, 2005), 264; Koskinen, *Mobile Multimedia in Action*; Villi and Matikainen, "Photo Messages as Communication".

28. Camera phone photography is closely affiliated with personal photography and snapshot photography; see Lisa Gye, "Picture This: The Impact of Mobile Camera Phones on Personal Photographic Practices", *Continuum: Journal of Media & Cultural Studies* 21, no. 2 (2007): 279–288; Lee, "Mobile Snapshots"; Villi, "Visual Mobile Communication".

29. Richard Chalfen, *Snapshot Versions of Life* (Bowling Green, OH: Bowling Green State University Popular Press, 1987), 8.

30. Chalfen, *Snapshot Versions of Life*, 71.

31. Joel Smith, "Roll Over", *Afterimage* 29, no. 2 (2001), 8–11.

32. Val Williams, "Carefully Creating an Idyll: Vanessa Bell and Snapshot Photography 1907–46", in *Family Snaps: The Meanings of Domestic Photography*, ed. Jo Spence and Patricia Holland (London: Virago, 1991), 186–187.

33. Heidi Rae Cooley, "Autobiographical Impulse and Mobile Imaging: Toward a Theory of Autobiometry" (paper presented at Ubicomp 2005 Workshop on Pervasive Image Capture and Sharing: New Social Practices and Implications for Technology, Tokyo, Japan, September 11, 2005); Gye, "Picture This", 84.

34. For a review of the research on photo messaging see Villi, "Visual Mobile Communication", 30–39.

35. Scifo, "The Domestication of Camera-Phone and MMS Communication", 367–368.

36. Fumitoshi Kato, Daisuke Okabe, Mizuko Ito and Ryuhei Uemoto, "Uses and Possibilities of the Keitai Camera", in *Personal, Portable, Pedestrian: Mobile Phones in Japanese Life*, ed. Mizuko Ito, Daisuke Okabe and Misa Matsuda (Cambridge, MA: MIT Press, 2005), 306.

37. Virpi Oksman, "Mobile Visuality and Everyday Life in Finland: An Ethnographic Approach to Social Uses of Mobile Image", in *Mobile Communications in Everyday Life: Ethnographic Views, Observations and Relections*, ed. Joachim R. Höflich and Maren Hartmann (Berlin: Frank & Timme, 2006), 103; Nancy Van House, "Distant Closeness: Cameraphones and Public Image Sharing" (paper presented at UBICOMP '06 PICS Workshop, Orange County, September 17–21, 2006); Nicola Döring et al., "Contents, Forms and Functions of Interpersonal Pictorial Messages in Online and Mobile Communication", in *Mobile Understanding: The Empistemology of Ubiquitous Communication*, ed. Kristóf Nyíri (Vienna: Passagen Verlag, 2006), 208; Koskinen, 2 *Mobile Multimedia in Action*, 135; Ling, "New Tech, New Ties".

38. Scifo, "The Sociocultural Forms of Mobile Personal Photographs", 191–192; Ling, "New Tech, New Ties".

39. The study consisted of an online questionnaire filled by 1,065 respondents. The main focus in the study was on the use of social media in Finland in general, but it provided information also on the preferred sharing mechanisms of photographs. I carried out the part of the study focusing on photography with my colleague Janne Matikainen. The study in full is reported (in Finnish) in Janne Matikainen, *Sosiaalisen ja perinteisen median rajalla* (Communication Research Centre CRC, Department of Communication, University of Helsinki, 2009).

40. Andrew D. Miller and W. Keith Edwards, "Give and Take: A Study of Consumer Photo-Sharing Culture And Practice", in *Proceedings of the SIGCHI Conference on Human Factors in Computing Systems*, ed. ACM Special Interest Group on Computer-Human Interaction, (New York: ACM Press, 2007), 347–356.

41. Chalfen, *Snapshot Versions of Life*.
42. Miller and Edwards, "Give and Take", 347–355.
43. Patricia G. Lange, "Publicly Private and Privately Public: Social Networking on YouTube", *Journal of Computer-Mediated Communication* 13, no. 1 (2008): 361–380.
44. Lee, "Mobile Snapshots", 163.
45. Lasén and Goméz-Cruz, "Digital Photography and Picture Sharing", 213.
46. Castells et al., *Mobile Communication and Society*.
47. Facebook, S-1 Registration statement, filed on February 1, 2012, accessed March 15, 2012, http://www.sec.gov/Archives/edgar/data/1326801/000119312512034517/d287954ds1.htm.
48. Ling and Stald, "Mobile Communities", 1135.
49. Most of the apps that I discuss in this paper have been first introduced for the Apple iOS platform.
50. Jennifer van Grove, "The Mobile Photo Sharing Boom Is Here", *Mashable*, December 5, 2010, accessed 29 March 2011, http://mashable.com/2010/12/05/mobile-photo-sharing-boom.
51. Pierre Bourdieu, *"Photography: A Middle-Brow Art"* (Cambridge, UK: Polity Press, 1990).
52. Scifo, "The Sociocultural Forms of Mobile Personal Photographs, 185, 191.
53. Steven Levy, "The 'Path' to Social Network Serenity Is Lined with 50 Friends", *Wired*, November 15, 2010, accessed February 15, 2011, http://www.wired.com/epicenter/2010/11/the-path-to-social-network-tranquility-is-lined-by-50-friends.
54. Jennifer Mason, *Qualitative Researching*, 2nd. ed. (London: Sage, 2002), 62–63.
55. Kasper, Lotta, Joakim, Mikael, Anja, Kjell, Ulla and Bengt.
56. Jari Eskola and Juha Suoranta, *Johdatus laadulliseen tutkimukseen*, 8th ed. (Tampere: Vastapaino, 2008), 174–180.
57. E.g., Koskinen et al., *Mobile Image*; Tim Kindberg et al., "The Ubiquitous Camera: An In-depth Study of Camera Phone Use", *IEEE Pervasive Computing*, 4, issue 2, 42–50; Rivière, "Mobile Camera Phones"; Scifo, "The Domestication of Camera-Phone and MMS Communication" ; Goggin, *Cell Phone Culture*; Koskinen, *Mobile Multimedia in Action*; Ling, *New Tech, New Ties*.
58. E.g., Scifo, "The Sociocultural Forms of Mobile Personal Photographs; Ling and Stald, "Mobile Communities".
59. Petersen, "Common Banality", 90.
60. Petersen, "Common Banality".
61. Silverman, *Interpreting Qualitative Data*, 83.
62. It has to be noted that in the case of MMS, technical and financial limitations play a big part in restricting the magnitude of sharing. It would be very cumbersome and quite expensive to share a photograph to a hundred contacts by using MMS.
63. Miller and Edwards, "Give and Take".
64. Lapenta, "Locative Media", 2–3.
65. Habuchi, "Accelerating Reflexivity", 178.
66. Mark S. Granovetter, "The Strength of Weak Ties", *American Journal of Sociology* 78, no. 6 (1973): 1377–78; Ling and Stald, "Mobile Communities", 1133.
67. Livingstone, "Taking Risky Opportunities", 404.
68. This practice is often portrayed in the commercials advocating video calling, e.g., those on using FaceTime on Apple iOS devices.

# Contributors

**Tracey M. Benson** is an Australian artist and researcher who has focused on notions of identity, tourism, borders, access and power as themes within her work. Primarily, she uses the online environments in conjunction with installation, digital data projections and video as mediums in her creative projects. Since 1995, she has been working creatively with the World Wide Web, focusing on developing hypertextual works, video projects and digital animations. Her digital work has been presented in many online galleries and projects in Australia and overseas. In 2010 Benson was awarded a Ph.D. at the Australian National University, which explores online communities and social networking tools. She is currently an adjunct fellow at the ANU School of Music, where she is researching semantic Web and geolocation technologies and their application to genealogy and Indigenous kinship systems.

**Troels Fibæk Bertel** is a Ph.D. fellow at the IT University of Copenhagen. His background is in informatics and media studies and his research focuses on the social uses of new media among youth. He has a special interest in processes of change associated with the convergence of mobile media and Internet services and content.

**Cecile Bezuidenhoudt** is currently doing her master's degree in operations research at the University of Cape Town (UCT). Her focus is on the optimization of complex simulation models, with the focus being on optimizing a simulation model demonstrating the operation of the South African electricity provider Eskom's coal stockpiles. She completed her undergraduate degree, followed by her honor's degree, at UCT as well, majoring in statistics and doing research on mobile Internet users in certain African countries.

**Jakob Bjur**, M.S., Ph.D., is research director at TNS-SIFO, Sweden, and affiliated researcher at the University of Gothenburg. He is heading methodological development of audience measurement systems to capture patterns of cross-media consumption. Bjur has previously held positions as researcher in residence at the Swedish Television and the Swedish Radio studying the digital transition of broadcasting and journalism. He serves as vice-chair in the COST Action Transforming Audiences, Transforming Societies, with 270 researchers from thirty countries, and as vice-chair of the section Audience and Reception Studies of ECREA. Bjur has, apart from his dissertation, "Transforming Audiences: Patterns of Individualization in Television Viewing" (University of Gothenburg, 2010), published a number of chapters in edited volumes.

**Kelli S. Burns,** Ph.D., is an associate professor in the School of Mass Communications at the University of South Florida. Her research interests include the use of social media in public relations, the intersection of social media and popular culture, and user-generated advertising. She is the author of the 2009 book *Celeb 2.0: How Social Media Foster Our Fascination with Popular Culture*(Praeger). Her research has been published in the *Journal of Advertising, Journal of New Communications Research, Newspaper Research Journal,* and the *International Journal of Interactive Marketing and Advertising* and as chapters in several edited volumes. Burns received a doctorate in mass communication from the University of Florida, where she was a presidential fellow, a master's degree in mass communication from Middle Tennessee State University, and a bachelor's degree in mathematics and business administration from Vanderbilt University.

**Kathleen M. Cumiskey (editor),** Ph.D., is associate professor in the psychology department and the women, gender and sexuality program at the College of Staten Island—City University of New York. She is recognized internationally as an expert on the social consequences of the uses of mobile technology. Her latest publications focus on the role that mobile phones play in changing people's perception of the social environment and how this results in public risk-taking. Her research has been published in *Feminist Media Studies* and *Psychology* as well as in edited volumes such as *The Mobile Communication Research Series: Volume II, Mobile Communication: Bringing Us Together or Tearing Us Apart?* (ed. R. Ling and S. Campbell, 2011; Transaction Publishers) and *Mobile Communications: Re-negotiation of the Social Sphere* (ed. R. Ling and P. Pedersen, 2005; Springer).

**Meng Di** is a Ph.D. candidate in School of Creative Media, City University of Hong Kong. Her interests include new media communication, women's studies, culture and technology, and visual representation.

**Jonathan Donner** is a researcher in the Technology for Emerging Markets Group (TEM) at Microsoft Research India. With research focused on the economic and social implications of the spread of mobile telephony in the developing world, his projects at TEM include Microenterprise/MSE development, Mobile Banking, Mobile Health and Wellbeing, and "first time/mobile-only" Internet use. He is the author, with Richard Ling, of *Mobile Communication* (Polity, 2009). His research also appears in the *Journal of Computer-Mediated Communication, The Information Society, The Journal of Information Technologies and International Development, The Journal of International Development,* and *Innovations: Technology, Governance, Globalization.* Jonathan is based in South Africa and is a visiting academic at the Hasso Plattner Institute for ICT4D Research at the University of Cape Town. Further details on Jonathan's research are a: http://research.microsoft.com/people/jdonner.

**Karen Freberg, Ph.D.,** is an Assistant Professor of Strategic Communication at the University of Louisville. Freberg also serves as an adjunct faculty member in the IMC Graduate Online Program at West Virginia University. Her research interests are in public relations, crisis communications, and social media. Freberg received her Ph.D. from the University of Tennessee, Knoxville.

**Larissa Hjorth (editor)** is an artist, digital ethnographer and associate professor in the games programs, School of Media & Communication, RMIT University. Since 2000, Hjorth has been researching and publishing on gendered customizing of mobile communication, gaming and virtual communities in the Asia–Pacific—these studies are outlined in her book, *Mobile Media in the Asia-Pacific* (Routledge). Hjorth has published widely on the topic in national and International journals in journals such as *Games and Culture* journal, *Convergence* journal, *Journal of Intercultural Studies, Continuum, ACCESS, Fibreculture* and *Southern Review,* and in 2009 coedited two Routledge anthologies, *Gaming Cultures and Place in the Asia–Pacific region* (with Dean Chan) and *Mobile Technologies: From Telecommunication to Media* (with Gerard Goggin). In 2010 Hjorth released the textbook *Games & Gaming* (Berg). As an artist, Hjorth has been awarded various prestigious awards, such as Gyeonggi Creation Center art residency (2010); Hjorth has had over ten solo exhibitions, participated in over fifty art exhibitions and curated many cross-cultural projects. In 2010 she had a solo exhibition, *Still Mobile,* at Gyeonggi Museum of Modern Art in Korea. http://www.larissahjorth.net/.

**Nandita Kapadia-Kundu** has a Ph.D. in public health from the Johns Hopkins School of Public Health and a M.A. in mass communications from Marquette University. Currently, she is a senior researcher with JHU CCP and is based in India. She has experience in grassroots-level health communication programs and worked as an additional director for a leading NGO for fifteen years. Her research interests include applications of the ancient theory of communication Sadharanikaran in the development of innovative, culturally appropriate response measures for attitudes, behavioral intentions, quality of life, emotions, and client satisfaction. Dr. Kapadia-Kundu has extensive experience conducting both qualitative and quantitative research in topics including: HIV stigma, gender and nutrition, adolescence reproductive health and poverty. She is also currently working in the area of mHealth, where she is involved in a project to promote contraceptive use via cell phones.

**Veronika Karnowski, Ph.D.,** is a research associate at the Institute for Communication Studies and Media Research of Ludwig-Maximilians-University Munich, Germany. Her research and publications focus on diffusion processes, appropriation, and usage of new communication technologies, mobile communication, and web navigation and searching.

**Ditte Laursen** is a postdoctoral researcher at DREAM (Danish Research Centre of Advanced Media materials) and at State Media Archive, State Library, Denmark. She earned her Ph.D. in media studies from University of Southern Denmark, specializing in young people's mobile phone communication. Her major research interests are social interaction in and through mobile media across formal, semiformal and informal learning sites. As a conversation analyst and ethnographer, her primary data are audio and video recordings of naturally occurring interaction and conduct, combined with participant observation and semistructured interviews.

**Michael J. Palenchar, Ph.D.,** associate professor and managing director of the Risk, Health and Crisis Communication Research Unit at the University of Tennessee, has more than two decades of professional and academic public relations experience. His research has been published in the *Journal of Public Relations Research, Public Relations Review, Public Relations Journal, Environmental Communication, Management Communication Quarterly, Journal of Contingencies and Crisis Management,* and *Communication Research Reports,* and his first book with coauthor Robert L. Heath titled *Strategic Issues Management* (2nd edition) was published by Sage in 2009.

**Claudia Riesmeyer, Ph.D.,** is a research associate at the Institute for Communication Studies and Media Research of Ludwig-Maximilians-University Munich, Germany. Her research interests and publications focus on journalism, public relations, qualitative methods and science as a profession.

**Basil Safi,** M.P.H., P.E., C.H.E.S. (JHU CCP Asia Regional Director) is a multidisciplinary professional with over ten years of international and domestic experience in the design and implementation of public health and integrated communication programs. Basil is a registered professional engineer, serves as an associate in the Department of Health, Behavior and Society at the Johns Hopkins Bloomberg School of Public Health, and is an Environmental Public Health Leadership Fellow at the CDC's National Center for Environmental Health.

**Raz Schwartz** is a postdoctoral researcher in the Social Media Information Lab, part of the School of Communication and Information at Rutgers University. Schwartz studies social media usage in urban settings and focuses on examining local social interactions through applying social computing methods to both big and small datasets. He completed his Ph.D. in the STS program at Bar-Ilan University and was a visiting scholar in the Human Computer Interaction Institute at Carnegie Mellon University. Raz holds a master's degree in law from Bar-Ilan University and a bachelor's degree in communications and economics from Tel-Aviv University. His research work on location-based social networks was presented in various academic settings and was featured in media outlets such as the *Wall Street Journal, Wired, Rhizome,* and *The Atlantic.*

**Gitte Stald** is an associate professor at the IT University of Copenhagen. She participated in the European project *Children and Their Changing Media Environment,* 1995–1998, in the research program *Global Media Cultures,* 1999–2001, with the project *Global Media, Local Youth,* and in the EU Kids Online project from 2006 to 2014. She has conducted a number of studies on digital children and youth media cultures, e.g., an ongoing repeated study of young Danes' uses of mobile media (2004, 2006, 2009, 2011). She also participated in research and development projects, e.g., MIL—Mobil Indholds Lab, on qualitative content for young Danes mobiles; MELFO, 2006–2007, a project on mobile solutions for dyslexics, and Mobity, 2008–2009, on the development of a user driven mobile media community.

**Tara M. Sullivan,** Ph.D., M.P.H., currently serves as the knowledge management director for the Knowledge for Health (K4Health) Project and as an assistant scientist in the Department of Health, Behavior and Society, Johns Hopkins Bloomberg School of Public Health.

**Marian Stewart Titus** is a Ph.D. Candidate in the School of Communication & Information at Rutgers University, New Brunswick, NJ. Her adviser is Dr. Vikki Katz. She holds a B.A. in English and a diploma in mass communication from the University of the West Indies, Mona, Jamaica, and an M.A. in communication from Stanford University. Her research interests are in mediated mobile communication and mobile telephony between developed and developing countries. She is also a lecturer in English at Bronx Community College of the City University of New York.

**Geetali Trivedi**, JHU CCP, has been guiding strategic health communication programs over the past eight years, making significant contributions to the implementation of the National Rural Health Mission (NRHM) in the state of Uttar Pradesh. As Senior Program Officer at ITAP, she was responsible for the visioning and spearheading the development of the comprehensive behavior change communication (BCC) strategy for NRHM for the state of Uttar Pradesh, which has been accepted nationally as a blueprint for planning BCC activities under the NRHM.

**Sanjanthi Velu**, Ph.D., has over fifteen years of experience spanning the communication field, from health communication and education, to quantitative and qualitative research, to multimedia design and production. Dr. Velu has built a vision for JHU CCP's India presence and translated its goals to action by designing robust and effective public health initiatives in response to local needs and in collaboration with a wide range of national and international partners, donors and governments.

**Mikko Villi**, Ph.D., works as a postdoctoral researcher at Aalto University School of Business in Helsinki, Finland. Villi's background is in communication studies. His research interests focus on the borderland between the new and old media, in particular the effects of new communication technology on established practices of communication

**Oscar Westlund**, M.S., Ph.D., holds a joint appointment as postdoctoral researcher at the University of Gothenburg and the IT University of Copenhagen. Westlund researches usage patterns and organizational practices emerging from the changing relationships between old legacy media and new digital and mobile media. He serves on the editorial boards of *Digital Journalism* and *Mobile Media & Communication*. Westlund has authored *Cross-Media News Work—Sensemaking of the Mobile Media (R)evolution* (University of Gothenburg, 2011), and served as guest editor for a recent special issue of *Information, Communication & Society* (15, no. 6, 2012) titled "Transforming Tensions: Legacy Media Towards Participation and Collaboration". His work has also been published in more than a dozen different international journals, among which recent work on news and mobile media appear in *Digital Journalism, Journalism Practice, Observatorio OBS* Journal, Northern Lights, International Journal on Media Management, Behaviour & Information Technology* and *New Media & Society.*

# Glossary

| | |
|---|---|
| GPS | Global Positioning System |
| IM | Instant Messaging |
| LBS | Location-Based Service |
| MMS | Multimedia Messaging System |
| SMS | Short Messaging System |
| SNS | Social Network Site |
| UCC | User Created Content |
| UGC | User Generated Content |

# Index

For Product Safety Concerns and Information please contact our
EU representative GPSR@taylorandfrancis.com Taylor & Francis
Verlag GmbH, Kaufingerstraße 24, 80331 München, Germany